HURRICANE
THE LAST WITNESSES

PILOTS TELL THE STORY OF THE AIRCRAFT THAT WON THE BATTLE OF BRITAIN

BRIAN MILTON

ANDRE
DEUTSCH

THIS IS AN ANDRÉ DEUTSCH BOOK

This edition published in 2015 by André Deutsch
A division of the Carlton Publishing Group
20 Mortimer Street
London W1T 3JW

A CIP catalogue record for this book is available from the
British Library.

ISBN 978 0 233 00454 9

Printed and bound by CPI Group (UK) Ltd, Croydon, CR0 4YY

AUTHOR NOTE
This book would not have been possible without the help of the
last witnesses, whose courage and humour aroused my deepest
admiration.

PICTURE CREDITS
Plate Section 1 in order of appearance: 1. Getty Images, 2. Imperial War
Museum (CH 1934), 3 & 4. courtesy of Billy Drake, 5, 6 & 7. courtesy
of Peter Ayerst, 8. courtesy of Peter Hairs, MBE, 9. courtesy of Bob Doe,
10. courtesy of Bob Foster, 10 & 11. courtesy of John Ellacombe, 12 &
13. courtesy of Graham Leggatt, 14. courtesy of Tom Neil, 15. Imperial
War Museum (CH 1406). Plate Section 2 in order of appearance: 1. Getty
Images, 2. Imperial War Museum (A 1126), 3. Imperial War Museum (COL
186), 4. Imperial War Museum (CR 141), 5. Getty Images, 6. courtesy of
Bill Swan, 7. courtesy of Terence Kelly, 8. courtesy of Graham Skellum, 9.
courtesy of Colin Ellis, 10, 11 & 12. courtesy of Tom Adams, 13. Imperial
War Museum (TR 869), 14. Getty Images, 15. Imperial War Museum (CH
18134), 16. Alamy/Tony Hobbs

CONTENTS

PREFACE

Knighthoods have been part of the English honours system since the age of chivalry, when knights were honoured for showing prowess in war, with great skill on horseback, and dexterity with the sword, lance and bow. They were courteous and eloquent, magnanimous in victory and defeat. Their raison d'etre was to protect the weak, defenceless and helpless, and to fight for the general welfare of all.

The young men who mounted their modern steeds in the summer of 1940 – Hurricanes and Spitfires – to fight skilfully as 'The Few' in the Battle of Britain, exactly fit the description of young men who actually earned their knighthoods by sacrifice and courage. Their 'sword, lance and bow' were Browning .303 machine guns.

Of those 2,946 young men who took part in the Battle, 537 were killed, and before the war ended a further 791 of the Few had lost their lives.

In April 2010, the 70th anniversary year of the Battle of Britain, there were fewer than 100 left alive, and of them – as a survivor put it – 'about 17 of us are still standing'. In the next few years there will be none left, and their voices and presences will be as crumbly paper and dust.

Those left today, all of them, should be knighted.

There is a precedent. In 1857 Queen Victoria honoured 62 men in one ceremony by awarding them the Victoria Cross, the country's most prestigious medal for bravery.

Knighting the remaining 'Few' is not just honouring them. It is restoring honour to the honours system.

Brian Milton, 2010

Chapter One

TUCK'S LUCK

S hooting people in the back is perfectly acceptable behaviour for a fighter pilot on any side in any war. Catch the enemy napping, 'bounce' him out of the sun, a quick squirt of the guns – it is all part of the game. With luck the victim will explode or go down in flames for a certain 'destroyed'. In the early months of the Second World War, some British pilots thought it unfair to make a kill this way, although in May 1940, when the Germans strafed refugees in order to cause panic and clog up the roads to prevent the movement of Allied troops, this sporting instinct began to die.

Certainly a year later, and in a Hawker Hurricane of all aircraft, one of the greatest of British fighter pilots, Bob Stanford Tuck, then just 24, seemed to go right out of his way to invite a bunch of German Messerschmitt pilots to shoot him in the back. In fine summer weather on Saturday 21 June, 1941, three of them decided to take up Tuck's invitation, a decision that they would not live to regret.

There was a curious scarcity of *Luftwaffe* fighter pilots at the time, eight months after the official end of the Battle of Britain. Where once there had been swarms of German fighters and formations of bombers, just two fighter units or *Jagdgeschwader*, JG-2 and JG26 which had been Adolf Galland's high-scoring *Geschwader* during the Battle of Britain, were left to face RAF Bomber Command. Totalling between 150 and 200 aircraft, they saw the RAF bombers as a nuisance rather than a threat.

Tuck seemed deliberately to be looking for trouble when he set off alone, with no wing man, from RAF Coltishall, home of 257 Squadron, the Hurricane squadron he commanded. He flew south along the coast, past Lowestoft and Clacton-on-Sea to his old hunting ground over Southend.

Tuck, along with the South African 'Sailor' Malan, and the legless ace, Douglas Bader, was already a legend. Slim, just under six feet tall, Tuck was a 'Dandy' who had his suits and uniforms made in Savile Row. He sported a thin, 'Errol Flynn' moustache, with his cigarette holder adding to his suave image. 'Tuck's Luck' was also a part of this legend.

He had amassed an odd collection of skills that were later to save his life, including fluency in written and spoken Russian – taught by his parents' housekeeper – proficiency at boxing, gymnastics and swimming, and the art of being able to throw knives. He was also a rifle marksman, the defining skill of a great fighter pilot.

Tuck had made a poor start in the RAF. Too tense and unable to co-ordinate hands and feet on the joy-stick and rudder, he had come close to being 'washed-out' of flying training in October 1935. Then it suddenly clicked for him. Within a year he was famous as an aerobatic pilot, graded 'above average', sometimes 'exceptional', but also 'apt to be over-confident'. But his life could have easily ended on January 18, 1938, flying aerobatics in 65 Squadron's Gloster Gladiators, tough little biplanes that were front-line fighters at the time. Tuck was flying in close formation at 3,000 feet over Uckfield in Sussex with a second experienced pilot, Flying Officer Adrian Hope-Boyd, and a new sergeant pilot named Geoffrey Gaskell. Flying line-astern with Gaskell in the middle, they hit rough air and Gaskell was caught in Hope-Boyd's slip-stream. Gaskell may have over-corrected and then broke right, straight into Tuck's propeller, which killed him. The engine fell out of Tuck's Gladiator, and his wings folded around him as he began to spin out of the sky.

For long seconds, Tuck struggled to find a way out of his doomed aircraft, standing on the bucket seat, kicking in his instrument panel and heaving on the cockpit canopy without effect. The spinning increased, tearing away the wings and the canopy but when Tuck stood up the force of the air pinned him to the rear of the cockpit. Then he was suddenly plucked out of the doomed aircraft, finding himself in a slow forward somersault, pulling at his ripcord, convinced the parachute would not open before he hit the fields he could see in such detail rushing up at him. With around 300 feet (100m) to spare, his parachute opened. He then realised that he was wet through and discovered it was blood from what seemed to be his throat, before he hit the ground, twisting one ankle.

When he reached up with his right hand to feel his face, he found a loose tooth which he grasped and pulled out through a gaping hole in his cheek. His face had been cut in a straight line – probably by a loose strutting wire – from the top of his ear almost to his chin. Tuck left hospital six days later (he was back in the air three days after that), with a long, permanent scar on his face, and may have grown his moustache to draw attention away from the disfigurement. Three months after that he was to survive another mid-air collision while flying in close formation, again in a Gladiator. Tuck's Luck was being sorely tested.

Tuck established his reputation as a fighter 'ace' – a French term, technically five confirmed 'kills' – during the Battle of Britain, when he destroyed 14 German aircraft while flying Spitfires with 92 Squadron out of the most battered of RAF bases, 11 Group's Biggin Hill in Kent. He would have been happy to stay there as flight commander, but on 12 September he was promoted to Squadron Leader and sent to Debden to take over 257 Squadron, which had lost 11 of its original 20 pilots since May. Both its flight commanders had been killed the previous day. The squadron was not lacking in good pilots, but its morale was at rock-bottom. It also flew Hurricanes.

'My first reaction wasn't good. After the Spitfire, she was like flying a brick – a great, lumbering, farmyard stallion compared with a dainty and gentle thoroughbred. The Spit was so much smaller, sleeker, smoother – and a bit faster, too. It nearly broke my heart, because things seemed tough enough without having to take on 109's in a heavy great kite like this.

'But after the first few minutes I began to realise that the Hurricane had virtues of her own. She was solid, obviously able to stand up to an awful lot of punishment … steady as a rock, a wonderful gun platform … just as well-powered as any other fighter in the world, with the same Merlin engine I knew and trusted so well.

'The pilot's visibility was considerably better than in the Spit, because the nose sloped downwards more steeply from the cockpit to the spinner. This, of course, gave much better shooting conditions. The undercart was wide and, I think, stronger than the Spit's. This made landing less difficult, particularly on rough ground. The controls were much heavier and it took a lot more muscle to haul her around the sky and yet, you know, after that first hop, after I had got the feel of her, I never seemed to notice this, or any of the other differences any more.'

By force of personality and by example, within three days Tuck was leading his previously demoralised Hurricane Squadron into the most significant day's fighting of the Battle of Britain – September 15, now known as Battle of Britain Day. They shot down three 'confirmed' kills and a 'probable', with no loss, and 257 went on to become one of the highest-scoring of the RAF squadrons that year. Tuck made Pete Brothers, one of the exhausted and despairing pilots he met on his first day, into a flight commander. Brothers went on to survive the war, as one of the RAF's most successful aces.

Tuck also showed his mettle by threatening two of his Hurricane pilots with a revolver after they broke and dashed for home instead of flying alongside the rest of 257 Squadron's 12 Hurricanes as they hurled themselves into battle against hundreds of *Luftwaffe* fighters and bombers. He did not fire the pistol, although it was touch and go, but gave one of those who had fled a second chance that was gratefully accepted, the pilot in question later earning a commission. The other pilot, charged with LMF ('Lack of Moral Fibre'), a pitiless RAF term for cowardice, was stripped of his rank but retained his pilot's wings. He was later seen cleaning out a control tower. The wearing of those once much-coveted wings must have compounded his humiliation.

By the end of 1940 Stanford Tuck had two DFCs (Distinguished Flying Crosses) and a DSO (Distinguished Service Order), winning a third DFC in March, 1941, a rare achievement. He received two of his medals on 28 January from King George VI, watched by the King's two young daughters, Princesses Elizabeth and Margaret, who had followed Tuck's career. That same day, 257 Squadron was equipped with Hurricane IICs, each armed with four 20mm cannons. The arming of the Hurricanes with 20mm cannons represented a personal triumph for Tuck, who had engaged in a fierce and heated 30-second, face-to-face shouting match with Douglas Bader on the issue. Bader insisted, as if there was no point to argue, that eight 0.303 inch machine guns were perfectly adequate, ridiculing Tuck and the top-scoring ace, Sailor Malan, in front of the C-in-C Fighter Command, Sholto Douglas, for demanding cannons.

Afterwards, they apologised to each other, but Bader left shouting 'You're wrong, you know! You're both bloody well wrong!'

'Exit the Demon King', said Malan.

'Why does he have to be so obstinate all the time?' said Tuck.

'Because if he wasn't so bloody obstinate, he bloody well wouldn't be here!'

It was at the controls of one of the Hurricane IICs that Tuck flew off to tempt the *Luftwaffe* that summer's day on 21 June.

Tuck's Hurricane IIC, powered by a 1,200hp Merlin XX engine, was about at the performance limit for Hawker's great fighter. It was capable of 330 mph (531 kph), which meant that its main German fighter rival, the Messerschmitt Bf 109E, was 30 mph (48 kph) faster, giving the German pilot the choice of whether or not to join battle. The Bf 109 had a slightly higher service ceiling at 36,500 feet (11,000m) but, crucially, the Hurricane could out-turn both the Bf 109 and the Spitfire. A classic German tactic emerged called 'Dive-and-Zoom', dive on a Hurricane, shoot at it, and then zoom upwards at a faster speed, because Bf 109 pilots did not want to take a chance of being out-turned. The 109's could not do the same to a Spitfire.

It was later said that Bob Stanford Tuck was looking for a fight after he reached Southend around 1.50 pm, and then turned left and set out across the sea. German-occupied Ostend was about 100 miles (161 km) away on a course of east-by-south, and a prudent pilot would have gobbled up all the height he could before getting near the *Luftwaffe* bases spread all along the coast. In Sailor Malan's definitive 'Ten Rules of Air-Fighting', height is everything, because with it comes control and the initiative in a fight. 'Beware the Hun in the Sun' is another of those rules. The canniest, and longer-lived, aces also chose their moment when to fight and when to flee – but Tuck had a reputation for never refusing combat.

So what was he doing, down at a thousand feet in what one German ace called 'a slow old puffer' (although that ace, Hans-Otto Lessing, was ultimately shot down and killed by a Hurricane) except trailing his coat?

The first German Bf 109 should have got him on its initial pass. Tuck's biographer, Larry Forrester, wrote the story 15 years later, describing a number of 20mm cannon shells bursting through Tuck's Hurricane:

'At last the din and the shuddering did stop, his mind was instantly clear and his reflexes working smoothly and swiftly. A 109 flashed by close underneath him. He put the stick forward. The sight dropped on to a flat-topped canopy. He checked the turn-and-bank in the space of a heart's beat – to ensure he wasn't skidding – and squeezed the button. The Messerschmitt waggled angrily under the blast of metal. The canopy crumpled like melting cellophane. It gave itself up to gravity and the deep, dark sea.

'The moment he was sure it was going down he threw the Hurricane into a steep turn. Somehow he knew there were others behind him.

'As he banked, bright tubes of tracer burnt through the air scant feet beyond the Perspex. He twisted his neck and saw another 109 very close. It had a yellow spinner, hallmark of a crack squadron. It was travelling too fast to get inside his turn. He let it go by underneath, slammed the stick over and cart-wheeled after it. He had not been in a real 'split-arse' dog-fight for months – he would soon discover if the old hound could still bite…!

'The German dived to about a hundred feet, went over on its side and pulled right for all he was worth. Nice flying. Tuck hauled hard and followed round. Round and round. The sea was a flashing vertical wall rushing past his starboard wingtip. The poles span and the sunlight dimmed, a tremendous pressure on the top of his head and his shoulders rammed him down in his seat. The engine screamed. His eyes ached. The red lines of his gun-sight were blurred and bent.

'Then the 109 took off a little of its bank. Tuck followed suit and everything came back into sharp focus. The Hun was trapped in the sight. They were still in a steep turn, less than 50 feet off the sea, nevertheless he checked his turn-and-bank needle and centred it with a tiny adjustment of the rudder before he fired. Two seconds worth of 20mm sent the Messerschmitt straight into the water. Tuck flew through the plume of spray it raised.

'He pulled up quickly, aileroned the opposite way, then throttled back. Immediately he was hit from the left. The throttle lever was blown out of his hand. The kick of it numbed every fibre of his left arm, like a high-voltage shock. The reflector plate in the firing sight exploded and a chip of it embedded itself in his forehead. The door and the hood of the Hurricane flew off, and a tornado raged in his cockpit.

'The third German flashed underneath and made a wide circle. The Hurricane's engine was missing badly and he had no throttle so he could not chase it. He just climbed slowly and watched the Bf 109 come round and start towards him, head-on. It was toe-to-toe stuff now.

'The sunlight made the 109's yellow nose shine like a golden bulls-eye – an archer's 'gold' he thought with mild, irrational amusement. He hoped there was enough ammunition to give the bastard one more good smack on the snout. He was being wistful now. In his heart he was pretty sure this really was the end of the road; the Hurricane just couldn't take any more punishment. He had pushed his luck too far this time – this was the dreaded moment when Fortune would desert him.

'He had no gun-sight but the turn-and-bank was still working. He wiped a trickle of blood from his left eyebrow and made himself relax.

'Charging through the summer sky at a composite speed of around 600 mph (965 kph), the two fighters slugged it out for perhaps five or six seconds. Marvellously, the German missed, Tuck's shells shattered themselves deep amid the whirling steel parts of the Daimler-Benz.

'The Messerschmitt made a shaky turn and disappeared eastwards in a shallow dive, bleeding glycol, without which the engine would soon over-heat and seize. The German did not have many miles to go, he would probably make the coast all right. Tuck knew he would never make his own coast.

'The Hurricane's engine was spluttering, crackling, cutting out altogether for seconds at a time. Temperatures and pressures were climbing fast. The radio was dead. The speed was falling steadily, 130, 125, 120. Something back towards the tail was flapping madly. Oil and glycol drenched his legs. The wind tore at his clothes, beat in his face. Blood filled his left eye and ran down the side of his nose into his mouth. His left arm had no feeling in it, and the whole arm was a frigid ache.

'Yet as he coaxed the Hurricane's nose round to the north-west, he was full of deep, warm gladness. Two victories, one damaged.

'The old hound was still in form!

'And he was still alive!

'The wrecked Hurricane did her best for him, stumbling through the shimmering air for an incredible time, until he could actually see a smudge of the south-east coast of England. Then the starboard aileron fell off and dull-roaring flames started coming through around his boots. He had about eight hundred feet. Ah, well, over the side it would have to be….'

Though quite battered, Tuck successfully parachuted into the sea, and was found two hours later, asleep in his dinghy, by a coal barge on its way from Gravesend to Brightlingsea, south-east of the Roman town of Colchester.

In effect, that day's fight marked a high point for the Hurricane as a front-line fighter. From that time they faded as the principal fighter opponent to the Germans, as new marques of Bf 109s and FW 190s came on to the scene. Hurricanes were sent to do their work in other theatres of war, the Middle East, Greece, Burma, Singapore, and Russia. In defending Britain's airspace during the Battle of Britain, however, the Hurricane had established its legend. The period would be referred to as the 'Spitfire Summer' but it had, in fact, been the Hawker Hurricane pilots who had won the Battle of Britain, shooting down more German aircraft than all the other British fighters put together.

These heroic pilots, and their neglected aircraft, deserve far more recognition.

Chapter Two

LAST WITNESSES

The glory days for the Hawker Hurricane lasted from the beginning of the Second World War in September, 1939, through the Battle of France to the end of 1940, about two months after the official end of the Battle of Britain. During that period, the Hurricane starred as a front-line fighter, able to compete against any other fighter in the world. It was virtually the only British fighter not annihilated during the Battle of France, though losses were heavy, and Spitfires had been held back by the head of Fighter Command, Hugh Dowding, despite immense pressure from Winston Churchill.

In the Battle of Britain, Hurricanes scored the highest number of RAF victories, accounting for 1,593 out of the 2,739 total claimed. By the beginning of 1941 German pilots had their measure. It did not do for a Bf 109 to get into a dog-fight with Hurricanes because the Hurricane could out-turn it, but the Bf 109 pilots' 'dive and zoom' tactics put Hurricane pilots at a severe disadvantage.

Yet those crucial months in 1939/40 were everything.

Without the Hurricane, the Battle of Britain would have been lost.

There is an exact figure calculated, 2,946, for the number of young men who flew fighters and fought in the Battle of Britain. Those eligible for this elite list must have made an operational flight against the enemy in Britain between 10 July and 31 October 1940. In February, 2010, fewer than a hundred of those once-young warriors were still alive, and the obituary pages seemed weekly to carry accounts of more of their deaths.

In putting together this story, I met ten former Battle of Britain Hurricane pilots to look back over 70 years, to make judgements and tell stories about the aircraft they flew, the last of the old-fashioned fighters.

Some were captured and made prisoners of war, and many went on to fly Spitfires, the Hurricane's great stablemate. Three were among the highest-scoring fighter aces of the war. One was shot down twice in a week during the Battle of Britain, once by our own anti-aircraft guns, a second time by a

Bf 109. He went on to be shot down a third time flying one of the 'children' of the Hurricane, this time by an American fighter in a 'friendly fire' incident.

I was conscious, coming face-to-face with each of them (18 in total, including Hurricane pilots who fought later in the war) that they are among our few remaining knights of the air. I have called them the 'Last Witnesses', men able to give a modern generation the last live insight to the air war between 1939 and 1945. In a few years all will be gone, and then such evidence as is found in museums and memoirs will be all that remains to tell their stories.

Three of them flew Hurricanes in the Battle of France, from the first day of the war until France's surrender on 25 June 1940. Though exhausted by the effect of the German *Blitzkrieg* victory, they went on to fight through the Battle of Britain. Among the others are individual stories from Hurricane pilots who defended Malta, fought in the Western Desert, were captured in the bitter aftermath of the Japanese advance through the Dutch East Indies (Indonesia) and took the fight back to the Axis powers when the tide of war turned in Burma against the Japanese. The Hurricane then had to find new roles away from aerial combat, concentrating on ground attack.

These are their early years; first the three who fought in the Battle of France:

BILLY DRAKE

Known as 'Shark Leader' in ECR Baker's *Fighter Aces of the RAF*, Billy was born in London on 20 January 1917. He was 92 years old when I met him, and had given up skiing only in 2008. An only child and son of a GP, he was educated at Stroud Grammar School, but expelled after a fight with another boy. His parents sent him to a school in Switzerland, where be became fluent in French and German. His parents were against him joining the RAF, but he signed on in 1936 for four years on a Short Service Commission at £400 a year. The RAF was in the middle of a recruiting drive by then, desperate for a bigger pool of pilots. Most existing RAF pilots came from a privileged background; as one Warrant Officer put it to a would-be flyer at the time, 'You've got to be a Gentleman to fly, my lad!'

Drake did 50 hours flying at Hamble on a biplane, open-cockpit Avro Tutor, which replaced the ancient Avro 504K. He was commissioned an Acting Pilot Officer on probation, and went to RAF Netherhaven – 6 FTS (Flying Training School) – for nine months flying on Hawker Harts and Furies.

Drake was posted to 1 Squadron, and flew 250 hours on the biplane Hawker Fury, in which he nearly went to war during the Munich Crisis of

1938. Number 1 Squadron was among the last of the period to be converted to the Hurricane Mark 1, but one of the first four Hurricane squadrons sent to France, leaving on 5 September, just two days after war was declared.

Billy Drake, one of the main characters of Paul Richey's classic book, *Fighter Pilot*, had amassed 110 hours on Hurricanes when he was thrown into the Phoney War.

He was 22 years old.

Drake:

'We had quite a few hours already in the aeroplane and had been advised that we were nearly as good as the 109s, the chief enemy we were up against. We came to this belief because the man who advised us just before the war – after the Munich Crisis – was the British Air Attaché in Berlin. He lectured all the RAF fighter squadrons on what he knew about the German Air Force.

'We had no armour plating behind our seats to begin with, but did not even think about it. We became aware of the need for armour when we were in France. Then we heard that a very senior officer had said "Don't give them any armour because the one thing that they will attempt to do is to bale out if they're ever attacked." That attitude was common in the First World War when senior officers said "Don't give pilots parachutes" because the one thing they would do is use them to avoid any contact with the German Air Force. That senior officer was subsequently sacked.'

PETER AYERST

Only surviving member of 73 Squadron which accompanied 1, 85 and 87 squadrons to France at the beginning of the war, was born in Westcliff on Sea on 4 November, 1920. He was 88 years old when we met. Subject of the book *Spirit of the Blue* and an RAF poster-boy in 1940, Peter's father was a City gent, while his mother's grandfather had made a great deal of money in construction. Peter went to a grammar school, Westcliff High, leaving at 17, not an academic but good at sport. He played rugby as a centre three-quarter and favoured the quarter mile as a runner. He went into the export business in the City, a job arranged by his father, then saw one of the frequent RAF appeals to become a pilot, offering short-service commissions. He applied, passed and started flying Miles Magisters on 6 October 1938, on a small grass airfield called Gatwick.

After three months and 62 hours training on the Magister, he was sent as an Acting Pilot Officer to Grantham in Lincolnshire for the first course on North American Harvards at 12 FTS, where he amassed 95 flying hours, including 2 hours 20 minutes solo night flying.

Ayerst made his first Hurricane flight just ten days before the war started, and after two more flights for a total of 3 hours 30 minutes, was sent into battle with 73 Squadron. His section leader was the briefly famous 'Cobber' Kain, first RAF ace of the Second World War. Ayerst was 18 years old.

Ayerst:

'We had the old 2-bladed airscrew, as all the squadrons did in those days. It seemed to take quite a long time on take-off to get airborne, but once in the air it was okay. We didn't envy Spitfires because they hadn't come in then – there were only two squadrons of Spitfires and they were both at Duxford – 19 and 66 Squadrons. We didn't know much about the Spitfire to be quite honest.

'Hurricanes were a very strong and solid aircraft. Of course, in those days it had the fabric fuselage and ailerons, and the outer portions of the wing were fabric. At the time we thought it a good aircraft, and it proved itself in the four squadrons that were sent to France.'

PETER HAIRS

Who worked throughout the Great Depression, earning up to £50 a year in Barclays Bank in 1933, was born on 10 July 1915 at Thornton Heath, South London. He was 93 years old when we met. His father was a Merchandise Manager at Dickens and Jones. Peter left school at 16, worked for two years as an apprentice estate agent, and then for Barclays. In 1936, convinced there would be war with Germany, he wrote to the adjutant of 601 City of London Squadron, unaware that it was, in fact, a gentleman's club whose members saw flying as a form of aerial fox hunting.

Not coming from one of the prominent families that supplied such Auxiliary squadrons, he was rejected, and joined the RAF Volunteer Reserve (RAFVR), which was actively recruiting. He started flying at Gatwick grass field in 1937, buying an engagement ring with his £25 retaining fee. Hairs learned first on Tiger Moths, then flew Hawker Harts, Furies and Hinds, all predecessors of the Hurricane. He was awarded his full wings on 10 December 1939. Commissioned as a Pilot Officer, he was sent to an 11 Group pool – the RAF group that bore the brunt of the fighting in 1940 – for a conversion course to North American Harvards. He then completed 30 hours on Hurricanes before being posted to RAF Tangmere on 25 January 1940, to join 501 Squadron. He made his first operational patrols the day the German *Blitzkreig* started, 10 May, when 501 Squadron was sent to France.

Hairs:

'The Hurricane had a pretty good name at the end of 1939. It was a thrill to sit in one, having been told what to press, which levers to pull and so on. To take off and fly what was at that stage the best fighter in the world, was terrific. It was at least 70 mph (120 kph) faster than anything I had flown before, a stable aeroplane, far more so than a Spitfire. The fore and aft control on a Spitfire was sensitive, while in a Hurricane lateral control was very sensitive, so it could roll very well. I can make this comparison because I did fly Spitfires later on in the war.

'Coming up against a 109, they were faster than us and we did feel disadvantaged, but that was usually because we found that we were lower than the 109s when the fighting began. At one stage of the war, they used to come over and protect their bombers. We attacked the bombers, to break them up as far as possible, and then pick individual targets.

'In the meantime the 109s came down and sorted us out.'

The Battle of Britain officially started on 10 July and ended on 30 October 1940. Another seven Last Witnesses fought in it, among them two of the higher scoring pilots.

BOB DOE

Credited with the third highest score of victories in the Battle of Britain, initially on Spitfires, and author of *Bob Doe – Fighter Pilot*, was born in Reigate in Surrey on 10 March 1920. He was 89 years old when we met. His father was a gardener, and, after leaving school at the age of 14, Bob entered the difficult employment conditions of the Great Depression. He secured a job through his father's boss's connections as an office boy on the *News of the World*.

Despite a complete lack of education, Bob Doe joined the RAFVR in March 1938, making his first solo flight on 4 June, clocking up 85 flying hours on Hawker Harts. He applied for and won a short service commission to join the RAF in January 1939. He trained with 15 E&RFTS (Elementary & Reserve Flying Training School) at RAF Redhill, in Surrey and did his combat training with 6 FTS at RAF Little Rissington.

Bob Doe:

'It was very difficult as an office boy to get in, but I persisted. I walked into the old Air Ministry building and told them, "I want to be an officer, please, and a pilot." Every time they realised I had no education they passed me to a different office, and I finished up with a very senior man. I knew he was senior because he had a hat on the desk with lots of scrambled egg on it, and I was with him for over half an hour. We got on very well, he liked me, and eventually he said, "Because of your lack of education you are going to have to sit an exam here in the Ministry, which I will set for you. Can you come back in two weeks time?"

'He then took a book out of his drawer, marked a paragraph, and said, "Before you come, learn that paragraph by heart." It was a paragraph about the "moment of an arm", where you put your foot on the pedal of a bicycle and its forces work on the fulcrum. I learned that by heart, went back for the exam, which was very simple and basic, apart from one question.

'This was, "What is the Moment of the Arm?" I knew that answer verbatim, and that's how I became an officer in the RAF.'

BOB FOSTER
Later Chairman of the Battle of Britain Fighter Association and author of *Tally-Ho*, was born in London on 14 May 1920. Bob was 89 when I met him. His father had been a Sapper – an engineer – in the Great War, and won a DCM at great cost. He was out in no man's land near Ypres in 1915, cutting barbed wire, when he was shot in the right leg. He lay there in great pain for 24 hours before being rescued, but the whole leg was lost and he was on crutches for the rest of his life.

What happened to his father – a real horror of trench warfare – influenced Bob Foster's decision to join the RAF. He learned to fly on a primitive Avro Tutor before going on to fly Hawker Harts and Audaxes, which he thought wonderful aircraft to fly but useless as far as the war was concerned. They had fixed undercarriages, open cockpit, biplane, just a basic aeroplane.

Bob Foster:
'Before converting to modern fighters we did a five-hour course on North American Harvards, which had all mod-cons, including retractable undercarriage and flaps and was a monoplane. I made my first flight on a Harvard at the beginning of June 1940, and went to a place called Sutton Bridge, a Hurricane OTU, on 18 June 1940. The Battle of France was over by then. The French signed an Armistice at about that time. At 20 years of age I was learning to fly a Hurricane, which I thought was only just a cut above the Audaxes and Harts I had learned to fly on.'

MIKE CROSKELL
Who found the love of his life the day he was shot down at the height of the Battle of Britain, was born on 13 September 1920, in York. He was 88 when I met him. The younger of two boys, he came from a railway family, a

'reserved occupation' during the war. Mike had three ambitions while at St Peter's, a public school in the City of York; to drive a car at 100 mph, to fly an aircraft solo, and to make a century at cricket for his school. He left at the age of 16 to become an apprentice on electrical signalling on the railways, then an apprentice draughtsman for Blackburn Aircraft, joining the RAFVR in 1937.

As a sergeant pilot he flew Harts, Hinds and Audaxes, all biplanes. He was called up when the war started and posted to 213 Hurricane Squadron in December 1939. The squadron flew fighter patrols over the North Sea and in May 1940 sent a detachment to France as part of Churchill's doomed attempt to save the French. They moved south early in June, first to Exeter with 10 Group, then to the embattled 11 Group airfield at Tangmere early in September. Mike fought throughout the rest of the year.

Croskell:
'The CO said, "Have you flown an aeroplane with flaps and retractable under-carriage?"

'I said, "No, sir."

'He said, "Better go to Aston Down and learn how."

'So I went to Aston Down and then came back and joined 213 Squadron. I was 20 years old. I remember being shown the Hurricane. The flight commander took me out to his own aeroplane and showed me the cockpit. I sat in it, he stood on the wing and said: "Now this is my aeroplane, if you break it I will break your bloody neck."

'I did fly it. I just did a circuit and landing. It was an easy aeroplane to fly. The Harvard wasn't difficult, the Hurricane was a bit hairier but otherwise quite a friendly old thing.'

JOHN ELLACOMBE

Born in Northern Rhodesia (now Zambia) in southern Africa on 28 February 1920, into a well-to-do family, and 89 years old when I met him. He went to a public school, Dionysian College in Cape Town, and was one of four boys from the school selected for the RAF in 1939. He arrived in Europe with his mother, who was intent, at that fraught period, on a grand tour of Europe which she made with her son.

John was inducted in the RAF in August 1939 at Jesus College Cambridge, where he learned navigation, then trained at RAF Yatesbury in Dorset to amass 100 hours on Tiger Moths. He was judged among the best of his course, which included Canadians and New Zealanders, and sent in early July 1940 to North Weald and 151 Squadron, which had been badly battered

in the fighting in May over France. His station commander was the famous
Victor Beamish.

Ellacombe:

'I was taken to Victor Beamish's office, and he said: "I don't know anything
about you, but I am delighted to see you. I'll get you converted and we will fly
together very soon, because I am flying with the squadrons."

'I came to regard Beamish, a 38-year-old Irishman well beyond the
accepted fighting age range yet constantly in battle, as one of the truly great
men of the war.

'We converted there to fly Hurricanes, on one of the most active
fighter fields in the country, and about three weeks later, with just 25 hours
experience on type, I was in my first combat.

'The Hurricane was a very stable aeroplane, quite easy to land once you
got the feel for it. You had to land in a semi-stall position, otherwise you
would start bouncing, but once you learned all that it was a delightful aircraft
to fly.'

BILL GREEN

Son of a professional soldier who had been invalided out of France in 1916
with terminal sugar diabetes and died within a month of Bill's birth, was
born in Bristol on 23 April 1917, his father's only child. He was 92 when I
met him. His mother had to scrub floors and work in a milliners to make
ends meet. He left school at 14, working as an errand boy and then for his
stepfather, whom his mother married in 1922, before joining the Auxiliary
Squadron, 501, at Filton as an aero engine fitter with the rank of LAC, Leading
Aircraftsman. In 1938, just after Munich, the aircraft fitter he worked with
applied to become a pilot with the RAFVR.

Green:

'Of course, I was absolutely green with envy – that's not a pun – and so I
wrote to my CO and said I wanted to do the same. This was ridiculous,
audacious and stupid, because had he said, "Okay, get on with it," they would
have said, "At what age did you leave school?"

'That would have been the end of it, because I was not educationally
qualified. The CO said to me, "Wouldn't you want to stay with the squadron
and fly? I am getting an establishment for six NCO pilots. Wouldn't you
rather stay with us and be one of them with 501 Squadron?" That was in
December, 1938.

'I started flying in January 1939. In March 1940 I was sent to 3 FTS
at South Cerney where I did another 100 hours on Hawker Harts and the

Audax. I never fired guns, never used oxygen, never used the radio, and flew with no enclosed cockpit, no flaps, no retractable undercarriage, no VP (Variable Pitch) airscrew.

'In the middle of our training, France collapsed.'

GRAHAM LEGGATT

Who was to take part in the 'Great Italian Turkey Shoot' late in 1940 after the official end of the Battle of Britain, was born in London on 14 February 1921. He was 87 when I met him. He served a year's studentship before the war started at the main Hawker Aircraft manufacturing plant at Brooklands, where Sydney Camm did his design work. Leggatt joined the RAFVR when war broke out, was trained at RAF Montrose in Scotland on Masters, and then was asked by the Chief Flying Instructor – CFI – what sort of fighter aircraft he wanted to fly.

Leggatt:
'Since I had a lot to do with the Hurricane in the immediate pre-war days, I seized the opportunity get into a Hurricane squadron. I dare say others chose Spitfires back then, though it was not the glamorous aeroplane that it is today. Quite the reverse. We were totally content with our Hurricanes, both as an operational training unit, and as far as I know, in a squadron.

'I never heard anybody say anything against Hurricanes.

'It was a pleasing aeroplane to fly, not difficult, it would do what you wanted it to do. Initially, of course, it was just magic. The first flight was pure joy. There I was, having spent more than a year involved in the manufacture of Hurricanes, eventually sitting in one, flying over the Gloucestershire countryside where I did my conversion course. It was just incredible. It was difficult to believe that I was really doing this, actually flying a Hurricane. I doubt if many of the other chaps felt quite that way.'

One Hurricane had flown to Egypt during the Phoney War before France fell, and before Italy entered the game, but after the winter of 1940/41 hundreds of Hurricanes were being deployed abroad, packed in crates to be distributed by ship throughout the fighting zones, including the Middle East, Malta, and Greece. When the United States entered the war after the Japanese attacked Pearl Harbor on 7 December 1941, crates of Hurricanes were diverted to Singapore and Burma. The following Last Witnesses had the edifying experience of flying Hurricanes in the Mediterranean, Middle East and Far East theatres.

WILLIAM SWAN

Born in north London on 22 October 1920, Bill's father was a librarian at the British Museum. When he left Harrow County Grammar School at 18, he went into the British Museum, but when war broke out he walked from the Museum to the Air Ministry – a short distance – and said, 'I want to be a pilot.' They said, 'Everyone wants to be a pilot.'

Bill Swan said he designed aircraft, he built model aircraft and they flew, and 'if that doesn't warrant being a pilot, I don't know what does.' He trained at Babbacombe at Number 5 Initial Training Wing, Torquay, then at 4 ITW at Paignton, and finally at 19 Elementary Flying Training School – EFTS – at Sealand.

Swan:
'I came out of Sealand in April 1941 – too late to be in the Battle of Britain – and as a sergeant pilot I went to SFTS at Terne Hill, then 56 OTU at Sutton Bridge, which took me up to October 1941, when I joined 43 Squadron at Acklington. There was a great deal of organising and re-organising as the shape of the war developed that year. Within a month I was moved to Ouston, near Newcastle Upon Tyne with 232 Squadron, then being formed to go out and save Singapore.

'Eventually the Squadron was taken via boat to West Africa, by air across to Khartoum in a Pan Am Dakota, where we were connected to Hurricanes. We did practice deck landings on the outline of a carrier marked on the sand on an airfield just outside Khartoum itself, called Gordon's Tree.

'From there we flew in a Blenheim from Khartoum to Port Sudan, and on to the carrier HMS Indomitable, where I was taken ill with amoebic dysentery and refused permission to fly off with the squadron when we they were sent to the Far East.

'This decision almost certainly saved my life.'

TERENCE KELLY

Suffered three years as a Japanese PoW and was a few miles away when the atomic bomb exploded over Hiroshima in 1945. He was born on 13 July 1920 and educated at the City of London School. He was 89 when we met. He applied to join the RAF – 'there was a great queue' – and trained on Magisters and then Miles Masters at Montrose in Scotland, followed by Hurricanes at Sutton Bridge.

On 1 May 1941, at the age of 20, he joined 3 Squadron at Martlesham, and did 40 hours of Channel patrols on Hurricane IIs. More Channel sweeps, this time over France, followed his transfer to 258 Hurricane Squadron at Kenley in Kent, and in a dozen 'rhubarbs'; 'I shot at the Germans, they shot at me but they didn't hit me.'

Kelly had 220 hours flying time on Hurricanes when the squadron was posted to the Middle East, but then the Japanese attacked Pearl Harbor in December 1941 and they were diverted to Singapore.

Kelly:

'The first time I took a Hurricane up, coming in to land the wheels wouldn't come down. I could see from the lights indicating wheels down – they were not on. I had to go up and muck about, a flight of 90 minutes in total, much longer than a normal first solo, before finally getting it down. Not a serious threat to my life, but it was my first Hurricane flight.

'I thought it was a wonderful aeroplane. I never had any doubts or complaints about it, and it never let one down. I had more than 200 hours in Hurricanes before I went abroad, including the occasional exciting things, but nothing tremendous. All my real action on Hurricanes was overseas.'

ERIC BATCHELAR

Spent most of his fighting career flying Hurricanes against the Japanese in Burma, was born in Hammersmith, west London, on 7 September 1921. He spent much of his teens in poor health but was educated at Wembley County Grammar School, and signed on for aircrew training at Uxbridge in July 1940, without telling his parents. He was sent on the first flying course run by the RAF at Medicine Hat in Alberta, Canada – crossing the Atlantic in a huge convoy with battleship escorts. There he amassed 80 hours on Harvards before being commissioned and sent back to England to train on Hurricanes with 52 OTU at Debden.

He had one sortie against a German intruder – 'at last!' – flying a 12-gun Hurricane IIB, but failed to catch it. Flying with 135 Squadron, he was *en route* to the Middle East in a convoy when war was declared by Japan, and they were diverted to the Far East.

Batchelar:

'My CO was an Australian, "Bush" Cotton, who later wrote a book called *Hurricanes Over Burma*. Three Hurricane squadrons went to West Africa. We got off the ship at a place called Takarartee, a big airfield and base, and from there we had to get ourselves across to Cairo by whatever means. Chaps went different ways. I was lucky enough to get a seat in a BOAC Loadstar, which gave us a round robin tour through the Sahara Desert, and from there we did the rest of the journey up the Nile, partly by boat, and partly by train to Cairo.

'We picked up our Hurricanes at Heliopolis. At that time it was one of our front-line fighter aircraft. I always had a nice comfortable feeling getting into and sitting in the Hurricane. It had reasonable room in the cockpit, even for a long chap like me. It was nicely responsive on the controls and, above everything else, as was proved again and again, it had the wonderful ability to absorb battle damage and get you back to base. It became a good friend right from the start, and I loved it more and more.

'When it was our turn to go east, we left in batches of six, led by a Blenheim as navigator. Our Hurricanes had long-range tanks fitted. We went from Cairo to Lither, to Habanya, and then down the Gulf to Bahrain, across to a little place called Jawanyi, then Karachi, on via Jodhpur, Allahabad, Delhi, to Dumdum the airfield at Calcutta. From there we went to Toungoo in northern Burma, and then finally the last stage down to Diminglegon.

'At Bahrain, I do remember it was just a landing strip marked out by oil barrels, with great sandy dunes all around everywhere. Now, of course, it's a magnificent modern airport.'

GRAHAM SKELLUM

Father was a labourer in the Pottery industry and left his mother when Graham was six months old. Born in Staffordshire on 16 December 1922, Graham was 86 when I met him. Graham grew up with only an elementary education to become a Post Office apprentice engineer, a reserved occupation 'but I realised I would be called up eventually.' He joined the RAF as a sergeant pilot, called up on the 6 April 1942 – 'I remember the date because it was Easter Monday' – reporting to Lords Cricket Ground.

Skellum:

'I finished up being trained on Harvards as a pilot in South Africa. When we qualified, a certain percentage of us received a commission. I didn't set my store out to get one. I thought my Potteries accent would be against me, so why try? I think later in the war I earned the right to a commission, because I was good at my job, I suppose.

'I was delighted to be posted to fly Hurricanes in Burma. They were easier to control than Spitfires, but I was on ground-attack, not fighters. At that time of the war, the Hurricane was out of its league as a combat fighter.'

COLIN ELLIS

Born on 18 September 1923, the son of a small businessman in Plaistow, in the East End of London. He was 85 when I met him, youngest of the Last Witnesses. Ellis was 15 years old when war broke out, and evacuated to Woodbridge in Suffolk. He volunteered for the RAF in January 1942, was deferred service until he was 19 in September that year, and as a cog in the massive Empire aircrew training system, learned to fly in Rhodesia on Tiger Moths and Harvards.

He got his wings, was commissioned and was made an instructor. It was only after a 'fuss' that he was sent north, overland, to Hurricane training in Palestine. His first Hurricane solo of 50 minutes was on 24 April 1944, learning photo-reconnaissance, photography, spotting for guns 'and to avoid having a fight.'

Ellis:
'Four of the course were summoned to go to India to join 28 Squadron on tactical reconnaissance. Imperial Airways flew us to Karachi in an Armstrong Whitworth Ensign in June 1944. There we kicked heels for six weeks. We were sent to Bombay for another six weeks, which I spent by joining clubs, but it was 12 weeks off flying, so I was sent on a refresher course in Poona, a two-day train journey.

'We obviously had too many replacements for not a lot of casualties, so there was another two-day train journey to Ranchi for a low-level attack course of 5/6 weeks.

'I was now 21 years old and it was September 1944. I arrived at Imphal by lorry. Imphal and Kohima had been fought over and won, stopping the invasion of India. Kohima looked like the Somme. From Imphal in late September, 1944, I was posted with three friends to 113 Squadron at Palel, at the southern end of the Imphal Valley. I did a sector recce on 6 October 1944.

'On 8 October I had my first ops, flying a Hurricane IIC with four 20mm cannon and two 250lb bombs, to bomb and strafe Japanese bunker positions.'

GAWAIN DOUGLAS
Oldest of the Last Witnesses but one of the last to see action, was born prematurely on a train journey in England on 18 December 1914. He was 94 when I met him. His father, having run away to sea at the age of 16, was a senior marine surveyor in Hong Kong, and Gawain spent his early years in China, first Bejing, then Hong Kong. His family moved back to England in 1923, where he was educated at Elizabeth College in Guernsey, a public school catering for the children of the Empire. He was captain of cricket, hockey, football and was a boxer.

He won a Cadetship at Sandhurst in 1933, and in February 1935 he was posted to India, attached to the Royal Norfolk Regiment, 'a test of sorts, to ensure I wouldn't let the side down', and then 15th Lancers, an Indian

Cavalry regiment. He took up flying as a hobby while he was working as ADC to Lord Erskine, the British Governor of Madras.

Douglas:

'When war started in Europe in 1939, it felt a long way away, though we read about it in newspapers daily, even if out of date. In 1940 my cavalry regiment was posted to the Middle East, but after being an ADC, I had to go back for training first. A request went around, looking for qualified pilots, I volunteered, was seconded to the RAF on 17 November 1941, 20 days before Pearl Harbor. I dropped in rank from an Acting Major to Pilot Officer.

'I completed flying training in Audaxes and Harts in June, 1942. Then the Viceroy's youngest daughter, Bunty Hope, invited me to the Vice-Regal House, and at a cocktail party I went down with both malaria and jaundice. I was not able to get to a squadron for three years, and risked a court martial to do so.'

TOM ADAMS

Was to fly 'clapped out Hurricanes' in Burma. Born on 11 August 1922, Tom was 86 when I met him. The youngest of three children, his mother died when he was 12. His father sold vacuum cleaners and was later a bookmaker. Tom was a grammar school boy who left school at 16 and was an apprentice surveyor until being called up into the RAF seven days after his nineteenth birthday, on 18 August 1941.

He was trained to fly in the United States under the Arnold Scheme, but instead of being sent to a fighting unit he became an instructor, flying Hurricane IIs with eight machine-guns, and Hurricane IVs with four 20mm cannon, at the US Navy base at Pensacola, and then on a British base in Arizona. He managed a posting to India in 1945, for a refresher at Poona. His first operational flight was nearly a month after VE Day, 5 June 1945, flying ground attack on Army co-operation.

Adams:

'It was quite something to be a pilot of a Hurricane, after having been instructing for quite a long while. I think it was fun. You were aware you only had one engine. You went up in pairs, so to that extent, if anything happened, somebody else knew about it. There was no opposition in the air from the Japanese, that had all ceased probably four months before, around January 1945. That was not a worry.

'I thought Hurricanes were very reliable, even though they could be clapped-out. The ground-staff's mess was called the 'Clapped Hurric-Inn', but providing you were given a kite to fly, well, in my case, every time, they worked. I never had any worry about that Merlin engine. It always did what I wanted it to do. You're flying very low, a couple of trees high off the ground, and you do want it to keep going. The odd person who didn't come back wasn't there to tell the tale and you did not know what had happened to him. I thought it was a super engine.

'I have seen Merlins at Duxford recently, and they still sound beautiful.'

ERIC BROWN

Widely acknowledged as being among the greatest of all test pilots and known across the aviation world as 'Winkle' because of his diminutive size, was born on 21 January 1919, in Leith in Scotland. He was 90 years old when we met, the son of a balloon observer in the Great War, one of the most dangerous of all aviation jobs. Eric was a sports star at his school in Edinburgh, and a brilliant linguist in German and French – he actually interrogated Herman Goering after the war.

He amassed 200 flying hours at Edinburgh University Air Squadron before applying for the RAF. Instead, he went into the Royal Navy, was one of only two survivors in his squadron when his aircraft carrier *HMS Audacity* was sunk in 1941, secured a DSC after shooting down two 4-engine Condors, and went on to test-fly more different types of aircraft – 487 – than anyone in the world. He remains an adviser to the Royal Navy on the latest two British aircraft carriers.

> *Brown:*
> 'The wonderful thing about the Hurricane is that it arrived at an important moment for the country. We were just about to enter the war and here we had a fighter which was literally going to save the country in the Battle of Britain. You realise, of course, the tremendous part it played there. Indeed, not only there, but throughout the entire war.
>
> 'This aircraft really was a stayer. It operated in virtually every field of operations. If you tally up at the end of the war, it actually destroyed more enemy aircraft than the Spitfire, throughout all the theatres of war. This is not just in the Battle of Britain, this was throughout the war.'

The Last Witnesses are the main storytellers for the Hurricane's career, from its beginnings as an idea in 1933, through its glory days when it was among the greatest of all fighter aircraft, to the other roles chosen for it when it could no longer live with the foremost aerial fighters. Some of the storytellers are great Hun-killers, to use a Great War term, others are lucky to be alive. After the war the Hurricane disappeared with indecent haste.

But where did it begin?

Chapter Three

THE RAF BETWEEN THE WARS

Almost as soon as the RAF was founded on 1 April 1918, it had to fight for its life, not against the Germans, but against the Royal Navy and the British Army. It had been put together from the Army's RFC – Royal Flying Corps – and the RNAS – the Royal Navy Air Service, acquiring assets from each service, assets that it had to fight to retain. It is still conducting that fight in 2010.

Both Navy and Army argued that the RAF had no separate role in a fight, that it wasted resources, that it contributed little or nothing to their own theatres of war, and that it should, in any case, be under their command. The in-fighting was fierce and bitter, and that period of struggle continued until the rise of the German *Luftwaffe*, a different type of separate force from the German Army and Navy, from 1935 onwards.

The Royal Air Force had briefly been the largest air force in the world at the 11 November Armistice in 1918, but it quickly shrank. During a long, bleak decade, its major champion was Hugh Trenchard. Born in 1873, Trenchard served as a soldier in the Boer War and learned to fly at the age of 40, but became the founding father of the Royal Air Force. He fought much of the First World War as the head of the Royal Flying Corps in France and, like ground commanders of the time, he believed the massed offensive was the key to victory. In Trenchard's case, this meant offensive war whatever the odds. RFC aircraft were always fighting over enemy lines, taking the war to the Germans, even if grossly outclassed by better German aircraft and airmen. This killed a lot of Trenchard's young pilots – at one time the average life of a scout pilot in the RFC on the Western Front was 11 days – but the culture of heroic sacrifice was created, and seen as vital to victory.

When peace came Trenchard led the RAF for its first ten years, established its culture, and beat off skirmishing from British Army and Royal Navy rivals. His influence was enormous, long surviving his retirement in 1930. He had developed the RAF to believe that the key to victory in an air war was the bomber, and that bombing vital enemy industrial and communications targets would break his will to fight. This loss of will, he felt, would cause civilians to pressure their government into agreeing terms. Trenchard believed that the bomber would always get through, that offensive was the stronger form of war, and that air superiority was absolutely necessary for all other military operations. He came to the view that the RAF's role was primarily strategic, as the major arm of Britain's armed forces, rather than tactical, helping the army and navy do their jobs.

As a result, the RAF gave priority to bombing units, rather than fighters, and it is in this context that much of the way it evolved in the 1930s should be seen. The four RAF commands – Bomber, Fighter, Coastal and Training – were not formed until 1936. When war came three years later, despite having had the lion's share of resources, all RAF bombers were two-engined aircraft of unimpressive performance. Fighter Command did not have a great deal of support in the late 1930s from Trenchard, who deplored the fighter's defensive role.

Until about 1934 the RAF was run on a virtual shoestring, flying biplane bombers, fighters and transport aircraft. After the horrors of 1914-18, that 'war to end wars', there was a real reluctance to spend any money at all developing weapons. But the British public, like people in other parts of the world, flocked to see flying displays and followed record-breakers as if they were modern pop stars.

Aviation was the rage, with great flights being made across the world, the advanced nations competing against each other. The core aim of Britain's aerial adventures was to establish regular routes to the far-flung outposts of the Empire – London to Sydney, London to Cape Town, crossing the Atlantic, air links with India, routes that resonated with the Empire's history. Heroes were made overnight. John Alcock and Arthur Whitton-Brown were knighted in 1919 for flying a twin-engined Vickers Vimy bomber non-stop across the Atlantic, from Newfoundland to Ireland. An American, Charles Lindbergh, was the first to fly non-stop from New York to Paris in 1927 in *The Spirit of St Louis*. And then there was Amy Johnson – 'Wonderful Amy' – whose England-to-Australia flight in 1930 turned her into a world superstar.

But the British public, and most of the rest of Europe, did not want to know about warplanes, and politicians reflected this view. Hardship during the Great Depression meant that defence budgets were kept tight, and no one wanted to believe that another war was possible. As a result, racing aircraft became a lot faster, but the development of war planes lagged far behind.

THE SCHNEIDER TROPHY

The British had won the prestigious Schneider Trophy twice in succession, in 1927 and 1929, and a third win in 1931 would mean that Britain would retain the trophy forever. The race became key to the development of the Hurricane and the Spitfire, because of its role in the history of the great Rolls Royce Merlin engine.

The Americans had lost interest in this European event, the French did submit an entry, but neither Italy nor France were ready by September 1931, when the races were scheduled to be held near Southampton on the Solent. The Italians and French intimated that the British would race and win on a bluff, at no better speeds than the 1929 races were won.

The British resolved to win handsomely, facing no real physical opponents but racing against their best results from the past. The British Labour Government, however, fighting economic turmoil, resolved not to put another penny into going for that third vital win.

There is a serious argument that Britain would not have won the war without the Hurricane and Spitfire to defend us against Germany's *Luftwaffe*. We would not have had the same peerless aircraft without the Merlin engine. We would not have had the Merlin without the fabulous Lady Lucy Houston. One of the richest women in the world, she gave £100,000 of her own money to back the British team in the 1931 Schneider Trophy. This was a colossal sum, the equivalent of £4.9 million today. The widow of ship-owner Sir Robert Houston, Lady Lucy had several inherited millions to play with and, after rescuing the RAF Schneider Trophy team, posed for photographs surrounded by all those handsome and ardent young men. At the age of 81, Lady Lucy looked the picture of charm and contentment. 'I am proud to say,' she declared, 'that I have inherited the spirit of my forefathers. We are not worms to be trampled under the heel of Socialism, but true Britons with a heart for any fate.'

Britain won the 1931 Schneider Trophy flying at speeds of more than 300 mph, a remarkable feat considering that it was just 28 years after the Wright Brothers first flew.

John Boothman clinched the Trophy with a world record 340 mph in a Supermarine 6B. Later that month he twice set new world records in the S6B, the first aircraft to break the 400 mph barrier on 29 September 1933 at an average speed of 407.5 mph.

This was at least 150 mph faster than the front-line RAF fighter of the day.

Nobody remembers Lady Lucy Houston now but, through the Merlin, she made a significant contribution to Britain's war effort. A. F. Sidgreaves, Rolls Royce's Managing Director, said the work undertaken to win the Schneider Trophy 'collapsed ten years of research into two.' Lady Lucy died in 1936, without ever knowing how far her £100,000 went towards saving the nation.

HAWKER AIRCRAFT

The Merlin engine began to be developed in 1932, a year after the Schneider Cup races, as a private venture by Rolls Royce, with the Air Ministry eventually providing funding in 1933. Such funding was not easy to come by at a time when the Air Ministry was continually tinkering with its budgets and requirements to try to anticipate the growing threat from Germany and Italy.

Just as Rolls Royce had to lobby hard for funding, so too did the aircraft manufacturers. One such manufacturer was Thomas Sopwith, whose company had built the famous First World War biplane fighter, the Sopwith Camel. Sopwith had learned to fly at the age of 22 in 1910, winning a £4,000 prize – an enormous sum equivalent to around £196,000 today – for the longest flight from England to the continent in a British-built aeroplane just a month after qualifying. He flew 169 miles (272 km) in 3 hours 40 minutes, and used the winnings to set up the Sopwith School of Flying at Brooklands.

In June 1912, with Fred Sigrist and others, Sopwith set up The Sopwith Aviation Company. The company produced more than 18,000 aircraft for the allied forces, including 5,747 Camel single-seat fighters. Sopwith was awarded the CBE in 1918, but bankrupted after the war by punitive anti-profiteering taxes. He re-entered the aviation business again soon afterwards, creating a new firm named after his chief engineer and test pilot, Harry Hawker. They bought the assets of the bankrupt Sopwith company in 1920 and formed Hawker Engineering.

The company prospered. In 1933 it was renamed Hawker Aircraft Ltd and the following year it took over the Gloster Aircraft Co. In 1935, it merged with the engine and automotive company Armstrong Siddeley and its subsidiary, Armstrong Whitworth Aircraft, to form Hawker Siddeley, also incorporating A. V. Roe and Co, the manufacturer that went on to build the Avro Lancaster bomber. The key to the success of Hawkers was its chief designer, Sydney Camm, then 40 years old.

Chapter Four

SYDNEY CAMM'S INTERCEPTOR MONOPLANE

Sydney Camm was born 5 August 1893 in Windsor, a little town with a royal castle and the famous public school, Eton College. Camm's father was an excellent carpenter, and Sydney was a pupil at The Royal Free School, leaving in 1908 at the age of 14. Only five years after the Wright Brother's first powered flight in 1903, Sydney was obsessed with aviation, and founded the Windsor Model Aeroplane Club while still a schoolboy.

He and his brother, Fred, became sufficiently competent in building reliable model aeroplanes that they supplied Herberts' Eton High Street shop. Their models of biplanes and monoplanes were advertised as 'Will Really Fly' and 'Will Rise from the Ground'. They found they could get a better price by selling direct to the Eton boys, delivering at night via a string lowered from the boys' dormitories to avoid the attention of the school authorities. Herbert's were not amused to find out what was happening.

Sydney Camm and his friends went on to build a full-sized glider with plans to put an engine on it. Camm's father instilled in his son an interest in hard work, accuracy and quality. He used to spend hours whittling propellers for model aeroplanes.

During the First World War, Sydney worked for the Martinsydes Aeroplane Company as a woodworker, under one of the leading aircraft designers of the time, G. H. Handasyde. In 1923 Camm joined the Hawker Engineering Company. Two years later, at just 32 years of age, he was appointed Hawker's Chief Designer, a role he filled for more than 40 years until his death.

In 1925, with Fred Sigrist, by now Hawker's Managing Director, Camm developed the distinctive Hawker metal construction, using cheap and simple jointed tubes, rather than any alternative welded structure. In the late 1920s and early 1930s, Camm designed the classic Hart family of fabric-and-metal biplanes. The Hart's success put Hawker in the forefront of aircraft manufacture and its design was used by Camm as the basis for aircraft to meet other requirements. These included the Demon fighter, Hart trainer,

Audax army co-operation aircraft, the Hind, the Fury, the Osprey and the Nimrod Fleet Air Arm machines. This new generation of aircraft boasted performance far in advance of their contemporaries.

At one time in the 1930s no fewer than 84 per cent of the RAF's aircraft were of Hawker/Camm design. Having been lauded by many as the greatest of all fighter designers, it is easy to see, in such circumstances, how upset Camm became in later life at all the adulation of the Hurricane's great rival, the Supermarine Spitfire.

Although he had no formal scientific training, Camm had an eye for good design, his aircraft evolving logically, progressively and successfully from each other. He was said to have a masterful eye and an intuitive feel for a well-designed aeroplane. As a result, he produced a succession of aircraft that were not only extremely good-looking but also boasted excellent performance and handling characteristics.

With the Hawker Hurricane, Camm moved from the technology of the biplane towards contemporary monoplane aircraft design. The Hurricane bridged the gap between the sporting aircraft that the public had watched in glamorous air races, and the outmoded stalwarts with which many of the world's air forces were equipped. Modern designs like Camm's Hurricane meant that fighters flew faster and, with the improved engine technology of the time, they flew higher – they could also be made more deadly than ever. Last Witness Graham Leggatt worked as a young student at Hawker:

'Mr Camm was the sort of man who would appear out of nowhere. You would be doing something, and you'd find him breathing over your shoulder, trying to see what you're doing. He was a very hard man. Brilliant, for his time, a brilliant aircraft engineer.

'Some would say, probably, he should have gone for the new type of monocoque construction, but the fact was that the Hurricane, although it had steel tubes and fabric and dope, was a tough aeroplane that could stand quite a lot of punishment.'

The Hurricane was developed by Camm at Hawker in response to the Air Ministry specification F.36/34 (modified by F.5/34) for a fighter aircraft built around the new Rolls Royce engine, later to become famous as the Merlin.

At that time, RAF Fighter Command comprised just 13 squadrons, each equipped with either the Hawker Fury, Hawker Hart variant or Bristol Bulldog, all biplanes with fixed-pitch, wooden propellers and non-retractable undercarriages. They had open cockpits, and carried at most four machine guns, still capable of being man-handled by the pilot. RAF pilot culture was dominated by the biplane fighter, and the Hawker company supplied it with some of the most elegant and efficient examples of the breed.

Fighter pilots liked open cockpit aircraft, because there was no distorting canopy to get in the way of seeing an enemy aircraft. They liked bi-planes because they were always more manoeuvrable than monoplanes and would be better in a dog-fight. Pilots thought enclosed cockpits made it difficult to bail out which of course, compared to open cockpits, they did.

Yet speed was everything – fighters needed to be able to catch a bomber, and monoplanes were speedier than biplanes because they had less wing area. The specification for the new RAF fighter demanded that it must be faster than the fastest bomber, the Bristol Blenheim, capable of 300 mph (483 kph). It was believed, correctly, that future air battles would take place at speeds above 300 mph, where a nimble target might only be in another fighter's sight for the blink of an eye. A bright young RAF squadron leader, Ralph Sorley, had worked out that, so fast were modern aircraft that an enemy might only be in a fighter's sights for two seconds. There were not enough bullets in two machine guns to do him real damage. Sorley estimated that at least eight guns were needed, firing 20 rounds per second apiece, each gun carrying 300 rounds of 0.303 inch ammunition, enough for 15 seconds firing. A two-second burst meant hitting an enemy aircraft with 320 bullets, which, if accurate, was thought capable of doing the job.

Sydney Camm's original plans, submitted in response to the Air Ministry's specification, were rejected, apparently 'too orthodox,' even for the Air Ministry. Camm abandoned the initial proposal and set about designing a fighter as a Hawker private venture.

With economy in mind, the Hurricane was designed to use as many existing tools and jigs as possible. The new aircraft was effectively a monoplane version of the successful Hawker Fury, a factor that contributed to the design's success. Early design stages of the 'Fury Monoplane' incorporated a Rolls Royce Goshawk engine, but this was soon replaced by the Merlin. The design came to be known as the 'Interceptor Monoplane', and by May 1934 plans had been completed in detail. To test the new design, a one-tenth scale model was made and sent to the National Physical Laboratory at Teddington. A series of wind tunnel tests confirmed the aerodynamic qualities of the design, and by December that year, a full-sized wooden mock-up of the aircraft had been created.

One of Camm's priorities with the new fighter was to provide the pilot with good visibility. The cockpit was mounted reasonably high in the fuselage, creating a distinctive 'hump-backed' silhouette. Pilot access was aided by a retractable 'stirrup' below the trailing edge of the port wing. This was linked to a spring-loaded, hinged flap which covered a handhold on the fuselage, just behind the cockpit. When the flap was shut the footstep retracted into the fuselage. In addition, both wing roots were coated with strips of non-slip material.

Though faster and more advanced than the RAF's current front-line biplane fighters, the Hurricane still represented the last of the old-fashioned fighters and was already outdated as it swung into production. It employed traditional Hawker construction techniques from previous biplane aircraft. It had a Warren girder-type fuselage of high-tensile steel tubes, over which sat wooden frames and longerons that carried the doped linen covering. One advantage of this 'canvas, string and sticks' design, along with the steel-tube structure, was that cannon shells could pass right through the wood-and-fabric covering without exploding. Even if one of the steel tubes was damaged, the repair work required was relatively simple and could be done by the ground-crew at a fighter airfield.

By comparison, an all-metal structure like the Spitfire's, damaged by an exploding cannon shell required more specialised equipment to repair. The old-fashioned structure permitted the assembly of Hurricanes with relatively basic equipment under field conditions. In 1941 crated Hurricanes were assembled in West Africa and flown across the Sahara to the Middle East theatre. To save space, some Royal Navy aircraft carriers stored their reserve Sea Hurricanes dismantled into their major assemblies, and slung up on the hangar bulkheads for reassembly when needed.

Initially, the wing structure consisted of two steel spars. It was fabric-covered and known as 'rag-wing'. Several rag-wing Hurricanes were still in service during the Battle of Britain, although a good number had had their wings replaced during servicing or after repair. An all-metal, stressed-skin wing of duraluminium was introduced in April 1939 and used for all of the later marks. Changing the wings required only three hours' work per aircraft.

The great advantage of the metal-covered wings over the fabric ones was that the metal ones could carry far greater stress loads allowing a diving speed more than 50 mph (80 kph) faster than the rag-wings. Although very different in construction, the two wing types were interchangeable, one trials Hurricane even being flown with a fabric-covered port wing and metal-covered starboard wing.

Construction of the first prototype, K5083, began in August 1935, incorporating the Merlin engine. The completed sections of the aircraft were taken to Brooklands, where Hawkers had an assembly shed, and re-assembled on 23 October. Ground testing and taxi trials took place over the following two weeks.

On 6 November 1935, the prototype took to the air for the first time at the hands of Hawker's chief test pilot, Flight Lieutenant P.W.S. 'George' Bullman. It reached a maximum speed of more than 315 mph (506 kph) at 16,500 feet (5,000m), to become the first fighter plane to break the 300 mph barrier. The aircraft performed well, although the Merlin engine had to be changed after teething troubles. Engineers at Rolls Royce resolved the problems with the 'C' engine and later developed it into the Merlin II for full-scale production.

Development work on the new Hurricane monoplane had now taken on a greater air of urgency. On 10 March 1935, the former commander of Richtofen's Flying Circus, Hermann Goering, a First World War ace with 20 kills, was put in charge of the *Luftwaffe*. Germany had new aircraft designs underway and Hitler's aggressive posturing did not bode well. Britain was beginning to wake up from a very deep sleep. The flight of the prototype Hurricane was a symptom of the new thinking. The first flight of the Supermarine Spitfire, which flew four months later, on 5 March 1936, was another such sign.

When it became apparent that the new monoplane fighters would not be ready for squadron service before 1937, however, there was a stop-gap specification from the Air Ministry – F.7/30 – to get the best from biplane designs, with which all aviation manufacturers were experienced. This spec called for a performance increase of 25 per cent and an armament of four machine guns.

The Gloster Gladiator emerged as the successful F.7/30 contender, a biplane fighter with a fixed undercarriage, four Browning machine guns and an enclosed canopy for the pilot. But with a maximum speed of 257 mph (413 kph), the Gladiator was only 20 mph (32 kph) faster than the contemporary Hawker Fury, though 80 mph (129 kph) faster than the Bristol Bulldog IIA which was still in frontline service with eight fighter squadrons of the RAF as late as 1935. The Gladiator was an excellent aircraft, fearsome in a dog-fight with much faster opponents, but it was obsolete before it ever entered service.

In acknowledging that they had to begin preparing for war, the RAF also realised that they would need more pilots. A serious recruiting drive was instigated, bringing in fighter pilots in time for what became the first year of the war, including most of the Last Witnesses. Proper RAF officers still went to Cranwell College, but there were also short service commissions for officers, and the RAF Volunteer Reserve, many of whom were non-commissioned officers – NCOs.

It took an average of 15-18 months to train a pilot. A typical course involved 10 days kitting out, drill, aptitude tests, maths, general knowledge. Then 12 weeks was spent on ground work with an ITW – Initial Training Wing – which included lots of drill, PT, Morse code, Navigation, Meteorology, gunnery, aircraft recognition. Recruits went on to Elementary Flight Training School – EFTS – and if they did not go solo within 12 flying hours, they were rejected. Survivors went on to a Service Flying Training School (SFTS) and amassed up to 150 flying hours.

By Spring 1939 there would be 2,500 RAFVR pilots under training. Recruiters were sent to Australia, New Zealand, South Africa and Canada for aircrew, and 800 pilots signed on.

The Empire Air Training Plan, set up in December 1939, created teaching centres in Rhodesia, South Africa and Canada (Australia was too far away, except for Australians). An EFTS/SFTS course usually lasted 21 weeks, and when in full flow, trained 3,120 pilots and 1,050 observers a year. One downside of the overseas training schemes was their weather was too good, so little night training was done, and the terrain was completely different to wartime Europe. These deficiencies were rectified in the OTU, Operational Training Unit, back in Britain. In the whole six years of the war, 5,000 aircrew were killed in training, mostly training on bombers, before they had a go at the enemy.

Over the winter of 1935/36, improvements were made to the Hurricane prototype; exhaust ejector stubs were added to direct hot gasses rearwards, giving a useful increase in forward thrust. The complicated folding doors to the undercarriage were removed because they could be damaged when taxiing over grass airfields. To aid recovery from a spin, a small fin was added below the tail, and the tail wheel was locked in the down position. The wings were also modified. The leading edge aft of the joint with the centre section was swept gently rearwards to bring the great weight of the guns and ammunition closer to the centre of gravity. Handling trials were successfully completed in the first half of 1936 at the Aeroplane and Armament Experimental Establishment at Martelsham Heath.

On 3 June 1936 Hawkers received an order to build 600 Hurricanes for the new Fighter Command, the RAF undergoing re-organisation into four separate forces, Bomber, Fighter, Training and Coastal Commands. But with an eye on the international scene, Hawker geared up to build a thousand Hurricanes. It would take over a year before the first production aircraft was ready for flight testing, which eventually took place on 12 October 1937. The long delay was caused by the adoption of the Merlin II engine, which meant considerable redesign work to the engine bearers, internal fittings and cockpit controls.

A flight of three aircraft arrived at 111 Squadron RAF before Christmas, 1937. British newspaper headlines boasted of a remarkable 990hp monoplane fighter that could beat the world, but journalists were soon nervous at the news on 11 November that year that a Messerschmitt Bf 109 had set a new world speed record of 379 mph (610 kph) over Augsberg.

As a result, there was enormous publicity – and relief – when on 10 February 1938, an RAF Hurricane pilot flew from Turnhouse, a Scottish airfield near Edinburgh, to 111 Squadron's base at Northolt. This was a distance of 307 miles (494 km) in only 48 minutes, at an incredible speed of 408 mph (657 kph) and a world record at the time. What was not publicised was that there was a strong 50 mph (80 kph) tailwind blowing that day. Squadron leader John Gillan, the record-breaking pilot, though displaying fine navigation and airmanship skills in dangerous and icy conditions, was known ever after as 'Downwind Gillan'.

As the Commanding Officer of 111 Squadron, Gillan wrote the RAF's first appraisal of the Hurricane, one copy going to the Air Ministry, the other to Hawker's Chief Test pilot, F/L 'George' Bullman. In reading his judgements, one should bear in mind that Gillan was accustomed to the nippiness of biplanes. It became apparent in combat conditions that the turning circle, for example, which Gillan judged 'large', was the smallest of the principal fighters in 1940:

> 'The Hurricane is completely manoeuvrable throughout its whole range, though at slow speeds between 65 mph [105 kph] and 200 mph [322 kph] controls feel a bit slack.
>
> 'Owing to its weight and speed, some time is taken coming out of a dive and at high speed its turning circle is large.
>
> 'On the ground the Hurricane is as manoeuvrable as is possible, and has the added advantage of feeling secure across wind – or with a strong wind – owing to its high wing-loading.
>
> 'Cross-wind landings are particularly easy in the Hurricane.'

On the view from the cockpit, Gillan wrote:

> 'Taxiing with the seat full-up and the hood back is exceptionally good all round, better in front and above than in other RAF fighters, and just as good in all other directions.
>
> 'Taking off and landing, the view is considerably better than the Gauntlet and the Demon, both individually and in formation.'

Gillan wrote that pilots flying in formation with Hurricanes had a better view than with Gauntlets and Demons, with the hood open or closed. His pilots had not yet tried flying in formation in bad rain or cloud, and there was a fear that in an enclosed cockpit it would fog or ice up.

Turning to formation flying, Gillan wrote that at height, and at speeds above 200 mph (322 kph), formation flying was very simple. He thought the reason may be that air resistance at this speed was considerable, and that pilots could speed up or slow down 'very quickly indeed'.

At slow speeds, around 100 mph (161 kph), because of the clean profile, Gillan found it difficult to take off more speed, but could accelerate to gain speed easily. Landing in formation, he thought, was the same as with any other aircraft.

'Taking off in formation is simple, but immediately after leaving the ground, when pilots retract their undercarriages and flaps, aircraft cannot keep good formation. This is because they retract at different speeds in each aircraft. It is recommended that "take-offs" should be done individually in succession.

'The Hurricane is a simple aircraft to fly by night. There is no glare in the cockpit, either open or closed, from cockpit lights or luminous instruments.

'The steady steep glide at slow speed, a characteristic of Hurricanes, makes landings simple.

'The take-off run being longer than with earlier aircraft, it is recommended that the "leading light" should be at least 500 yards [457m] away from the beginning of the run, instead of the normal 250 yards [228m] on ordinary flare paths.

'The Hurricane without its engine running has a very steep glide, and to the pilot inexperienced on this type, judging the flattening-out may be difficult. It is recommended that on initial training, pilots come in with their engines running. Landing with the engine running lengthens the period of holding-off, making the landing easier. If a pilot flattens out too high, he still has time with a running engine to stop it hitting the ground heavily as the speed falls off.

'The cockpit is large and comfortable and there is room for the largest man inside with the hood shut. By using the adaptable seat, the smallest man can see everything comfortably.

'Having a selector box, and a lever, each of which must be moved to operate the undercarriage and the flaps, is unsatisfactory. A pilot can take 30 seconds using his right hand to pump up the undercarriage, while flying with his left hand, during which time he cannot move the throttle, also on the left. Taking off in formation, in bad weather, the difficulties are obvious. Two simple controls could be substituted, one to move the flaps full up, or full down, the other to operate the undercarriage.

'All other controls are easily accessible and efficient, and the instrument lay-out is good and not complicated.

'Operational Characteristics

As far as can be seen, the indicated air speed (IAS) at 2,000 feet [610m] is

270 mph [435 kph]. IAS at 10,000 feet [3,048m] is 260 mph [418 kph], and at 15,000 [4,572m] IAS is 240 mph [386 kph].

'Petrol consumption at 15,000 feet, cruising economically at 160 mph indicated – correcting to 200 mph [322 kph] – is 25 gallons [113.75 litres] per hour. Plus 2 ½ boost – the maximum permissible cruising speed – consumption is close to 60 gallons [273 litres] per hour.

'At 2,000 feet [610m] and an IAS of 200 mph [322 kph], petrol consumption is 30 gallons [136.5 litres] per hour.

'Among other characteristics, the windscreen shows no sign of oiling up, and the cockpit is weather-proof.'

By March, 1938, Gillan's 111 Squadron was fully equipped with Hurricanes. Numbers 3 and 56 Squadrons took delivery during 1938, though the latter was not operational at the time of the Munich Crisis in September, where war with Germany came so close. At year's end, 200 Hurricanes had been delivered.

On 1 November 1938, the head of RAF Fighter Command, Sir Hugh 'Stuffy' Dowding, boosted Spitfire and Hurricane fighter aircraft production, winning priority for fighters over bombers. The ratio of fighters to bombers was to rise from 1.7-to-1 to 2-to-1, a decision that went through despite bitter opposition from Lord Trenchard.

The first Hurricanes to be built, designated as the Hurricane Mk I, were modified several times during the course of production. The engine was first widely delivered as the 1,030hp (770 kW) Merlin II in 1938, and production was quickly stepped up. The fabric-covered outer wings were replaced on the assembly lines with wings of all-metal construction, the first model of which took flight on 28 April 1939. Other improvements included changing over to the Merlin III engine, and the addition of increased pilot protection, such as armour behind the seat and a bullet-resistant windscreen.

At this point in time, the Spitfire was still very much an unknown quantity. The Hurricane was exactly what the RAF needed. It had a classic pedigree, already tested, and a proven lineage. It was vice-free, easy to fly, with a strong tubular steel frame that made it easy to build and to repair. Its eight guns fitted into two groups of four inside a thick wing, grouped closely together in a steady gun-platform. It was easy to handle on the ground because of its wide undercarriage, and it could operate off rough airstrips.

The major downside, though it was not apparent at the time, was its propensity to catch fire because of the fuel tanks either side of the cockpit. The Munich crisis sent a shock wave throughout Europe; there were few people who now believed that war could be avoided. Friendly nations turned to Britain to buy modern fighting aircraft. Belgium, Romania and Yugoslavia wanted Hurricanes for their own defence. Hawker had already established a new production line at Langley, Buckinghamshire and was able to enter into contracts to supply Hurricanes abroad without reducing the flow of machines to their main customer, the RAF.

Modifications being introduced during production included the introduction of a de Havilland variable pitch, constant speed, three-bladed propeller. The new propeller installation was 250lb (113kg) heavier than the Watts 2-blader, but gave the Hurricane an improved climb and cruise performance. A height of 15,000 feet (4,600m) was now achieved in 6.2 minutes and top speed in level flight was now 328 mph (528 kph). The de Havilland unit required further modification to the engine and again Rolls Royce were able to accommodate the changes into the Merlin III.

The scale of the rapid introduction of the Hurricane into the home-based Fighter Command squadrons at this time can be seen in the table below:

11 Group	Squadron Location	12 Group	Squadron Location
1 and 43	Tangmere	46, 73 and 504	Digby
3, 32 and 79	Biggin Hill	85 and 87	Debden
17, 56 and 151	North Weald	213	Wittering
25 and 111	Northolt		
501	Filton		

On the eve of the Second World War, 17 squadrons were fully operational, a total of 457 Hurricanes having been delivered. The aircraft were all Mark Is, all armed with eight 0.303 inch machine guns but with a variety of propeller installations. The mix included Merlin II engines driving a Watts two-blade fixed-pitch wooden propeller, or a Merlin III of similar power having a standardized shaft for de Havilland or Rotol three-blade metal propellers. The Hurricane I, at 7,127lbs (3,239kg), possessed a maximum speed of 325 mph (523 kph) at 17,500 feet (5,334m); a range of 700 miles (1,126 km) at 200 mph (322 kph) at 15,000 feet (4,572m); a service ceiling of 36,000 feet (10,973m), and the ability to climb to 20,000 feet (6,100m) in nine minutes.

Only seven RAF squadrons had Spitfires, four others had the fighter version of the Blenheim light bomber and six were still flying Gladiators, Gauntlets or Hinds.

Production of Hurricanes was established in Canada, with a licence issued to the Canadian Car and Foundry Company. At home the Gloster Aircraft Company also opened a Hurricane production line. The first Gloster-built Mk I took to the air on 27 October 1939.

By then, Britain was at war with Germany.

Chapter Five

THE BATTLE OF FRANCE

The war started badly for the Hurricane. Two of them were shot down *by Spitfires* on September 6, with one pilot killed. It became known as the 'Battle of Barking Creek'. The early warning radar system that day detected six German bombers, He 111s, approaching the Thames Estuary but they turned back because of bad weather. Twelve Hurricanes from 56 Squadron took off from North Weald to begin patrolling, and they were joined by two late-comers. These two were wrongly identified as enemy aircraft and a number of other Hurricanes, as well as some Spitfires, were scrambled to intercept. The Spitfires saw the two detached Hurricanes against the rising sun and fired at them, causing them both to crash.

P/O Montague Hulton-Harrop was killed, P/O Frank Rose escaped unhurt. Rose's Hurricane was repaired and thrown into battle, but lost when there was another disaster the following June on *HMS Glorious*.

A Spitfire was also lost that day to 'friendly' anti-aircraft fire, but the pilot survived.

The Sector Controller, Group Captain Lucking, was sacked over the incident, and the two Spitfire pilots who did the shooting were court-martialled. Lucking received a cursory punishment and was later promoted, while the two pilots were exonerated and went back into battle.

It was hardly a good omen.

In September 1939, when war was declared, the RAF had 536 bombers and 608 fighters. The Germans had 2,130 bombers and 1,215 fighters, but they were to lose a significant number taking Poland. RAF Bomber Command could contribute some 392 aircraft to operations in France. British bombers included Fairey Battles, Whitleys and Blenheims – all cut to pieces by the *Luftwaffe* when the real fighting started the following Spring.

It was not simply that the Allies were inferior to the Germans in the air; the French *Armee de l'Air* had 1,562 aircraft, but most of the Allied aircraft were obsolete. Only the Hurricane and the French Dewoitine D520 could cope with the German Bf 109. The French had an estimated *matériel* reserve of nearly

2,000 aircraft, but this fleet suffered a chronic lack of spare parts. Only 29 per cent (599) of the French aircraft were serviceable. Of these, 170 were bombers.

By 27 September 1939, Hawker had delivered 497 Hurricanes to the RAF, enough to equip 17 Fighter Command squadrons, against the initial order of 3,500. Despite the need to bring Britain's fighter strength to its potential peak, Hurricanes were exported to other countries; 15 went to Turkey, another 15 to Finland, 12 to Romania, and 1 went to Poland.

Hawker also put out tenders for the construction of the Hurricane overseas. One successful bidder was the Canadian Car and Foundry Works (CCF), which won a licence to build both the Hurricane and the Sea Hurricane. A total of 1,451 machines were to be built by CCF and, of these, 60 were flying by 10 January 1940. The Canadian company built the Hurricane in a number of different versions.

The original accepted design of the Hurricane Mark I in Canada became the Mark X, powered by the Merlin 28 engine and built by the Packard Car Co. The Mark XI was built with Canadian equipment, while the Mark XII's were powered by the Merlin 29 engine and armed with 12 Browning guns. The Mark XIIA reverted to the more efficient eight-gun format.

During this period, 24 Hurricane 1s were delivered to Yugoslavia. Belgium was granted a licence to build the fighter, and physically acquired 20 Hurricane 1s from Britain. Only 15 of these had been delivered before the Germans turned up, uninvited.

Last Witness Eric Brown:

'It was lucky we got the Hurricane. We got a shock, of course, when we found that the Germans had a Messerschmitt Bf 109 – that was a very severe shock to us. Dowding, head of Fighter Command, was very pro the Hurricane. He felt that it was proven by the time the war started, whereas the Spitfire really had just arrived, but was pretty unproven as a combat aircraft. The Spitfire was proven as a flying aircraft, but there's a difference between having a fine flying aircraft – for doing aerobatics – and having a good combat aircraft. That was why the Hurricanes were sent to France first.

'There was no feeling at the time that the Hurricane was inferior to the Spitfire. The Spitfire really had to prove itself. It turned out to be magnificent, but the fundamental point was that it was not as manoeuvrable as the Hurricane, which made a difference when it got into combat. It was thought that the Hurricane had better harmony of control than the Spitfire, and a better rate of roll, but was just not as fast.'

The French Government wanted ten RAF fighter squadrons immediately to be based in France, but Sir Hugh Dowding was alarmed that the request could fatally weaken the defence of Britain. He sent just four squadrons of Hurricanes, Numbers 1, 73, 85, and 87 Squadrons, keeping Spitfires back for 'Home' defence.

A little later, Numbers 607 and 615 Hurricane Squadrons joined them. These squadrons assumed a protective role over the British Expeditionary Force as they settled down to what, for the next eight months, was called the 'Phoney War'. Flights of three Hurricanes conducted daily patrols along the lines.

Most of the German aircraft crossing into Allied airspace at the time were there just to keep track of the French and British Armies. All the active German units were in the east, mopping up in Poland. Whenever there was combat between Hurricane and Bf 109s, the Hurricane pilots felt they had the measure of their opponents, and confidence in their aircraft.

Eric Brown:

'If a pilot is going to bond with an aeroplane, it has to have good harmony of control. That usually means that you have very light ailerons, moderately light elevators and a reasonably heavy rudder. You do not want too light a rudder, otherwise you pick up a lot of skid. These are three qualities you look for to get harmony of control. The Hurricane was absolutely wonderful in that respect, particularly in the ailerons, it had very light ailerons indeed.

'The other great thing was that it was very robust. Generally speaking it could accept a lot of punishment in combat. It had an Achilles heel because it had fabric covering that was a bit susceptible to incendiary bullets, so it could more easily burst into flames.

'The view from the cockpit was much better than from the Spitfire, and it was an easy aeroplane to land. The major problem was, you did not want to get too slow. A Hurricane had a very nasty stall. It dropped a wing very quickly in a stall, and it gave little indication it was going to happen, that is, hardly any buffeting. This characteristic was not that important in land operations with standard runways, but it did matter in carrier operations later in the war.'

The first RAF confirmed 'kill' of the war was scored on 30 October by Pilot Officer 'Boy' Mould of 1 Squadron, who caught and shot down a Dornier 17 over French soil. Billy Drake, flying with 1 Squadron, was then 22 years old.

Last Witness Billy Drake:

'A lot of us fighting in Hurricane squadrons at the time had not seen much about Spitfires, so we only had a vague idea what a Spitfire was, that it was a comparable aeroplane to us. We could only judge our own aeroplanes through familiarisation. What we found was that we were flying an aeroplane with a sound engine that seemed to go on forever, with eight machine guns that should be very lethal, a gun-sight that worked, and that we were personally as good an aviator as anybody we would meet on the enemy side.'

Peter Ayerst is the only surviving member of 73 Hurricane Squadron. It is an indication of the lack of flying action against the Germans that it took two months before the first serious combat occurred. 'Boy' Mould could claim the first German aircraft, but on 6 November, Ayerst was the first RAF pilot to offer combat to the key German fighter, a Bf 109.

Last Witness Peter Ayerst:
'I was doing aerodrome defence. We sat in the cockpit on the ground, all dressed up and ready to go at a moment's notice. Down the side of the airfield – all grass, no runways, of course – there was a French Army unit. They had a powerful pair of binoculars, and they were looking east, trying to check on German aircraft. There was no radar.

'Then I heard shouting, "The flag's waving! The red flag's waving!" These French chaps had seen a Dornier and used the only warning system we had, waving a red flag. I took off with the old two-bladed Watts airscrew and started climbing. He must have seen me take off and decided to turn for home. I thought I would try and catch him. With the Hurricane climbing, I wasn't gaining any distance on him very much, but I was sticking with him. I got up to about 20,000 feet [6,100m], and was getting nearer, but we were going in an easterly direction all the time.

'We had no radio aids whatsoever, apart from the radio in the aircraft which worked at a distance from our base, up to 25 miles [40 km]. I carried on flying east and I had got within two miles of him when he dived into cloud at a lower level and I never saw him again.

'As I turned for home I saw nine aircraft, line astern below me. I thought they must be 1 Squadron. They had come to our airfield, we were further forward than they were, and they were going to put up a joint Hurricane patrol with us. I thought these were their Hurricanes, saw them pull up in front of me and thought they wanted me to join on.

'I did just that and then got up close and saw black crosses! They were not quite what I thought they were going to be. I pulled up and gave a quick squirt at the chap at the tail end. I don't know whether I hit him or not, but I think I did, I claimed a "damaged" later.

'After that, I did not wait around to see. I was at about 18,000 feet [5,486m] and went straight down. We had no armour plate back then so I was vulnerable to shots from behind. There was broken cloud at a lower level. I was whipping in and out of that cloud, flying west, trying to get into a safe area. I had no idea where I was, apart from the fact that I had been farther into Germany than I ever anticipated.

'Unknown to me, there were another 18 109s in the air at the same time – 27 of them all together! I dropped down as low as I could and, still not knowing what I was doing, led them through a flight of French fighters – Moraine 406s and Curtis Hawks – who shot nine of these Germans down!

'The Germans were concentrating so much on me, they were not looking after their own backsides. This was the first big air battle of the war. I was dubbed "Decoy".

'After a bit I realised that I was over France, because I saw a factory with the glass roofing painted – always painted in blue paint, I don't know why. I throttled back to save fuel – I had been using quite a lot of fuel – and then I saw some aircraft circling ahead of me. I realised there must be an airfield there and sure enough it was a French airfield. I landed, finished the landing run and my engine cut, out of fuel. What luck!'

That winter, 1939/40, was particularly cold, especially wearing on Hurricane pilots doing patrols. Peter Hairs flew with 501 Squadron, thrown into the Battle of France when the *Blitzkrieg* started.

Last Witness Peter Hairs:
'Hurricanes had no heating. On one occasion when we had a call to scramble, I jumped out of my seat and went to pick up my gloves – we had silk gloves with yellow gauntlets over them. I couldn't see my inner gloves, so I went without them. I jumped in, we took off and got to about 20,000 feet [6,100m], and my hands froze. I could do absolutely nothing with them. I throttled back and came down to a lower altitude. As I came down they warmed up, and as they defrosted they were frightfully painful so I opened the hood to let the air play on them. It did surprise me at the time that it was so cold, and how effective those inner gloves were.'

The tactics used by RAF fighters in the early stage of the war were very formal, and known as 'Fighting Area Attacks'. They involved flying in tight formations, one wingtip just feet away from another, the 'eyes' of the flight being the leader, and the 'weaver', often the most inexperienced pilot, flying at the back. Fighting Area Attacks were governed by rigid rules, designed to take out lone bombers, a sort of formal ballet to bring guns to bear on the enemy in an ordered way. But they also meant that most pilots, flying in vics of three, had eyes only for each other, and not the enemy.

The Germans called the tight vics *Idiotenreihen,* that is, rows of idiots.

It was not just that RAF pilots were discouraged from showing initiative. They were actually forbidden to do so. There was a dreadful logic to the Darwinian outcome of these tactics; those using them died early, and survivors went on to invent new tactics, essentially based on the German

schwarme formation of four aircraft developed by *Luftwaffe* ace Werner
Mölders during the Spanish Civil War.

Last Witness Billy Drake was one of those survivors:

'We had been taught about Fighting Area Tactics, able to fly in close
formation and going that way into battle. In retrospect, they were extremely
dangerous. Our idea was to fly in vics of three, and nobody was really looking
after each other.

'We flew this way until halfway through the Battle of Britain, and saw
that the Germans were not flying this way. They were flying in "finger fours",
and everybody was looking after everybody else. It was not until the end of
the Battle of Britain and later on that we accepted that this was the right way
to formate operationally.

'We found that we had to respect the Germans. We had been advised that
they were not fools and that they had much more experience than we had.
Their leaders, particularly, had started in Spain before 1939 in the Kondor
Legion. As far as we were concerned, they were as good as ourselves. We did
not consider ourselves to be inferior in any way.

'I was invariably a leader, as a Flight Lieutenant, as a flight or squadron
commander, and I had two jobs. One was to lead properly and then,
having got within close range of an enemy aircraft, to shoot him down at a
reasonable range, not to shoot way out of range and waste bullets. It was all
over within minutes, if not seconds.'

'There were two theories about how guns should be aimed. One was to
harmonise for all eight machine guns to meet at a point, and that was the
way I liked it, to get the maximum number of bullets if you aimed straight, at
a point 250 yards [228m] away. The other theory – known as the "Dowding
Spread" – was for those who were not as good a shot, where the guns were
harmonised at 400 yards [365m] but spreading the bullets. The first method
was favoured by those who were good shots. Johnny Johnson, the RAF ace,
and myself, we had both been brought up by our fathers to shoot at birds,
and we understood deflection shooting.

'We were very young. We did not do a great deal of thinking. We
expected our seniors to be able to talk to us and teach us about air
fighting. But very few of them themselves had any idea of tactics. We were
the ones who went to France, met the enemy for the first time, worked in
operational units through the Battle of Britain and learnt through bitter
experience.'

Peter Ayerst, flying a Hurricane with 73 Squadron and having survived the
first fighting encounter with a Bf 109, was learning from his flight leader,
'Cobber' Kain, now in regular combat.

'We used to see the odd German aircraft, and when we did we made a bee-line for it. With old Cobber Kain in the lead, you knew you had a good leader. Before the actual war started on 10 May Cobber had already shot down five Germans and won the DFC. So whenever we saw an aircraft we would go down and have a pass at it.

'We used to patrol up and down these fronts daily. But I had to leave France earlier than the rest of the squadron because I got severe headaches. They didn't last long but I was off a few days. Old Bill Kain ("Cobber") was suffering as well. I went on to hospital in England at the end of April 1940, before the *Blitzkrieg* began. I was there for five weeks through July and August, according to the doctors, "worn out".'

In the period 23 April to 12 May 1940, Billy Drake notched up 35 hours operational flying, and was starting to show success at knocking down German aircraft:

'I remember one of the first, a 109 that we had seen flying in our direction. The only way we knew that they were probably enemies was the condensation trails. That was the only early warning that we were ever given when we were in France. We were sitting at readiness, saw the con-trail, I was detailed to take off and intercept the con-trail and when I got fairly close to it I saw that it was a German 109 and that he hadn't seen me.

'When I got within a reasonable range of him he did see me. He dived away at a very great speed back to his base. I followed him and could not catch him at all. I found myself at 20 feet [6m] from the ground still chasing him and saw that he had ducked under a high tension cable. He thought I hadn't seen this cable, and probably that I had hit it. He pulled up, something he shouldn't have done because the moment he pulled up he lost speed. I was able to shoot at him and shot him down. I saw him crash, and the confirmation came from the intelligence service, Y-Service. That was my first recognised kill.

'Quite a few of us had similar incidents. We never thought in terms of destroying a person, we were just destroying a piece of machinery. It was my job to do this.'

On 9 April 1940, the Germans, anxious not to be bottled in by the British Fleet, and also not to be forced into the terrible trench warfare in France that marked the First World War, invaded Norway and Denmark. The RAF deployed a single Hurricane Squadron to Norway's defence, along with the Gloster Gladiators of 263 Squadron. The Hurricanes of 46 Squadron were sent to Norway in May 1940, selected to form part of the Expeditionary Force.

The Mark 1 Hurricanes were lifted – rather than flown – on to HMS *Glorious*, one of the Royal Navy's seven aircraft carriers. Despite doubts that a Hurricane could actually take off from a carrier flight deck in a flat calm, they all got away without difficulty, thanks to the efforts of the ship's engineers who managed to get the *Glorious* up to a speed of 30 knots.

Hurricanes began operations in Norway on 26 May, with standing patrols over the British land and naval forces at Narvik, some of the pilots going without sleep for more than 48 hours. In its brief campaign 46 Squadron claimed 14 enemy aircraft, probably destroying many others. On 7 June the Squadron was ordered to evacuate immediately and, on the night 7/8 June, the seven Hurricane survivors were successfully flown back to HMS *Glorious*. This was an astonishing feat at the time, considered virtually impossible, because none of the aircraft were fitted with deck arrester hooks.

The Hurricanes were sorely needed; the Dunkirk retreat had just ended but all the aircraft and eight of the ten pilots were lost the following day when HMS *Glorious* was sunk by a German battle group led by the battleship *Scharnhorst*. Only 45 of the 1,474 of the crew of HMS *Glorious* and its two defending destroyers *Acasta* and *Ardent* survived the attack; 46 Squadron was re-formed around the two remaining pilots, who survived the war and went on to senior rank.

On 10 May 1940 the German onslaught against France and the Low Countries began. The *Blitzkrieg* attack swept around the static defences of the Maginot Line in which the French had placed so much faith. Ju 87 Stuka dive-bombers accompanied the advancing columns of Panzers, while medium bombers ranged further afield to attack airfields and troop concentrations. They were protected by an umbrella of single and twin-engined Messerschmitt fighters.

The ten Bristol Blenheim and Fairey Battle squadrons in France mounted repeated attacks against the advancing German columns in a frantic attempt to stem the enemy's progress. They suffered appalling losses for little gain. The RAF light bomber force was massacred. The Battles faired particularly badly, being poorly armed and under-powered – though with Merlin engines – they were easy prey. The Hurricanes fought desperately to defend the bombers and gave good account of themselves against the Messerschmitt Bf 109E and Bf 110 fighters of the *Luftwaffe*. But they could not prevent the decimation of the bomber force, with 72 of the 135 Blenheims and Battles destroyed in three days.

By 17 May, the end of the first week of fighting, only three Hurricane squadrons in France were near operational strength. Despite their heavy losses the Hurricanes had claimed nearly double the number of German aircraft. F/O 'Cobber' Kain, having been responsible for 73 Squadron's first confirmed victory in France, the RAF's first fighter ace of the war, was credited with a total of 15 kills by early June.

Kain's kills, and his brief fame, along with the other young RAF pilots in the four French-based squadrons, had a vitally important effect among fighter pilots back in England. It proved they could cope with the aircraft they had against what had been trumpeted as the most powerful air force in the world. They added to the aura surrounding the Hurricane, and there was no inferiority complex about not flying Spitfires.

Billy Drake:
'This thinking emerged after the war. We were never told that. If we saw something we went for it. We never felt at a disadvantage if we were flying Hurricanes. It depended entirely on where we were, what position we were in the sky, where the enemy formation was. Our idea was, if we were in a certain place, and we saw a formation of Germans, we went for that.

'Morale was high. The fact that we lost companions meant nothing, really. It was just an accepted fact that, as long as it wasn't oneself that was shot down, the fact that Joe Soap was shot down was hard luck. We were young and we were doing a job of work, and that job was warfare. We accepted that there would be losses, and hoped they would not be us. The fact that the whole nation was at war was part of it.'

Last Witness Peter Hairs, a 24-year-old pilot officer with 501 Squadron, went to France on 11 May. Two days later he was one of three 501 Squadron Hurricanes attacking Dorniers, claiming one or two 'probables'. He disclaimed responsibility, saying, 'My shooting wasn't very good, I started firing too early.'

On 27 May 1940, 13 aircraft from 501 Squadron intercepted 24 Heinkel 111 bombers escorted by 20 Bf 110's. In the fight, 11 Heinkels were claimed as 'kills' and others damaged, with little damage to the Hurricanes. The initial engagements with the *Luftwaffe* showed the Hurricane to be a tight-turning and steady platform, but the Watts two-bladed propeller was clearly unsuitable. One pilot complained that a Heinkel 111 was able to pull away from him in a chase, yet by this time the Heinkel was obsolescent.

Hurricanes equipped from the outset with Rotol constant-speed propellers were delivered to RAF Squadrons in May 1940 with deliveries continuing throughout the Battle of Britain. The Rotol constant-speed propeller enabled a pilot to select an optimum pitch for take-off, climb, cruise and combat, and also prevented the engine overheating in a dive. It transformed the Hurricane's performance from 'disappointing' to one of 'acceptable mediocrity'.

Last Witness Bill Green had chalked up an impressive tally of solo hours before the British Army was evacuated from Dunkirk:

'By that time I had become a corporal pilot UT – under training – and I was sent for and told, "This is your third stripe, Green, you're a sergeant now, go back to your squadron." I went back to 501 Squadron which had just come back from the Battle of France and was based at Middle Wallop. They had been fighting from day one to the end of the battle, the only squadron in Fighter Command to be in the thick of it all the way through, both the Battle of France and the Battle of Britain, and were badly bashed around.

'The CO asked me what I had done, I told him, he said, "Oh, you're no earthly good to me, I'm going to send you off to an OTU – Operational Training Unit."

'I found myself on attachment to 32 Sqdn at Biggin Hill where they had a training flight with a Miles Master which was unservicable. Because of this, I was flown over to Hornchurch which had a serviceable Master. After one dual circuit the instructor said, "You're okay, back to Biggin you go, there's no time to go solo tonight."

'This I did and presented myself to the training officer, F/O Flinders, with all the experience of one dual flight on a Miles Master, ready to learn to fly Hurricanes.

'He said, "501 Squadron have got Hurricanes. You'll know all about them. See that one over there with a P on it? Go and sit in it and when you feel happy, whack it off."

'That was my training – one flight in a Hurricane.'

Last Witness Mike Croskell had joined the RAFVR in June 1938. He was called up in September 1939, and posted to join 213 Squadron at Wittering on 26 January 1940:

'I had no fears about going into battle with the Hurricane. When we got the de Havilland three-bladed propeller, it did improve the performance. We did a lot of patrols in the winter of 1939/40, not seeing very much, wandering about over the convoys in case they got dive-bombed. We used to go off from Wittering, near Peterborough, to an airfield called Sutton Bridge nearer the coast, and do our convoy patrols over the North Sea from there. This was in 12 Group, under Leigh Mallory.

'And then we came south.'

In May 1940, 501 Squadron sent a detachment to France to assist the hardpressed squadrons of Air Component of the BEF for a few days. Croskell took part in the Battle of France and the operations over Dunkirk in May 1940, where he probably destroyed a Ju 87.

But luck had already run out for Billy Drake, three days into the *Blitzkrieg*:
'I had four or five confirmed kills before I was shot down on 13 May. I went off in a formation of four aeroplanes. When I got to 18,000 feet [5,486m] I realised

that I was getting no oxygen. My own aeroplane was unserviceable and I had got into this aeroplane, and they obviously hadn't completed the necessaries. I called the leader and said I had no oxygen. He told me to go back to base.

'On my way back I came down to 10,000 feet [3,048m] and I saw these three Dorniers. I looked around and couldn't see any 109s covering them, and got behind number three, and shot at him, quite successfully. I found out later he had been confirmed as destroyed by the British Army. Then I got behind the leader of this formation, and just as I was getting in range there was an almighty bang. A Messerschmitt had got behind me. I thought I had verified that he wasn't there but in fact he was there.

'My Hurricane was in flames, I was covered in petrol and glycol anti-freeze. I undid my harness and tried to bale out, but I had not released the hood, which probably saved my life. Had I opened the hood the flames would have come straight into the cockpit, on to my petrol-soaked flying suit. Just before I released the hood I turned the aeroplane upside down and then baled out. As a result the flames went underneath the wing and not into the cockpit.

'I jumped at 10,000 feet [3,048m]. This Messerschmitt was still trying to shoot at me as I was descending by parachute. I could hear the guns going but nothing hit me. At that time that sort of thing was considered unsporting. It depends entirely where the battle was taking place. If it was taking place where the enemy was over his own territory it was reasonable to have a shot at him, because you're trying to kill the pilot as well as the aeroplane, to stop him from getting into another aeroplane to shoot at you once again. But I never thought about doing this. I don't think anybody else in Fighter Command thought about shooting people down once they were on the end of the parachute.

'When I landed, bear in mind that I was very young and very blonde, all I saw was a whole bunch of French farmers with pitchforks and scythes.

'When they saw the RAF wings they could not have been more helpful. I was in a hospital within the French medical system for about a week. My friends were not quite certain whether I was alive or dead, until Paul Richey came to see me and reported back to the squadron that I was all right. But the squadron did not tell the Air Ministry and the Air Ministry did not tell my parents that I was still alive, and they thought I had been killed.'

From Paul Richey's Fighter Pilot:

'I found him in a room with a French officer – and by God, it was Billy! He was lying painfully on his stomach, having been operated on that morning. He told me he had left the flight because he'd run out of oxygen. On the way back to the airfield he saw four Dorniers and attacked them without realising they had an escort. He got one Dornier, maybe two, but a moment afterwards he was shot up to glory by 110s from behind. He got two bullets in the leg, one in the back, and cannon-shell splinters in the back, too. His aircraft caught fire and he baled out. He passed out on the way down but came to, quickly to see tracers whistling past him from the 110s. But as he heard a hell of a battle going on overhead, it is possible that was where the bullets came from. He felt pretty lousy and spoke with difficulty.'

Richey's book, the first RAF fighter pilot classic of the war, exhibits throughout an old-fashioned English manner, concerned with playing fair. He went out of his way to play down the fact that Billy Drake might have been shot at while descending in his parachute.

There is a famous revelation scene two days later, five days into the *Blitzkrieg*, when weary surviving pilots of 1 Squadron are talking, and the subject comes up of German fighters deliberately strafing refugees to clog up French roads and make it harder for British and French to move and fight on the ground. This had happened to Richey on his way back to his squadron after visiting Billy Drake:

> 'There was a stony silence in the mess when we told our story. Then a disillusioned Johnny Walker, flight commander to the Squadron CO, "Bull" Halloran, almost reluctantly said: "They are shits – after all."
>
> 'From this moment our concept of a chivalrous foe was dead.'

Drake had been operated on with no anaesthetics in the French hospital system, which was overwhelmed with refugees. He went from northern France to Chartres. There, an American girlfriend called Helen Ahrenfeldt, working with Spears Ambulance Service, picked him up in her private car. But the French Police arrested him – blond, young, wounded, trying to get away – clearly suspecting he was a German.

Helen called Paris to get help from the British Embassy, but the Embassy staff had already been evacuated. Helen called the U.S. Embassy which got him un-arrested, but also said to him, 'Get out of France.' Helen gave him a car and fuel with which he drove to Le Mans. He came home in a three-seat Fairey Battle, as one of the walking wounded.

Billy Drake:
'They sent virtually every fighter pilot who survived the Battle of France to go and teach RAF squadrons new tactics, which we had learned in the battle. We taught them what we knew about air warfare, which was still fairly basic. I taught them what the Hurricane was all about, what you could do with the aircraft, and if attacked by a 109 how to evade him. In a Hurricane you could out-turn a 109 below a height of about 12,000 feet [3,657m].

'In a circle you watched him very carefully, either in the mirror, or by turning your head. I don't think I ever used a mirror seriously. I used my eyesight, and also, if you were flying in the correct formation, we were looking after each other. That way we were able to suggest to the leader that he turned either left or right.'

When Billy Drake's fellow 1 Squadron member Paul Richey was wounded in combat, he sat in a French hospital totting up the pros and cons of how his Hurricane squadron had done against the Germans. From 30 October 1938 to 9 May 1940, 1 Squadron claimed 26 Germans destroyed, with the loss of just one new pilot. From 10 to 19 May, the squadron claimed 114 kills, losing two pilots presumed dead, two wounded and one a PoW. These figures filtered back to Britain and heartened Richey's colleagues in other Hurricane squadrons. It meant they could cope.

Almost all the RAF pilots of that period seemed to have the insouciance of the very young. Peter Hairs' description of being shot down reads almost as if he had fallen off a horse hunting foxes, rather than having had a close encounter with death:

'We were flying as a squadron, line astern, and I was some way in the middle. Suddenly I felt a thump underneath the aircraft. I looked down, thinking I might see French anti-aircraft gunners having a shot at me. It turned out that a 109 had come swooping down underneath us and fired at me. Why he chose me I don't know. The oil pressure dropped down to zero, and there was a fuzzy feeling in the cockpit, a bluish haze, which must have been a mixture of glycol and oil, along with a nasty smell of burning.

'I thought I had better get out and prepared to jump, but the aircraft seemed to be flying well, so I throttled back because I did not think the engine would last very long with no oil pressure. I chose a field and went down to land with my wheels up. It was a nice sensation, and you had not got too far to go to the ground when you got out of the cockpit.

'At the far south of the field there was a wooded area, and people came out from there. A French chap, a soldier, young chap, came towards me from the other side of the field, looking a bit scared and brandishing his rifle. I told him to put it down, and almost immediately a Jeep came through a gap in the hedge. It contained two English army officers. I was very pleased to see them, because my French is not very good.

'They took me aboard and drove me to the farmhouse where they were stationed, to eat lunch, then gave me a railway warrant, took me to the railway station, and put me on a train to Paris.

'I got there in the evening and booked myself into a hotel. My only luggage was my parachute. I went down to the bar and found an RAF officer there – I don't know what he was doing – but he showed me around the city that evening.

'I got up fairly early and got a train which took me to Chateaudun, where the squadron was based. When I arrived, I found they had moved on to Le Mans. I can't remember how I got to Le Mans, but they were quite pleased to see me because they didn't know what had happened to me.'

Back home, the defence of Britain was the responsibility of the Head of Fighter Command, Air Chief Marshall Sir Hugh Dowding, who divided his forces into four groups, each headed by an Air Vice-Marshal.

10 Group covered SW England, was led by the South African, Sir Quentin Brand.
11 Group, where the bulk of the fighting was to occur, covering south east England and London, was headed by a protégé of Dowding's, New Zealander Keith Park.
12 Group covered the Midlands, and was led by Trafford Leigh-Mallory, brother of the famous mountaineer George Leigh-Mallory, lost on Everest in 1924.
13 Group covered northern England and Scotland, and was led by Richard Saul.

As the fighting intensified into the Battle of Britain, squadrons were moved to the south east to be thrown into the fray, then, after being savaged, survivors were allocated to relatively quiet areas on 10, 12 or 13 groups to re-build.

Dowding was the oldest man ever to lead Fighter Command, and would normally have expected to retire in 1942 at the age of 60. Born on 24 April 1882 in Moffat, south west Scotland, the eldest son of a schoolmaster, he was brought up in a Victorian middle class household. He was educated at Winchester, like his father, and was accepted into the Royal Military Academy at Woolwich in 1899. He wanted to become an engineer, but failed his exams and was accepted as a gunner instead.

He spent ten years in various army posts abroad, and when he returned to England he took flying lessons at Brooklands in 1913, leading a RFC squadron on the Western Front in 1916. After the Battle of the Somme, Dowding clashed with Trenchard, commanding the RFC, over the need to rest pilots exhausted by non-stop duty. Dowding wanted them rested, Trenchard did not see it as necessary. Dowding was sent back to Britain and, although promoted to the rank of Brigadier, saw no more active service during that war.

He rose through the ranks in the 1920s – Chief Staff Officer for RAF Iraq Command in 1924 – but he was struck by personal tragedy. His wife of just two years died, leaving him to bring up his son alone. He withdrew into himself, and was seen as a loner, and to some, arrogant. In 1930 he was transferred from planning the technology of air defence, which eventually included the introduction of radar and the Royal Observer Corps, to commanding Britain's fighters in the field. He became an expert at plotting enemy raids and the radio control of aircraft, seeing the Hurricanes coming under his command, and later Spitfires, as having a profound effect on fighting tactics.

Known as 'Stuffy', he was knighted in 1934, promoted Air Chief Marshall in 1937, but was passed over as Chief of Air Staff that year. Among his fellow senior officers, his cards had been marked.

He must have been under nearly intolerable strain. Having been passed over, he was told in August 1938 that he would be retired in June 1939. But a newspaper leak with this news meant he got a letter on 20 March 1939 saying he would not go that June. He was now expected to stay on until March 1940. With the country now at war, he was recognised as the most qualified of all the senior officers to lead Fighter Command into what everyone knew would be a fight to the death. Dowding's retirement deadline was extended – at one day's notice – until 14 July. On 10 July, ironically, the day that the Battle of Britain is considered to have begun, he was told he would not be given the push until 31 Oct, even more ironically, the official end of that battle.

His 'enemies' within the RAF included Air Vice Marshall William Sholto-Douglas, who, though two ranks below Dowding, held a powerful position as Assistant Chief of Air Staff, and one of Dowding's own Air Vice Marshalls, Trafford Leigh Mallory. Their problem in opposing Dowding was that no one had his qualifications and, as crisis followed crisis, he was so obviously the perfect candidate to direct Britain's young fighter pilots. Yet he had strong opinions, and crossed Churchill more than once, becoming more and more politically isolated throughout the Battle.

Dowding had chosen Keith Park over other candidates to lead 11 Group, where the real fighting would occur. This incurred the deadly enmity of the very ambitious Leigh-Mallory, whose speciality was the co-ordination of air/ground attacks, just the thing the Germans were doing in France, but not a skill required for the first great aerial battle in history. This enmity turned out to be fatal for Dowding, and Park, though their downfall thankfully came too late to change history.

One cause of Leigh Mallory's ire was his demand after the Munich Crisis of 1938 for 29 of Fighter Command's 41 squadrons to be allocated to 12 Group. His argument was that all the vital manufacturing resources in Britain were in the midlands and that would be the natural target for the Germans. This was not an unreasonable argument, but Dowding refused. A year later, after the war had begun, Leigh-Mallory again asked for another disproportionate division of squadrons. Again, Dowding refused.

In retrospect, like many other of his decisions, Dowding was correct in focusing his defensive efforts on Keith Park's 11 Group, but that was not so obvious at the time. Park has since drawn comparison to history's great captains, like Wellington at Waterloo. Wellington's tactics, also much criticised by his contemporaries, are now seen as brilliant. So it is with Park. Leigh-Mallory, leading 12 Group, Park's greatest critic and the man who engineered the downfall of both Park and Dowding after their terrific victory, was later described – by the Germans – as 'The Flying Sergeant'.

On 9 March 1940, the headquarters of RAF Fighter Command was established at Bentley Priory near London. On 20 April, Park took over 11 Group. Twenty days later, France was attacked with great ferocity in the end to the 'Phoney War'.

The French had a large air force, with more fighters available after their formal surrender on 25 June than they had when the *Blitzkrieg* started on 10 May. Yet they seemed paralysed, almost frightened to death by the myth of the *Luftwaffe*. As the Germans blasted their way into France, the French Government daily pleaded with Winston Churchill to throw his precious RAF fighters into battle, and continued to make these urgent pleas even while secretly opening negotiations to surrender to Hitler's forces.

On the morning of 15 May, only five days after the German onslaught began, French Prime Minister Paul Reynaud telephoned Churchill. Reynaud wanted ten RAF squadrons immediately. 'We have been defeated,' he wailed, 'We are beaten; we have lost the battle.' This alarmed Churchill, a great Francophile, who flew to Paris the following day, intending to bolster the fighting spirits of the French. He was willing – it seemed back home to Dowding – to sacrifice any number of Fighter Command's Hurricanes to save France from its own defeatism. Dowding fought for every squadron, against more demands each day. It took two more days, until 18 May, before it became obvious, even to Churchill, that the French were looking for someone to blame for their impending defeat.

Perfidious Albion was an obvious candidate.

In total, 261 Hurricanes were sent to France. Of these, 195 were either shot down or were so badly damaged that they were destroyed on the ground by retreating RAF personnel, figures that fully vindicate Dowding's earlier decision not to send more aircraft to the continent. The remaining RAF fighters were eventually withdrawn to Britain from where they re-engaged the enemy over the massive evacuation of the BEF from Dunkirk which began on 30 May.

One of the great aces of the Battle of Britain, leading 74 'Tiger' Squadron from Hornchurch, the South African 'Sailor' Malan (his given name was Adolf, not then popular locally) discussed tactics with two other squadrons – 65 and 54 – after fighting over Dunkirk on 4 June. They agreed to abandon official RAF tactics, opting for 'finger four', a loose formation of four fighters just like the *Luftwaffe schwarme*. Malan also coned his machine guns at 250 yards [228m], instead of using the 'Dowding Spread'. These lessons were spread very slowly.

Some 330,000 British and French servicemen were plucked to safety from the beaches of Dunkirk by the Royal Navy and a flotilla of little ships. Not every soldier could be saved. Many were left behind, captured, wounded or dead. The Hurricane squadrons lost many of their most prominent pilots.

Peter Ayerst:

'Cobber Kain got killed in a silly way. The squadron always "beat up" airfields in the early days, often in formation. It was a leftover from the carefree days of the 1930s. In the first few days of June, Cobber was due to come home. The rest of us had already left, there were not many of us alive anyway. Cobber Kain was at the squadron base at Echemines, south-west of Paris.

'He had finished operational flying, but he said he was going to have one more flight before he went back to England. He went up, and was doing a "beat-up" of the airfield but he came across too low, did two slow rolls and attempted a third with insufficient speed, and he went in. He was the highest-scoring RAF fighter pilot at the time.'

In the retreat back to England, great efforts were made to rescue fighting aircraft, because every one counted.

Peter Hairs:

'We had moved on 18 June from Le Mans to Dinard on the coast – near St Malo – and one of the Hurricanes had been left behind because they could not start its engine. The CO asked me to go there and fly it back. There were some ground crew left behind, to help me. Gibby – John Gibson – had liberated a French two-seater aircraft, so he flew me over. We got to Le Mans, landed, and he flew off, leaving me behind with the ground crew still working on the Hurricane. They had all the panels and cowlings off the engine, but they still couldn't get it to work.

'Then my flight commander, Pat Cox, flew over in his Hurricane, and said, "Look, if you can't get this thing going, we'll both fly back in my Hurricane. You can sit on the seat and I will sit on your lap." He was shorter than I was.

'Then the men got the engine to fire, hastily put the panels back on, and I was able to get the Hurricane into the air and fly it back. The ground crew had a truck there to drive back to a place of safety.

'I must admit when I crossed the coast, the engine seemed to give a little blip, which was a bit worrying because I am not a swimmer. One of my fears was coming down in the Channel, or coming down in flames. I don't like fire and I didn't like the idea of coming down in the water. Thankfully, neither of these things happened to me.'

Paris was occupied on 14 June, the French Government having fled to Bordeaux. On 22 June, an armistice was signed between France and Germany, marking a spectacular German victory. With so many men and so much of its equipment having been lost in France, the British Army was in dire straits and the RAF was seriously short of fighters, making it truly fortunate that Germany was unprepared to mount a cross channel invasion close on the heels of the Dunkirk evacuation.

In fact, for much of June, Hitler thought he had beaten Britain, and was waiting for that fact to be acknowledged. The *Luftwaffe* was luxuriating in victory, occupying all those lovely French air force bases, finding billets and local pubs, eyeing the local talent, confident that Britain would surrender, or if not they could be easily beaten. On 22 June Hitler told the *Luftwaffe* to restrict their operations to the seas around the British Isles and not attack English cities, thus buying the RAF a few weeks to reinforce their fighter arm.

There was still intense development work underway to make the Hurricane a better fighter. On 11 June a Hurricane Mark I was fitted with a two-stage, supercharged Rolls Royce Merlin XX engine that at sea level was rated at 1,300hp rising to 1,460hp at 6,250 feet [1,905m]. After numerous tests, the aircraft was given the designation of Mark II, the improved power plant being the only difference from the Mark I. This first model of the Mk II was known as the Series I.

Further modifications took place as Sydney Camm made improvements, and the next model was given the title of Mark II Series 2. The fuselage was given added strengthening, needed to cope with redesigned wings that had attachment points for external stores.

By the time of the intense stage of the Battle of Britain, from 8 August, the RAF could field 32 fresh squadrons of Hurricanes and 19 squadrons of Spitfires. At the time, 60 Canadian-built Hurricanes were beginning to arrive as well.

Chapter Six

THE BATTLE OF BRITAIN BEGINS

A total of 1,715 Hurricanes flew with Fighter Command during the period of the battle, far in excess of all other British fighters combined. Having entered service a year before the Spitfire, the Hurricane was 'half-a-generation' older, and markedly inferior in terms of speed and climb. However, the Hurricane had proved itself a robust, manoeuvrable aircraft capable of surviving fearsome combat damage. Unlike the Spitfire, it was a wholly operational, go-anywhere, do-anything fighter by July 1940.

To put the supply of Hurricanes into perspective, ten days into the *Blitzkreig*, on 20 May 1940, Fighter Command had 30 operational Hurricane and Spitfire squadrons. It had six Blenheim squadrons – the fighter version – and one doomed Defiant Squadron. In terms of fighters actually capable of putting up a decent fight, that meant 247 Spitfires, and just 99 Hurricanes. One way or another, at Churchill's insistence, the rest of the Hurricanes had been sent to France.

Six weeks later, on 1 July, Fighter Command had 58 squadrons, of which 29 were equipped with Hurricanes and 19 with Spitfires – an increase of 60 per cent in effective fighters – with no increase in Blenheim or Defiant squadrons. This was despite an order from Deputy Chief of the Air Staff, Sholto Douglas, who told Dowding to create eight squadrons of Defiants, the Merlin-engined fighter with two crew, a four-gun rear turret and no forward armament. The fact that this suggestion was refused by Dowding cannot have done anything to help the latter's case when the political knives came out towards the end of the Battle of Britain, no matter how wise Dowding's decision was.

Dowding's problem was trying to find enough fighter pilots, but it was compounded by self-inflicted wounds. Three hundred fighter aircraft were being produced each week, but only 200 pilots. Hundreds of experienced pilots were 'flying desks', because almost all officer ranks in the RAF were expected to be filled by pilots. Despite Churchill's orders, only 30 of these 'flying desk' pilots were released to front line squadrons.

Drawing from regular RAF forces as well as the Auxiliary Air Force and the RAFVR, Fighter Command could muster 1,103 fighter pilots on 1 July. Replacement pilots, with little actual flight training and often no gunnery training whatsoever, suffered high casualty rates. Last Witness Bob Foster had more hours than most, and with the traditional insularity of an islander, the blind historical belief that they could never lose:

'Nobody ever thought we were going to lose this battle. Morale was always very high. It never crossed our minds that the Germans might defeat us, and destroy the RAF. Maybe it was ignorance, but I never really thought, and I know others felt the same way, that we would lose. We weren't losing. We lost odd chaps. There again, I have been asked, did you feel badly about losing friends? The answer is – I say this and it sounds a bit harsh – most of these chaps I had only known for three or four weeks. I joined the Squadron in July, and I had never met any of them before. July, August, we got together a bit, September ... they were fellow pilots. They weren't old buddies or friends.

'It was very sad when you lost chaps like Jock Muirhead or Ralph Hope, wonderful chaps, but ... it was a done thing, and you went on with your own job. I can tell you exactly who they were, even to this day, the friends I lost. George Forrester was the first to go, then later on Jock Muirhead went, then Charles English, and so on. I remember them as young men. I can see their faces. There were no great lasting friendships that were broken up. Charles English was with us only for ten days. He was a couple of years older than me ...'

The *Luftwaffe* could muster more fighter pilots, 1,450, than the RAF. Many had combat experience, having learned their trade during the Spanish Civil War. They had gone through comprehensive courses in aerial gunnery, as well as instructions in tactics suited for fighter-versus-fighter combat.

For a month after the fall of France, Hitler banned the *Luftwaffe* from flying in British air space. The Germans thought they had won and to Hitler it was obvious that Britain was beaten. He did not want to damage facilities on an island he confidently expected to dominate quite soon. Goering was told he might engage the RAF over the Channel, and sink British supply convoys, but nothing inland. This ban lasted until 25 July.

Nevertheless, on 4 July Hitler outlined four goals for the *Luftwaffe*:

Destroy the RAF
Destroy its supply system
Destroy British aircraft production
Damage the Royal Navy as much as possible.

But as the realisation grew that Britain would still not acknowledge German mastery of Europe, serious thought was given to planning an invasion. It was given the code-name 'Sealion'. The Sealion invasion front was targeted along a wide stretch of coast between Ramsgate and the Isle of Wight. The intention was to land 160,000 troops. The German Army considered the Channel crossing as 'a river crossing on a wide front' and waited to be offered transport.

The German Navy, the *Kriegsmarine*, consistently threw cold water on the whole idea. On 11 July Admiral Raeder told Hitler that an invasion could only be contemplated with full air superiority. The *Luftwaffe* reported that it would take between two and four weeks to establish air superiority over Britain. This claim was made with faulty intelligence. In fact, the German High Command knew very little about the logistics governing how Fighter Command worked. They under-estimated the importance of radar and the Royal Observer Corps, they knew little of British aircraft production, and not a great deal about the fighting qualities of the Hurricanes and Spitfires ranged against them. One result of their poor intelligence was that *Luftwaffe* High Command became increasing deluded about the effects they were having.

The first invasion date was pencilled in: 25 August 1940. The *Luftwaffe* was officially given five weeks to carry out its four goals, from 8 Aug to 15 Sept. Goering planned to use three air fleets.

Number 2, led by 'Smiling Albert' Kesselring, was to target south east England and London.

Number 3, led by Hugo Sperrle, concentrated on the west country, the midlands and north west England.

Number 5, led by Han-Jurgen Stumpff in Norway, targeted the north of England and Scotland.

As the battle developed, so Sperrle became responsible for the night-time *Blitz* attacks, while Kesselring took on all the daylight raids.

The period of fighting over the Channel was an early means of finding out how good individual pilots were; some reputations soared, while others plummeted. The careful, rigid system of rank had no significance at all in who was, and who was not, a good killer.

Billy Drake:
'One was always surprised at the activities of most pilots. Those who you thought were good turned out to be average. Some of those who you thought would be bad turned out to be absolutely first class. One had to fly with them on a number of occasions, and operate with them, to be able to assess. The views of the flight commanders were equally important in making such assessment; they had such jobs because they were classed slightly above the others.

'I had experience of one chap that I had to throw out in the end. What happened was that we were being attacked by 109s and we had a drill that, as soon as I saw them, I watched them come into our formation, and said "prepare to break", that is, break left or right.

'I did this on three occasions with this chap flying as my number two, and he broke the wrong way, that is, into me, every time. He missed, thank God. In the end I got hold of him and said, "I don't think you're enjoying flying with me, are you?"

'He said, "No, I don't want to be a fighter pilot anyway." I sacked him. He didn't like being a fighter pilot and he proved it.'

There were also problems with young RAF pilots who were often barely trained. It was not uncommon for youngsters with ten hours experience on Hurricanes or Spitfires to be thrown in to fight, and the first time they actually fired their guns was in battle.

Bob Foster:

'I finished training at Sutton Bridge by 18 July having done about 40 to 50 hours. We did a lot of formation flying in simulated attacks, useless when it came to the fighting, but that was the way it went. My instructor was a chap called Smallwood, who finished his career as Air Chief Marshal Sir Basil Smallwood. In those days he was a young flying officer, a regular RAF career man who survived a week's flying patrols over France in May, and was then instructing on Hurricanes.

'Our postings came through. I lived in London in those days, and I was posted up to a place outside Edinburgh. There was a Scotsman on the same course posted to Kenley. We went to see the station commander to see if he could swap the postings and, thank God, he said no. That chap went down in July to Kenley, and he lasted a few weeks and that was it, he was killed. In Edinburgh I got another 40 hours in – for a total of 90 hours in all – before we came down to Croydon into the battle proper.'

What was important for Keith Park, and his mentor Hugh Dowding, was not to make too many useless sacrifices. It was a question of how many losses the RAF could sustain and still achieve its goal. Bomber Command tolerated losses of 80 per cent in the first months of the war before they realised they were essentially doing no damage.

The crucial tactic in how Fighter Command approached the battle was exactly how to engage the massed formations of German aircraft. Hurricanes were generally directed at the bombers; they were a steady gun platform, and had a speed difference over Do 17 and He 111s that they did not have over Bf 109s. The Spitfires were directed at the German fighters.

John Ellacombe:

'I was posted to 151 Squadron in North Weald in early July, 1940. I had about 25 hours experience. Three weeks later, I was in my first combat.

'We were flying on patrol and saw a lot of bombers and dived down at them, straight through them. A couple of the chaps shot things down.'

On his next sortie, Ellacombe spotted a formation of enemy aircraft that his CO, Pete Gordon, had failed to see. They returned to base without attacking but when Gordon heard that Ellacombe had sighted the enemy, he insisted that Ellacombe fly as his number two from then on.

John Ellacombe:

'He was a very nice man. I was with him when he was shot down. He baled out of a burning Hurricane and landed in a river in Essex. As he walked out, I thought he was taking his gloves off, but it was the skin coming off his hands.

'From then on we all flew with our big gauntlets, which served me well, because later on when I was shot down, the only thing that burned my hand was where the fastening burnt in.'

Park was careful and intelligent about how he threw his fighters in, often in small numbers, squadrons or even flights. They constantly harried the Germans all the way to their targets, and all the way back again. Park was keen to attack before the Germans reached their targets, and break up their formations.

The rival view – which gradually destroyed Dowding's career and pretty well ruined Park's – was that it was better to shoot 50 aircraft down *after* they had bombed and were racing for home, than shooting 10 down *before* they got to their targets and scattering their formations. As far back as 1938 Sholto Douglas had said that the point of Fighter Command was not to stop the bombers getting through, but to shoot down as many of them as possible. This is the essence of the 'Big Wing' argument that was described time and time again by our Last Witnesses, all of whom were hostile to it.

The 'Big Wing' was the brainchild of the legless British ace, Douglas Bader, a protégé of the 12 Group Commander, Trafford Leigh-Mallory. At no time in this fierce tactical fight were the people of London and other British cities, who were much more likely to be bombed under Sholto Douglas and Leigh Mallory's tactics, involved in the debate. There is no question what their view would have been.

The definitive history of the Battle of Britain, *The Most Dangerous Enemy*, was written by historian Stephen Bungay, who identified six arguments against the 'Big Wing' philosophy:

'First, getting a single squadron into a fight was fast and simple. It would be airborne within two minutes of the 'scramble' order, under a single leader.

'Second, it was flexible enough to have its plans changed in the air, and this flexibility reduced serious losses.

'Third, unlike a "Big Wing", a single squadron was difficult to detect in the sky.

'Fourth, RAF pilots had a target-rich environment – get in, hit, get out. They may be greatly out-numbered, but virtually everything they shot at was a German.

'Fifth, the Germans suffered continuous attack as soon as they crossed the coast and from then on, which wore them down.

'Sixth, squadron claims were much more accurate than the gross claims made by "Big Wing" formations, which turned out to be almost as inaccurate as German claims.'

Bob Doe:

'I believed in going in bald-headed, not waiting to get into position. My view was, don't give them time to think, just go at them. The reason I had any success was I had been trained as a bomber pilot, and the only gunnery we did was right at the beginning of the war, where I did lots of shooting from the rear turret of an Anson. I knew the basics of deflection shooting. It's the shooting that matters in a dog-fight, rather than the flying.

'An average pilot could get more from a Hurricane than from a Spitfire. But if you were good you could get more from a Spitfire. A Hurricane was like a brick-built shit-house. It was sturdy and reliable, and it did not leap about when the guns were fired.

'I did get bashed around in the first year of the war, and I was very lucky. My official Battle of Britain score was 14 ½ – the ½ meant you shared a kill with another pilot.'

Tactically, Dowding and Park felt that the Germans would give up if they became convinced that they were not achieving their aim. It was perception that mattered, as much as the actual number of aircraft shot down.

All fighter forces over-claim. RAF pilots claimed more than they actually destroyed, probably by 1.5-to-1, but the Germans were not helped by their own huge claims against the RAF, which were threefold higher than their actual kills, and this distorted their tactics. They were constantly expecting to see fewer and fewer RAF fighters turn up – when this did not happen, they began to lose heart. There was a gradual realisation that, no matter how many attacks they launched, they were met every time by Hurricanes and Spitfires in never-decreasing numbers.

Bob Foster:

'Going into battle I had confidence in the aeroplane, though I think for the first few occasions you don't really know what is going on half the time. I fired at quite a lot of stuff but didn't register anything that I know of, because I didn't hang around in the danger zone. If you did, it was the last thing you would do. Everything was over so quickly.

'We had reflector sights, and were supposed to set the wingspan of the enemy aircraft within the sights, and when that filled the gap, you open fire. If you had time you did it but as far as I was concerned it was hit or miss and then get out of the way.'

British pilots like Bob Doe just had to keep punching, no matter what their losses, until the chill winds and cloudy skies of November, when there was time to lick their wounds, and the real threat of invasion was over.

John Ellacombe:

'The Hurricane had extremely good visibility, sitting high up in the cockpit. You had this big mirror on the top, a sort of rear-view mirror from a car. Twice, with the 109s I shot down, I saw them coming down at me through the mirror. The drill was, you do a flick roll – you put your left foot hard over and your stick to the right and the aircraft would do a flick roll – and the Messerschmitt would finish off in front of you. I was so close to one that I shot its radiators off before I pulled out and shot him down and he crashed into the sea.'

As the battle developed, it became more obvious that there was no, or inadequate, air/sea rescue for the RAF, yet it took a year to make such arrangements. By contrast, the Germans had an efficient system, picking up Germans and British alike. Going into the Channel was normally more fatal for British pilots than for Germans.

Of the 89 pilots killed in the period of 32 days after 10 July, ten died over the North Sea and 58 over the Channel, almost 80 per cent of the pilots lost. Only four wounded and three unhurt pilots were fished out of the sea. In all, some 200 RAF pilots and aircrew were lost at sea during the battle.

There was an ongoing debate about shooting down air/sea rescue aircraft flying under the Red Cross. The RAF saw these aircraft as spies, gathering intelligence, and felt that it was unfair to use the Red Cross to protect them, so they were shot at. The Germans felt aggrieved.

Bungay gave this summary of Fighter Command losses 10 July – 11 August.

By Bf 109 – 87 destroyed, 52 damaged, total 139.
By Bf 110 – 6 destroyed, 10 damaged, total 16.

By bomber – 13 destroyed, 38 damaged, total 51.
Collisions (4), flak (1), Friendly (1) and unknown accounted for the other 9
destroyed.

Accidents accounted for 47 destroyed, and 68 damaged! Pilot error accounted
for most accidents – five pilots forgot to lower their undercarriage, and 28
accidents occurred in night-flying practice.

During this period the Bf 109 damaged or destroyed 66 Spitfires, and 66
Hurricanes, and the bombers 25 of each. As two thirds of the fighters were
Hurricanes, were the Spitfires being worked harder? They certainly appeared
to have a better rate of survival. Of 66 Spitfires hit by 109s, only 31 were
destroyed rather than damaged. Of the 66 Hurricanes hit, 45 were destroyed.
The bombers were even more deadly to the Hurricanes. Of 25 Spitfires hit by
bomber fire, only 2 were destroyed. Of 25 Hurricanes, the figure was 11. Of
the total pilots killed, 51 flew Hurricanes, and 25 Spitfires. Bungay suggested
that Hurricanes were more vulnerable to cannon fire. They may also simply
have had more exposure to the enemy, especially in close encounters with
bombers. Figures can be interpreted in many different ways.

But Bungay thought the main fault of the Hurricane was with two of
its three petrol tanks, one in front of the pilot, but the more vulnerable one
either side:

> 'Once the wing tanks did catch fire, flames would spread very fast along
> the fabric part of the fuselage, which starts just behind where the tanks are
> and is in the path of flames blown back by the slipstream. The fabric was
> covered with highly inflammable dope. More importantly for the pilot, there
> was open space between the thick wings and the fuselage. The air flowing
> through gun-ports would feed the flames and take them directly from the
> wing into the floor of the cockpit. In such a situation, no pilot, who would
> at that moment be rather preoccupied with other very immediate concerns,
> would be likely to notice whether the source of the flames was from in front
> or the sides. As the fire would have erupted within a split second from the
> cockpit floor, even the most careful and detached of observers would have
> found it difficult to do so in any case.'

But under realistic combat conditions, if a Bf 109 stayed with a Spitfire in
a turn, a Spitfire could be on its tail within a shooting distance of 250 yards
(228m) after seven and a half turns. This would take about two minutes. A
Hurricane could do so in less.

The Bf 109 had other disadvantages. It was so difficult to fly that it killed
1,500 learner pilots in the first two years of the war, most of them taking off
or landing.

Last Witness Tom Neil assessed other German aircraft:

'If you hit a 109 over England, in the plumbing system, it wouldn't get home. If you hit a bomber, like a Dornier, badly, it probably wouldn't get home. If you hit a Junkers 88, the bugger would get home. They were as tough as boots.

'You saw aircraft every day that you were sure wouldn't get home. In fact, if you damaged an aircraft, we didn't even report it. You were damaging aircraft two or three times a day, but so what? You can't claim a "damaged". You knew you had hit him, there were things flying off, but that was it – it seemed to fly on after that.

'Other times you would say, "Well, I am sure I shot this chap down, but I didn't see him land" because he might have landed 50 miles [80 km] away. This is where all the over-claiming came in. By the time, as a German, you'd got to the ground 50 miles away, you had been attacked 4 times by different squadrons all the way down, each of which would have claimed a Hun.'

On 29 July, the German High Command agreed to commit 50 per cent of *Luftwaffe* bombers to destroying the RAF, leaving the other 50 per cent to cover – tactically – the invasion itself.

Goering claimed there were two main aims, to destroy the RAF and stop seaborne supplies. A key to both was the use of the fearsome Ju 87 Stuka, the dive-bomber which played such a large part in the defeat of France. It was planned to attack specific English targets with Ju 87s, forcing the RAF fighters to defend, and therefore enticing them up to be destroyed by Bf 109s. Goering believed that not only the Hurricane but the Spitfire was inferior to the Messerschmitt Bf 109. The Germans wanted to engage, fighter to fighter, but the RAF would not waste time doing this, going instead for the bombers.

A downside for the Germans was that, caught by either a Hurricane or a Spitfire having burst through the protective German fighter screen, Stukas were easy meat. Young RAF pilots talked of 'Stuka Parties', and relished getting into a fight with them.

On the other hand, approaching the peak of the fighting in the Battle of Britain, one of the greatest factors working in the favour of Hurricane pilots was the widespread belief among German pilots that the Hurricane was easy meat.

The Germans became over-confident, more open to mistakes. Hardly any Germans admitted to having been shot down by a Hurricane – it was always by Spitfires.

Being a snob could be fatal.

Chapter Seven

THE LEGEND OF 'THE FEW'

German generals were worried about the damage that the RAF could inflict on their invasion force, and Hitler agreed to their request that the invasion should be postponed until the RAF had been destroyed.

Going into the battle, the *Luftwaffe* had 2,800 aircraft stationed in France, Belgium, Holland and Norway. This force outnumbered RAF Fighter Command four to one. On paper, it looked a foregone conclusion, but German fighters only had the fuel to stay over England for half an hour before having to return to home bases.

The RAF had the benefit of nearby airfields, the advantage of an effective early warning radar system and secret intelligence information provided by Ultra, having cracked the German signals codes.

Last Witness Tom Neil, gave this assessment of the forces facing each other:

'The RAF had three types of aircraft, and this is where it differed from the German Air Force. The *Luftwaffe* started at square one. Your German is a land animal. The first thing you see about him is his army. He regards his other forces as ancillaries to his army. Their Air Force always was – what we called later – a tactical air force.

'They had short-range fighters to defend their dive bombers. Their Do 17s, the He 111, their Ju 88s, were only meant to fly and fight within a hundred miles of the forward line. The army was the important element. The Air Force was there to look after the Army.

'This is why the Bf 109 used to give them grey hairs. It was not really designed to carry out offensives over other peoples' countries. German pilots – whom I spoke to many times after the war – told me how much they hated flying over Britain. They hated the Channel, were aware of their short range, because their aircraft were not really designed to do it.

'At the time we had what was called the Strategic Bomber Force – they were supposed to be heavy bombers but in the beginning we didn't have any. Eventually we had Lancasters. We had the interceptor fighters to defend the country – Hurricanes and Spitfires. Then we had a whole mass of in-between aircraft which were meant to control the Empire. These were Vickers Wellesleys, all sorts of aircraft which were useless otherwise, other than manning the North West Frontier.'

There were four phases to the battle. Between 10 July and 12 August, it was all about running fights over the English Channel, the *Kanalkampf,* to establish *Luftwaffe* 'ownership'.

From August 13 to 23 August, it was the 'Eagle Attack', against fighter airfields near the coast.

From 24 August to 6 September – the critical phase of the battle – it involved attacking all the fighter airfields the *Luftwaffe* could find. In 33 heavy attacks against 11 Group's area, 24 were against airfields. Biggin Hill and Hornchurch were attacked four times, Debden and North Weald twice.

From 7 September, day attacks switched to British towns and cities, but especially London.

Last Witness Mike Croskell was early into the fight:
    'On 11 August, flying with 213 Hurricane Squadron, I chased a Junkers 88 and got a good old burst of shot into it. The chaps got out of it, sat on the wing and then slid off with their parachutes, which opened, and the aircraft went down.

    'Then I got tied up with five 109s, all chasing around in circles, until I got into the inner circle and shot the last one down. They all buzzed off but I was out of ammunition anyway. We only had ten or 12 seconds firing.

    'I was confident that in a scrap with Bf 109s, the Hurricane could always out-turn it. What the 109s used to do was stick the nose down good and hard, and dive down. We had the old float-chamber carburettor in those days, and the engine used to go "phut"when you stuck the nose down. Until we got the new carburettor we could not really follow them. They knew that if we were chasing them and they did a steep dive they would get away from us.'

The problem Croskell faced plagued Spitfires and Hurricanes in 1940 using the Merlin engine, fitted with an 'SU' carburettor. When they went into negative G by pitching the nose hard down, fuel was forced to the top of the float chamber. This starved the engine, which lost power for two or three seconds. If the negative G continued, the carburettor flooded and drowned the supercharger with over-rich mixture. This could shut down the engine completely, not the sort of thing you wanted in a fight to the death.

German fighter pilots, whose engines were fuel-injected, did not suffer this problem, exploiting their advantage in a fight by pitching steeply forward. RAF pilots could counter by half-rolling – so there was no negative G – but this took time and allowed the Germans to dive away.

It took a 'flaming Women's Libber' to work out a practical – if temporary – solution. Tilly Shilling, then 31 years old, was a bright engineer and well-known racing motorcyclist. Working at the Royal Aircraft Establishment in Farnborough, she introduced a simple flow restrictor, a small metal disc like a plain washer. The restrictor orifice was made to accommodate just the fuel needed for maximum engine power, the setting usually used in dog-fights. It was a stopgap solution, but it allowed RAF pilots to go through quick negative G without loss of engine power.

With a small team she travelled around the countryside in early 1941 fitting the restrictors, giving priority to front-line units. The device became known as 'Miss Shilling's Orifice.'

The Germans attacked RAF airfields on 12 August, starting with Hawkinge, two raids on Lympne, one on Manston, and the attacks went on through to 5 September on Biggin Hill and Hornchurch. Though causing a lot of damage, they were less effective than they might have been because of a far-sighted decision by Dowding in 1938 to order RAF aircraft dispersed in blast pens, not lined up like sittings ducks. The *Luftwaffe* also began mass bomber attacks on radar stations and aircraft factories.

Last Witness Bill Green had his first experience of flying a Hurricane around this time, never yet having flown solo in an aircraft with retractable undercarriage and never having flown any aeroplane armed for combat:

'I was frightened to death, of course. I went up to about 20,000 feet [6,100m], and thought I would do a loop. I pulled the stick back as I would have done in a Hawker Hart and immediately blacked out. I looked out of the side and saw the sky and realised I was upside down. I put the stick over to roll out and went into a spin.

'The buzz was, for us sprogs, that if you went into a spin in a Hurricane, that was it, you couldn't get out of it. I had been taught how to recover from a spin – opposite rudder, stick forward to unshield the rudder and let it get the maximum effect from the slipstream – and I was so relieved when I came out of the spin.

'Then I was called back because I was in the middle of the Battle of Britain fighting zone and any passing German Messerschmitt could have come along and shot me down. There were reports of 40 Bf 109s in the area and the intercom was abuzz with action. It was a brave new world for me.

'When I got back to Biggin Hill I was over-confident. I over-shot tremendously and ran out of runway, on to the grass, zig-zagging in and out of parked Hurricanes as best I could, and finished up within six feet [1.8m] of the edge of the airfield, looking at a hedge.

'I was relieved to have got it down without bending it, or me. Someone jumped on the wing – it was Squadron Leader Worrall, CO of 32 Squadron. He gave me a hell of a dressing-down. "Come to my office," he shouted. "You're confined to camp for two weeks!"

'This was in the middle of August. I was not judged quite ready to go into battle.'

By 13 August (*Adlertag* or 'Eagle Day') the weather was clear and the concerted attacks on the RAF's airfields began in earnest. Wherever possible Hurricanes were directed to intercept the enemy bombers, their tightly grouped armament and steady gun platform made them ideal for the role. Although generally outmatched by the Bf 109, they were capable of dealing with the fast but fragile, twin-engined Bf 110.

Mike Croskell:

'The 110s used to go into protective circles, because they had a chap sitting in the back with a gun. They used to try and entice you into the middle of the circle, then they all shot at you, which was a bit unsporting. I just took a quick poke at one of them at the outside of their turn, and shot one down and then buzzed off quick, and never thought to look in the rear-view mirror to see if any of his mates were following me.

'They were – there was me with two 109s behind me. Before they got off a shot I pulled the nose up and got into the only cloud in the sky, and lost them. I don't think fear came up at all. I can't say I remember being very fearful. The only time your heart missed a beat was when you were in the crew room and the telephone rang. I remember my flight commander – Operations rang us – he just picked up the phone and said, "City Gas Works."

'This amused us all, but we still went tearing outside.'

The Germans mounted a series of attacks on nine RAF airfields, and against the primitive but effective British radar systems. The raids were countered by the RAF and no radar station was permanently knocked out. Fighter Command managed to have the right number of aircraft in the right place and at the right time, to frustrate the German onslaught.

The weather forecast for 13 August turned out to be inaccurate, which caused a classic cock-up. Initially, Goering postponed the attack. The German fighters got the delaying signal, but the bombers didn't, because they didn't hear the recall. The bombers and fighters operated on different frequencies. One German fighter pilot slung his aircraft all over the sky to signal the bombers to turn back, but the bomber pilots thought he was showing off. Five German bombers were lost, though ten RAF fighters were claimed. In fact, only one British aircraft was lost.

Last Witness Peter Ayerst:
'I got a Heinkel on 14 August. All of the chaps in France with fighting experience were put on to instructing. I was sent to Sutton Bridge, and was there for a month. I had two Hurricane OTUs, one at Sutton Bridge, and one at Aston Down.

'Then the powers that be opened one at Hawarden, near Chester, and took some of the instructors – including me – as the nucleus. We had finished flying for the day and the airmen had spread our aircraft out and dispersed them around the edge of the airfield, packing them all up for the day. It was half past eight at night. In those days we had the extra hour of daylight.

'There was an aircraft overhead and shots were being fired. We looked out and we saw this aircraft in the distance, bombing RAF Sealand, only five or six miles from Hawarden. Three of us got into our flying gear and got airborne. I was the youngest and least experienced of the three. The other two had shots at the Heinkel 111 and then I had a shot, and I got him and he went down. It must have been a combination of the three of us, but my final shot put him out for good. He made a wheels-up crash landing in a farm field.

'The whole crew survived, they all got away with it. This German pilot was very good, and they were all taken prisoner and put into PoW camps. They expected to be released after a couple of months because, of course, any German invasion would succeed in setting them free. They were eventually sent to Canada until 1947.'

There was a plethora of *Luftwaffe* sorties on 15 August, including bombing raids against the North of Britain but German losses were turning out much higher than anticipated. Goering began to consider withdrawing certain aircraft from the campaign as their weaknesses were revealed – the Stuka being one notorious example. The German Riechsmarshall also never really understood the importance of the radar stations, nor how close they were to failing, and ceased the attacks on them.

On 16 August Winston Churchill watched the air battle from inside Keith Park's HQ at Uxbridge, gradually realising, to his horror, that all the reserves had been thrown in to the battle. This moved him greatly, and it was that evening that he formed the idea of 'the Few' to whom he would refer in his famous speech.

On 18 August the campaign saw a day of high casualties on both sides. The RAF lost almost 25 per cent of their pilots during these weeks and the survivors were exhausted from days when a few hundred pilots flew over 1,000 flights. Fighter Command strength stood at 551 Hurricanes and 275 Spitfires. A further 77 machines, of which 52 were Hurricanes could be available in 12 hours as the ground crews worked throughout the night.

Bill Green:

'I did about five or six hours on Hurricanes, some of which was ferrying aircraft to Northolt and Hornchurch, and meanwhile, the battle was going on around us. We were being bombed, we were fully at war, and Biggin Hill was a prime target at that time.

'I took an aeroplane back to Gravesend on 19 August, and ran into Hogan, the 501 CO who asked how I was getting on and how many hours I had done.

'I said, "About five or six hours."

'"Oh, they're too slow," he said. "You come back here, we'll train you a lot quicker than that."

'I said, "When do you want me back?"

'He said, "Tonight!"

'So back in the gloom I flew, and I was shown to a bed next to "Ginger" Lacey – on his way to becoming one of the great aces of the war. We went and had a cup of cocoa and a cheese sandwich, and that was it. I put my head down and went to sleep.

'At about four o'clock the next morning someone was flashing a light in my face.

'I said, "No, no, no, I am new, I'm Green."

'He said, "I know you're green, you're Green Three! Get up."

'Within ten minutes I was walking down to the Hurricanes, asking "Ginger" Lacey, "What's all this Green Three business?"

'He told me, "We're arse-end Charlie, we cover the squadron and stop them being bounced. When you see me do a turn to the right, you do a turn to the left. Don't go too far or too long or you will lose the squadron."

'So when we were in the air and Ginger signalled to turn, I did the gentlest turn in the Hurricane, and the shortest one of all time, but when I turned back, of course, they had gone. They had been doing 300 mph one way, and I had been doing 300 mph another way, so it was not surprising I ended up on my own.

'I found my own way down to Hawkinge and that was the start of my operational career.'

On 20 August, Winston Churchill made one of his most memorable speeches to the House of Commons: 'Never in the field of human conflict has so much been owed by so many to so Few.' As Churchill well knew, the word 'Few' had a deep resonance in British culture. It evoked the 'thin, red line', celebrated in numerous 'last stands' in British history, a small force fighting against overwhelming odds; Cawnpore in the Indian Mutiny in 1857, Rorke's Drift in Africa in 1888, the 'Contemptible Little Army' of 1914. Before Churchill it was most famously used in Shakespeare's Henry V's speech before Agincourt in 1415:

> 'We few, we happy few, we band of brothers, for he today who sheds his blood with me shall be my brother, be he ne'er so vile, this day shall gentle his condition, and gentlemen of England now abed shall think themselves accursed and hold their manhood's cheap whiles any speaks that fought with us upon St Crispin's day.'

It had an electrifying effect, not just on the country, but on the band of brothers doing the actual fighting.

John Ellacombe:
'Your friends were being killed, the place was being bombed, and we knew we just had to succeed. There was a tremendous spirit. We had this extraordinary man, Winston Churchill, making all his famous speeches. We were actually on the ground in our forward base in Essex when we heard his "Few". We all looked around at each other and said, "Chaps! That's us!"'

From 24 August onwards, the *Luftwaffe* concentrated their attacks on Fighter Command airfields. Barely trained young men took to the air in hastily assembled aircraft, only to be shot down in minutes. One bright note was that many of the RAF pilots were able to bail out. Since they were over England they could be rescued and returned to their units. Every RAF pilot who took to his parachute and lived was expected to find the parachute packer when he got back to base, and pay him ten shillings (now 50 pence). This was more generous than it looks because packers were paid a day rate of ten shillings and sixpence (52½ p). This day also marked the first of two shootings down of the absolute tyro, Last Witness Bill Green:

> 'The Squadron had been doing a lot of convoy patrols over the Dover Straits, and on 24 August we were vectored in on some Ju 88s who were about to bomb Manston. I put the gun button on to fire and was pulling in behind these Junkers, when – bang! – my aeroplane was hit by something and the whole of the windscreen was black with oil from my engine.

'I was pretty sure I had been hit by our own flak from the Manston gunners. The engine was spluttering, coughing in, coughing out, and I managed to put it down at Hawkinge Airfield, and finished up on my nose, looking at the ground.

'I went straight back into operations the next day'.

That night there was a raid by Heinkels which missed its target, the Thameshaven oil terminal on the north bank of the Thames near Tilbury. The *Luftwaffe* wandered on and dropped bombs on the East End of London, hitting St Giles, Cripplegate.

It was probably a careless accident, but the bombing of purely civilian areas was something that had been waiting to happen. The following night, 25/26 August, a pugnacious Churchill sent out two squadrons of Bomber Command Hampdens to bomb Berlin. Six crews failed to return, three having run out of fuel and dropped into the sea. The bombs hit the suburbs, and two Germans were injured.

On 27/28 August RAF bombers were sent out to bomb other German cities, and even Turin in Italy. The effect may have been frightening locally, but in reality they were just a nuisance.

As a result, a few more stray bombs fell on London. Churchill ordered another raid on Berlin, this time killing eight people and wounding 21. Hitler, who had wanted to negotiate but had now lost patience, lifted his ban on attacking London.

During August, 103 Fighter Command pilots had been killed and a further 128 were wounded. Although the Operational Training Units were able to prepare 260 men as replacements, they could not restore the lost knowledge and experience of the casualties.

John Ellacombe:

'We knew in the Battle of Britain that things were desperate and that we had to win. The terrible thing, when you look at it now, Bomber Command lost 55,573 men. You might say Bomber Command won the war, but the Battle of Britain saved the war. Had we been invaded in 1940, that would have been the end.'

Between 23 August and 6 September 1940 almost 300 Hurricanes and Spitfires were either shot down or written off and a further 171 were under repair. Deliveries of new fighters from the manufacturing base were not able to keep up with the terrible rate of attrition. Only 269 new machines reached the squadrons, a shortfall of about 200. If the state of available aircraft was becoming critical the losses of trained pilots was worse.

Dowding maintained the strength of No 11 Group by rotating squadrons and bringing fresh units in from the other three Groups. He felt that a fighter sector operated best when it controlled between two and four squadrons. He had to re-enforce and relieve squadrons, and conceived the idea of dividing his resources into three classes:

A – squadron in 11 Group, or close by, kept in the fighting by drafting in re-enforcements.
B – squadron outside 11 Group, kept together as a squadron when sent to 11 Group as re-enforcements.
C – squadron so savaged just a few survivors were sent to quiet areas, like 13 Group, to rebuild around the core of the squadron culture.

Even then, Dowding worried that squadrons with proud histories – like 32, 54, 85, 111 and 610 – which had been thoroughly bashed around, would take even longer to recover from being given a 'C' designation. The culture of an RAF squadron is vital to its fighting strength, as the culture of a regiment is to the British Army, and the name of a ship is to the Royal Navy. In each case – squadron, regiment or ship – it is not just the present participants doing the fighting. They have a real and vital responsibility to those who fought under the same numbers and names *in the past*.

A pilot in 56 Squadron, for example, was conscious that in the Great War, one of the squadron members was the legendary Albert Ball VC, and that Cecil Lewis, author of the classic *Sagittarius Rising,* was also a 56 Squadron member. All pilots fly with the ghosts of their squadron predecessors, making Dowding's fears all the more real.

There was no rotation of *Luftwaffe* squadrons, as there was with the RAF. Whatever the attrition, recruits were drafted in, numbers replaced, and the daily attacks went on. Individual aircrew were beginning to disbelieve the briefings they were given.

For his part, Dowding was coming to doubt whether organising squadrons into four sections of three was best for dog-fighting. He thought it should be replaced by three sections of four, allowing the four to split into two pairs, copying Molders' *schwarme* tactics. But he was not keen to make sweeping changes during the battle itself, because it would upset known standards.

In many cases it was done for him. 'Sailor' Malan – leading Spitfires of 74 Squadron – had already abandoned the RAF's standard rules, harking back to hard-won lessons which governed air fighting in 1918. Malan, who had to fly with the ghost of 74 Squadron's First World War hero Mick Mannock VC, developed 10 rules for fighter combat still taught today:

1. Wait until you see the whites of his eyes. Fire short bursts of one to two seconds only when your sights are definitely 'ON'
2. Whilst shooting think of nothing else, brace the whole of your body: have both hands on the stick: concentrate on your ring sight.
3. Always keep a sharp lookout.
4. Height gives you the initiative.
5. Always turn and face the attack.
6. Make your decisions promptly. It is better to act quickly even though your tactics are not the best.
7. Never fly straight and level for more than 30 seconds in the combat area.
8. When diving to attack always leave a proportion of your formation above to act as a top guard.
9. Initiative, aggression, air discipline, and teamwork are words that *mean* something in Air Fighting.
10. Go in quickly – Punch hard – Get out!

John Ellacombe:
'On Aug 30 we were bounced as we surfaced through a cloud, hit by 109s and we all broke left and right. When you do that, you turn around and you can't see anybody. There was North Weald calling – Bengal was their call sign – "This is Bengal, we have a large formation heading for our base." I didn't like large formations because they had twice bombed us when Douglas Bader's wing at Duxford didn't get down to protect us.

'I saw this formation in the distance, so I thought I would do a head-on attack. From about 2,000 yards out [1,829m] I kept the tit pressed and dived underneath a Heinkel 111. All his Perspex came off.

'As I went underneath my engine stopped. He had put one bloody bullet right through the spinner into my engine. I was going to bale out but I strapped myself in again, we were told don't bale out or you'll be shot, so I force-landed in this huge field.

'When I jumped out of the aeroplane, a man with a pitchfork started running at me, shouting, "I'm going to kill you, you bloody German."

'I was screaming at him, running around my Hurricane, saying, "I'm British, I'm British." Fortunately the army appeared from a big gun battery nearby and the sergeants disarmed him.

'They told me, "Your Heinkel crashed in that field over there."

A sergeant went across to look at the wreckage, then came back and said,

"Don't go and look, they're all in a horrible mess from your attack."

'In fact, the pilot died later on that night, so all five of the crew were dead. When I got back to North Weald, Victor Beamish said, "Go and find another Hurricane. You'll fly as my number two, there's another big formation coming in."

'I said, "Sir, I have had four pints of draught cider. I don't think I should be a good number two."

'He said, "Oh, dear," and we didn't fly on that occasion.

Dowding needed more pilots. He now had plenty of Hurricane and Spitfire aircraft, but he needed young men to fly them. He took 30 pilots from the doomed squadrons flying Fairey Battles, the single-engined light bombers with a crew of three that had been cut to pieces in the Battle of France. This was despite resistance from the Air Ministry, which thought using Battle pilots was 'unpalatable'. Sholto Douglas, no friend of Dowding's, believed they should be kept to attack Germans on invasion beaches in England. At the height of this tremendous fight, they thought Dowding was being too pessimistic about the numbers of pilots he would lose, yet they apparently did not believe that the battle would prevent an invasion!

The Royal Navy's Fleet Air Arm was also canvassed for fighter pilots, and their record illustrates the terrible attrition rate being suffered. There were 23 young volunteers, 17 went to Hurricane squadrons, five to fly Spitfires, and one was sent to a Blenheim fighter squadron. Eight RN pilots were killed in the Battle itself, three in July, four in August and one in October. Three went back to the Fleet Air Arm and were killed flying fighters there. Four remained in the RAF and were killed in the following four years. In all, 16 of the original 23 RN volunteers were killed, and just seven, all of whom flew Hurricanes, survived the war.

The Germans inevitably got Last Witness Bill Green on 29 August, along with a pair of his wife's hand-knitted socks. Barely trained, with fewer than 10 hours on Hurricanes when he went into battle, Green had already been shot down by his own flak on his first operation. Having left school at 14, Green had worked in a cardboard box factory. When he was 14 ¾ years old he walked up the stairs with a hundredweight of cardboard on his shoulder, opened the work-room door, and opposite him:

'There was this tall, beautiful, brown-eyed girl. Her name was Bertha Biggs, she worked at one of the cardboard box machines in the factory, and I fell in love with her. After I trained as a pilot, we married on 3 June 1940. We had the bans called in Bristol – St John's Church on St Luke's Road – then all leave was stopped because of the Battle of France collapsing.

'Bertha came up on the bus to Cirencester, and we had two days together in Cheltenham. I should have been sleeping after some night flying, but the CO gave me two days leave, so that was our honeymoon.

'Bertha had knitted me a new pair of socks, and on 29 August I was writing to her, thanking her for the socks – wearing them, too – saying, "You can breathe easy today, dear, cloud is down to 200 feet [61m], no chance of being scrambled." Then, at six o'clock we were scrambled and vectored to Deal – code-named Red Queen – at 20,000 feet [6,100m].

'We were orbiting our Hurricanes over Deal, buzzing around and around, looking out for two hundred Bf 109s coming in over Red Queen. For nothing more than self-preservation, I was covering every inch of the sky – or I thought I was. Suddenly – *bang, crash, broken glass* – I was covered in liquid, there was a hole in the windscreen as big as a baseball (it was supposed to be bullet-proof – I can still hear the crashing of that Perspex today) and the stick went slack.

'I was told later it was Bf 109s doing the firing, because my flight commander, Gibson, was hit at the same time as me. It was damn good shooting because we had been doing steep turns through 360 degrees. I saw nothing, Gibson saw nothing, but he assured me later that it was 109s that did it.

'They came out of the sun at lightning speed and it was all over in a split second. I realised the aeroplane was finished, and pulled the pin on the Sutton harness, got to my feet and then bang, I was out in space.

'I heard my flying boots go past my ears – *psst, psst* – they disappeared, and then I was patting everywhere on my body to find the rip-cord. I finally found it, yanked it and thought that was it. Then I saw something white going around in circles and disappearing from me, going up while I was going down. It had no significance until the main canopy, on which I sat, just fell out of its pack and I was rolling forward. Then I rolled into it.

'It wrapped itself around me so I could see nothing as I was falling. I started doing a breast-stroke, forlornly hoping I could push it back. It had to get the wind under one of its folds. I remember, I was not a Christian at the time – I am now – and I said, "Please, God, open this bloody parachute!" I had been married about twelve weeks and I was seeking my end through thoughts of Bertha. I wondered if she would wonder if I would have been pondering my end. I thought she would know that one minute it would be like this, falling in a shroud, and the next it would be black.

'Then there was a jolt, it must have been the wind under one of the folds. It kicked me back, there was a secondary jolt when the rigging lines were ripped away from their securing straps on the back. I grabbed those lines because I had already seen one part of the parachute go off into space, and thought the whole lot might go. The quiet that hit me had more effect than any noise imaginable.

'After 140 miles an hour [225 kph] falling through space, the wind noise – like if you stuck your head out of a car at 80 mph [128 kph] – suddenly ceased. There was this tremendous quiet. I thought, "My God, I'm alive!"

'I looked to the right and could see pylon cables level with me. I looked to the left and the trees were above me! I was in a valley, Elham Valley in Kent. I relaxed my legs. That was the only thing I knew about parachute jumping, none of us ever practiced, you didn't want to have stiff legs when you hit the deck. Then – *bang* – I was down on the ground.

'I sat in the middle of this field. It was full of cow pats and thistles. I had my new socks on and my boots had gone. I was thinking, "Do I really have to walk through this lot with Bertha's new socks on?"

'Two blokes came running down the field with shotguns, pointing them at me, and when they got nearer they said, "Oh, you're English."

'I said, "Yes, I'm English all right." I had no intention of being shot after all that had happened to me. I went to get up and, of course, I fell over, because I had been wounded in the right leg. I was hospitalised and non-operational for the rest of the Battle of Britain.

'I had only ten days in the fighting itself and I feel quite a fraud being a member of the Battle of Britain Association.

'I suppose ten days is longer than some.'

Polish fighter pilots, who became a legend in the battle, entered the Battle of Britain proper on 31 August when two Polish squadrons, both equipped with Hurricanes, were unleashed. They had been straining to get into the fight for weeks. There were 145 Polish pilots in Fighter Command, 66 in those two squadrons, already well-trained and not at all interested in the official RAF fighting rules.

Most of them had hundreds of hours of flying time, well trained before the war to fly in loose formations and to fire from close range during combat. Many were members of the Polish Air Force which had fought the *Luftwaffe* in 1939. One Polish pilot was to refer to the close formation flying and set-piece attack patterns practised in the RAF as 'simply suicidal.'

By the summer of 1940 some 35,000 Polish airmen, soldiers and sailors who had escaped the Germans had made their way to Britain, by far the largest foreign military force in the country. Of these, 8,500 were airmen. The Air Ministry and the RAF underestimated their potential value in fighting the *Luftwaffe* and posted most of them either to bomber squadrons or into the RAF Volunteer Reserve.

In July the RAF finally agreed to form two Polish fighter squadrons; 302 *Poznanski* Squadron and 303 *Kosciuszki* Squadron, with Polish pilots and ground crews, although flight commanders and commanding officers were British. Other Polish fighter pilots were integrated into regular RAF units.

The Poles gained a reputation for being 'fanatical' and inspired by hatred, prepared to ram German aircraft during the fighting, but their experience of air war had taught the Poles that the quickest, most efficient way to destroy an enemy aircraft was to open fire from close range. After a brief opening burst at 150 to 200 yards, just to get on the enemy's nerves, the Poles would close almost to point-blank range, where they did their real work.

These don't-fire-till-you-see-the-whites-of-their-eyes tactics led to accusations of recklessness. Yet the 303 Squadron death rate was almost 70 per cent lower than the rate for other RAF squadrons during the battle.

The 145 Polish pilots claimed 201 aircraft shot down. Squadron Leader Witold Urbanowicz of 303 Squadron was the top Polish scorer with 15 kills. Sergeant Tony Glowacki was one of two Allied pilots in the Battle to shoot down five German aircraft in one day, on 24 August (the other was New Zealander Brian Carbury). Squadron Leader Stanislaw Skalski became the top-scoring Polish fighter ace in the Second World War.

In all, 30 Polish fighter pilots were killed in the battle.

Many other foreign nationals, including large numbers of Czechoslovakians, found their way into the battle; the majority flew Hurricanes, as every new squadron formed during the battle was equipped with the type. This was because they could be produced quicker than Spitfires, and when damaged, they were easier to repair and return to operations. Of the 88 Czechs in Fighter Command, the core was the foundation of 310 Squadron in July, and 312 Squadron in September. They were very disciplined, with a fierce CO.

One Czech youngster landed a Hurricane heavily and wrecked it – its wheels buckled – and they had an informal court martial. It was resolved to take him behind the hangar and shoot him. They were told it was not the English way.

The leading Czech fighter ace was Sergeant Joseph Frantisek, with 11 victories in Poland and with the French before joining 303 (Polish) Squadron. He was credited with 28 kills, 17 on Hurricanes, before dying in a landing accident at Northolt in October, 1940. At the time he was the highest-scoring pilot in Fighter Command.

Of the 2,946 official 'Battle of Britain' pilots, these were their nationalities (the numbers don't add up):

Great Britain	2,344
Poland	145
New Zealand	126
Canada	98
Czechoslovakia	88
Australia	33
Belgium	29
South Africa	25
France	13
United States	11
Ireland	10
the Rhodesias	3
Newfoundland	1
Jamaica	1

The Battle of Britain approached its peak on 30 and 31 August 1940, with RAF losses of 50 aircraft over those two days, compared to the Germans' 41. RAF pilots were close to being overwhelmed until Hitler changed his tactics and ordered the *Luftwaffe* to switch its attack from British airfields, factories and docks to civilian targets. This decision was the result of the 25/26 August bombing attack on Berlin that had been ordered by Churchill.

John Ellacombe:

'I was shot down on 31 Aug. On the first sortie that morning I shot down a 109, but we lost our Polish pilot, Frank Czajkowski who I got to know very well later on. The second sortie was rather uneventful, we didn't find anything. The third sortie we found a big formation heading out to sea. I was attacking a Ju 88, when the rear gunner, I could see the tracer coming at me, hit my gravity tank and that burst into flames.

'I baled out immediately. We had practiced the drill – pull the hood back, undo your strap and go. You didn't undo your intercom cord, that was expected to break. As I was falling I was standing upright watching to see that I was getting well clear of all the German fighters. Then my face suddenly started feeling funny. I took my helmet off and realised that it was badly burnt in the front. I threw the helmet away, sadly, because it would have been a nice souvenir.

'Then I looked down and realised that I hadn't any bloody trousers on!

'I waited a little longer until there were tiny little aeroplanes up there and then I opened my parachute. I landed in Essex, and as I came down I saw a bloody Home Guard running around pointing his rifle. He fired two shots at me and I shouted, "Don't shoot, I'm British!" He came up and was very apologetic. He took me to a farmhouse and the dear lady looked at my legs and said, "Oh, I'll go and get a bottle of vinegar, we pour that on burns."

'I said, "No thank you, just get me a sheet." I put that on and was waiting when the door suddenly burst open and two policemen appeared. One of them came up and hit me. The Home Guard said, "Look, he's got his RAF wings on!"

'They took me to Southend General Hospital. While I was in the farmhouse I asked for a drink of water. The chap gave me a pint of water, but he put a brandy in it, which was a silly thing when you've been shot. I drank the damned thing, and when I got to the hospital the doctor looked closely at my face.

'"Well, you're burnt," he said, "and we'll go and treat you. Do you always fly pissed?"'

Going into September, the Germans were living with fancy illusions, believing the RAF was down to its last few reserves. Because of the 3-to-1 difference between claims by fighter pilots, and reality, and because they had no idea how many Hurricanes and Spitfires were being produced, by 30 August Goering was told the British had lost 800 aircraft out of a front line strength of 915.

The Germans reckoned the replacement rate was 200 or 300 a month; reality was closer to 500 a month. They expected to wipe out the last 200 RAF aircraft by 15 September. In fact, going into the height of the battle after 6 September, Fighter Command had 750 Hurricanes and Spitfires, 200 more than it had when the *Luftwaffe* set off on 10 July to wipe out the RAF.

Chapter Eight

LAST WITNESS – TOM NEIL

E very now and again in life, a natural story-teller appears, someone absolutely exceptional, able to look over a span of 70 years and pull together thousands of experiences into a coherent tale as if they all occurred yesterday.

Such a man is Last Witness Tom Neil, whose story covers the whole history of the Hurricane in three of its major fields of battle – Britain, Malta and Burma – but had Tom's story appeared earlier in this book, would have pre-empted history.

In 2001, Tom Neil published an account of his experiences in the Battle of Britain – *A Fighter in My Sights* – that should have been a runaway best-seller. Sadly, it wasn't, although it bears direct comparison to Geoffrey Welham's *First Light*, which was a best-seller. If anything, Tom Neil's book had more action.

Neil was born, an only child, on 14 July 1920 in Bootle, Lancashire. I met him on his 88th birthday, having been shocked by his first comment to me: 'The Hurricane was a disaster!'

As one of the higher-scoring pilots in the Battle of Britain, with a dozen victories, all in a Hurricane, this seemed an ungenerous judgement for Tom Neil to have made. It transpired that his remarks applied to the 1941/42 period of the war, when he was sent to be part of the desperate defence of Malta. By then the Bf 109 had a distinct advantage over the Hurricane, and Neil was furious that there was a generous supply of much faster, late-model Spitfires available, which were not sent out to Malta for months.

Neil's experiences, along with the odd fact that he became an honorary member of the Hitler Youth on a visit to Germany in 1937, and the sheer vivacity of the tales of his youth, make it an affront to reason not to devote a special chapter to his story.

'My father started in lowly capacity on the Lancashire and Yorkshire Railway, but rose to one of the senior positions. We travelled in great style all over Europe, red carpets everywhere.

'I went to a grammar school and then into the RAF, after some months working in a district bank in Lancashire, because my father wanted me to know something about money and cheques. My salary was 18 shillings a week. I paid more in fares to get to the bank than I received in take-home pay.

'I went to Hendon and the pageants there, from around 1935, when I was 15. Hendon in those days was a little grass airfield surrounded by fields. We sat in the fields and watched all these gay coloured aircraft. I remember the commentary used to go on about 601 Squadron – the Auxiliary Squadron – and this chap always said, "And, of course, these aircraft are flown by butchers and bakers and candlestick makers." In fact it was nothing of the kind. Each of those pilots must not have been worth less than a million, Max Aitken among them, son of Lord Beaverbrook.

'I tried to join 611 Auxiliary Squadron, the West Lancashire Squadron, while I was living in Manchester, about 35 miles away from their airfield. I went for my interview and they were frightfully toffy-nosed.

'They turned me down because I lived too far away and didn't have a car. Eventually I was pushed into 17 Elementary Reserve Flying Training School. The Air Force took me on in the RAFVR when I was 18.

'When I joined the RAF in the summer of 1938, I didn't expect there to be a war. Nobody expected a war. We thought Chamberlain would pull it off. He came back from Munich waving this piece of paper saying, "Peace for our time." I had already been to Germany in 1937 and I was fascinated by that country. The visit had been arranged with another grammar school in Germany, and we stayed in Koblenz and Wiesbaden.

'It was the most wonderful experience of my young life. I made many German friends, including one or two very nice girls with whom I kept in touch. I enjoyed Germany. I was an honorary member of the Hitler Youth, and I ran in their races. I hope I upheld the honour of England by always coming second in the race, not first. I always felt I could win, but tactfully, came second.

'Then, of course, I started flying in 1938. We began on Gypsy 1 Moths, much earlier than a Tiger Moth. I remember the first aircraft I flew was K-1900, which, as I walked out to it (I had never been in the air before in my life), I surmised was something to do with the day it had been built.

'To me the engine was just a black mass up front. I didn't know what happened to an engine or how it worked. I didn't know anything serious about aircraft. It took a long time for me to go solo, because the weather was filthy. We only used to fly at weekends. My instructor almost despaired of me because he had just got me ready to go solo and then there would be an interval of eight weeks before the weather was good enough to fly again. It was a brutal winter, 1938/39.

'We changed on to Tiger Moths from Gypsy 1 Moths, and thought, what hot ships these are! The new Tiger Moth arrived in the Spring of 1939, and I was never taught thereafter. Instructors used to take you for a five-minute go in the morning to see if you were in a fit state of mind not to damage the aeroplane, and you were let go. The only thing you had to do to go solo was to cope with a spin and do a stall, and know what to do in the event of fire (stop the engine).

'The only thing I used to be able to do in my hours and hours of solo was loops. My stall turns were terrible, and my rolls even worse. Rolling a Tiger Moth is not easy. My parents lived near a rather up-market club in Worsley, and I used to roll my Tiger Moth over the bowling greens and tennis courts of this club until I got a letter, saying please would I go somewhere else? People were taking to their heels as they watched me spinning towards them.

'At the end of the peace, August 1939, I was 19 years old and was called up. I left the bank for good. Even as an airman I would have got much more money than I got at the bank. As a sergeant I was so rich I can't tell you, £12 a week! I had never seen such money in my life.

'We were called up on 1 Sept 1939, and assembled at our town centre. There were 60 of us. A bloke in a round hat turned up and said, "Look, we don't know what to do with you chaps. Would you mind going home for a bit?"

'I stayed home for quite a few weeks. I didn't mind a scrap. I had nothing to do and I had this massive amount of money to spend. I drove around to see all my relations in Lancashire and Wales, and then I was sent, with others, to 17 Elementary Reserve Flying Training. By this time I had done about 60 flying hours, and we had just been about to go on to Hawker Harts.

'I was then sent down to 4 ITW – Initial Training Wing – at Bexhill on Sea. It was a glorious time and I loved the discipline. We lived on the sea front at Bexhill in the Sackville Hotel, a tremendous 4-star establishment, especially gutted so we might live in the greatest possible discomfort. They took the lifts out so we had to walk. I was on the fourth floor so I had to walk 108 steps, up to eight times a day. I had muscles on my legs like onions.

'We were there for two weeks, and then they posted us to 8 FTS – Flying Training School. I was sent to Montrose on the east coast of Scotland between Aberdeen and Dundee. I was to spend from the end of November to the end of April 1940 up there, and came to love it. The Scottish Highlands were wonderful. We started flying Hawker Harts, and then we were supposed to fly Furies, but they were taken away. We flew Hawker Harts and Audaxes – all biplanes, of course – and I flew a hundred and something hours. I finally finished at Montrose at the end of April, shortly before Dunkirk.

'At this stage of the war we were being beaten to a frazzle by the Germans. I can honestly say that during these terrible, dismal days, it never occurred to me, or indeed anybody else, that we were going to be beaten. Not for a second. I was British, wasn't I? The British weren't beaten. They won all the wars. We had been winning wars since forever. We fought the French at Crecy and Agincourt. Britain did not lose wars. We made very hard work of it from time to time, but we never lost.

'So it never occurred to me that we would lose, and then, of course, the Hurricanes which had already been in France for a time – despite the fact that they didn't perform other than adequately – the pilots came back with wonderful stories about how they were better than the enemy.'

'I had first seen Hurricanes in 1936 when they came to Hendon. Then in 1938 the RAF Pageant came to an end and it was superseded by Empire Air Day. The RAF used places like Ringway, a field in Manchester which became Ringway Airport, to show us modern aircraft. All the new aircraft were there – a Spitfire, a Hurricane, a Hampden and a Whitley – one of each, always tremendously impressive.

'I had experience of Spitfires at Montrose, because 602 and 603 Squadron – two Scottish Auxiliary squadrons, one based in Glasgow, the other Edinburgh – had small formations at Turnhouse and Montrose, three aeroplanes at the time. I had seen the Spitfire, but I hadn't flown it. We used to go out and touch it reverently, it was the Spitfire I. I hadn't seen Hurricanes close up at all.

'Then I was commissioned. When I left school I had had no training whatsoever in being an officer. In fact, I never did get any training to be an officer. The RAF took the view that if you were a grammar school boy and a prefect, it automatically fitted you to command men. So I was made an officer. This was despite the fact that I could not have moved one file from one office to the next. I didn't know anything about being an officer.

'I went home on leave in Manchester for a couple of days, then had a letter which I read in front of my mother and my father. It said, "Post Pilot Officer T. F. Neil to 249 (H) Squadron, with effect from 15 May 1940, at RAF Church Fenton."

'I did not know what (H) was but surmised it was Hurricanes. To go to a Hurricane squadron was something else. I went to Church Fenton by train – everybody went by train in those days. It took about three trains to get there, and I arrived in the early afternoon. I was still mentally tuned to earning 18 shillings a week, so I carefully enquired as to how much the taxi was going to charge to get me to the airfield. It was within my means, so I set off for Church Fenton RAF Station.

'It seemed newly built and absolutely beautiful. The officer's mess was immaculate. There were no aircraft there, except, believe it or not, a Whitley. I went into the officer's mess, knees trembling, passing a group of officers with their ladies, playing tennis. They had tea around the tennis court. They were partaking of tea and we were being thrashed by the Germans!

I thought, "This is the way to run a war."

'We were already at the stage where Dunkirk was happening, and yet here you would never believe the war was on.'

'I was the first officer in 249 Squadron to turn up at Church Fenton. It was a resurrected squadron in May, 1940, brand new. When I arrived I thought I had come to the wrong place, because nobody knew anything about me, or about the squadron.

'Then a chap turned up, delightful man, the adjutant of 249 Squadron. He was Flying Officer Ewart Lomar, he had been in the First World War as an observer and he had a DFC. We were there for two days. After the second day he said, "The squadron is gathering and we are moving to Leconfield," which was seven or eight miles up the road, towards Hull. "You are in charge of the squadron – all the transport and 180 men, including senior NCOs."

'The place had been newly built and the officer's mess was delightful, but our sergeants didn't have any accommodation at all. They had to live on the airfield in tents. Then we learned that, instead of being 249 Hurricane Squadron, we were going to get Spitfires! We were asked, "Who can fly a Spitfire?" One or two people put their hands up. They had come from other squadrons to join us, either as flight commanders or designate flight commanders, and so they went off and brought back one or two Spitfires. Others were brought in by ferry pilots, and eventually we had 18 to play with.

'They were all different. The Spitfires came in various stages of completion. We all had three-bladed metal propellers. Some had retractable undercarriages that worked on their own, which did not need to be physically pumped up by the pilot, but no two aeroplanes were the same.

'Before we had even flown, Air Marshal Saul turned up. He was in charge then of 13 Group. He stood us all in a row, and he said, "It's jolly nice of you chaps to come and help us out. You have about five weeks to get yourself in full flying trim, to take on the *Luftwaffe*."

'We all looked at each other and said, "We haven't even flown one of these things yet!"

'The authorities said, "Right," to most of us, "you have never flown anything other than a biplane, you had better go into the hangar here and we'll sort you with a Spitfire." They had one there on trestles.

'I was put in a cockpit with a blindfold around my eyes. They said, "If you feel around the cockpit, you will find the controls. We will point them out to you and you will sit there for half a day, raising the wheels and lowering the wheels, putting the flaps down and raising the flaps, and by lunchtime, you should be able to fly a Spitfire."

'By lunchtime I came out and took the blindfold off my eyes and my flight commander, a chap called Boosey Kellop – he was about 30, terribly old – he came from 616 Squadron, and he said, "Right, get in. Off you go, and don't damage it."

'I didn't even know how to start the engine. I remember sitting there, I had a sergeant I had never seen before, and the rigger and the fitter were there, and there were chocks underneath the wheels. I had my face mask on. I had never worn a face-mask before, I had never used oxygen, I had never used radio, so I took the mask off and called the sergeant over.

'I said, in a whisper, "How do I start this thing?"

'"That thing there, the primer," he pointed at it, "you pull it out and squirt it six times and that primes the engine. Then you do this and do that, and then you open the throttle and stand back ..." and the engine started! The engine was started electrically, then they had to take out the starter battery and I had been given some very stern information about what I was to do. On the Spitfire, the radiator was not in the direct airflow, it was to one side under one wing, so the engine overheated very quickly. Once you got to the point of take-off it could go beyond 100 degrees centigrade, in which case it boiled and you got a lot of steam under the front end, and you had to stop.

'The other thing I was warned against was not to apply the brakes too hard, otherwise you would tip it on its nose. There were lots of damp parts of the airfield that were a danger to me. I taxied very carefully, zig-zagging from side to side so that I could see forward over the big nose, and I went to the end of the airfield, 90 degrees to the wind with the windsock on my right.

'I turned into the wind and opened the throttle. It set off like a startled Dervish across the grass, bumping and bumping. I got it into the air and prayed that the engine wouldn't stop. I had never been this fast in my life before! My Hawker Hart only went at 120 mph [193 kph] flat out. Here I was doing 180 mph [290 kph] before I was even beginning to climb. Then I raised the wheels, and there were two positions on the hood, either open or closed. I didn't want to close it because I was fairly big, but I climbed away, closed the hood, and before you could say anything I was at 6,000 feet [1,828m], through broken cloud. I got used to the thing, circling the airfield at about 15 miles [24 km], keeping it in sight, and flew for 20 minutes, then came in to land. I felt absolutely on top of the world.

'I had flown a Spitfire and landed safely.'

'From that day onwards I flew five hours a day on Spitfires until I had done almost a hundred hours in three weeks. It introduced me for the first time to oxygen. It climbed to 25,000 feet [7,620m] ... I had never been that high in my life before ... I learned about radio. Half the instruments in the cockpit, I never knew what they meant.

'Almost directly afterwards, 12 Group was extended to the north and we came under Trafford Leigh-Mallory. Then, suddenly, we were transferred to Hurricanes. We had 18 Spitfires and 18 Hurricanes turn up. We had 36 aircraft in the squadron, and stepped out of one aircraft into another. It was no problem transferring from one to the other.

'The Hurricane came with the reputation that it was slower than the Spitfire, and we knew all about Spitfires, which we had flown at 450 mph [720 kph]. When I climbed into a Hurricane I came to the conclusion that I was flying my Hawker Hart again. If you look at a Hawker Hart, take off the top wing, and put on a retractable instead of a fixed undercarriage, you got a Hurricane.

'In certain respects the Hurricane was nicer than the Spitfire, because you sat higher in the cockpit and saw more outside, over a sloping nose. You didn't have a cockpit in the strict sense of the word. You just sat in space, and if you dropped something down it disappeared under your feet, and you lost it for good. You couldn't carry gloves or a torch and drop them because they would just disappear.

'In a Spitfire you had a cockpit which had a floor and you could retrieve them. The Spitfire was more gentlemanly, better-built, while the Hurricane was an 'old-fashioned' aircraft which had been renovated. But in many respects it was better. The ailerons were better – the Spitfire tightened up at high speed, as the speed mounted it got very stiff indeed. All the ailerons on all our aircraft were fabric covered. Eventually, on Mark V Spitfires, they were changed to metal and worked so much better. They were also changed on the Hurricane.

'The Hurricane was a lot slower than the Spitfire because it was bigger and with the same engine – the Merlin III engine developing 1,030 HP if you really pushed it. But the Merlin engine was really quite small, 27 litres, which we began to see as much smaller than the German engines. The Daimler-Benz 600 series engine, which they had in the Bf 109, was 39 litres, nearly half as big again as a Merlin. Indeed, when we had the Griffon in the Spitfire in 1942, it was only 37 litres. Our engines were smaller than the German ones.

'The Hurricane was not as light on the elevators as the Spitfire. The

Spitfire was largely unstable, and you could black out any time of the day or night, using one finger on the control column. On the original Spitfires we had to hang a weight of lb [11.4kg] on the elevator to make it difficult for the pilot to apply the elevator and blacken himself stupid. When you flew the original Spitfire 1, you spent half the time unconscious. Every time you did a turn you lost your vision.

'Similarly, every time you pushed the nose down the engine stopped. It was a carburettor-driven engine, and the floats drained away the fuel; we had that problem on the Hurricane as well.

'In certain respects the Hurricane was an easier aircraft to fly than the Spitfire. Going around the countryside, it was about as fast, but it didn't have the legs of a Spitfire at all when you piled speed on, because it had this thumping great high-lift wing – the wings were about 18 inches [46 cm] in depth – which meant it climbed more slowly than the Spitfire – at 140 mph [225 kph] rather than 180 mph [290 kph]. This meant that operating from North Weald, 25 miles [40 km] north of Leicester Square, which we eventually did, if you took off from North Weald and climbed nearly flat out we could just about get to 13,000 feet [4,000m] when we crossed the Thames. It took us to Maidstone, south of London, before we got to 16,000 feet [4,877m], the height the Battle of Britain took place, in the main.

'We used to read, cynically, headlines in the *Sunday Pictorial* and various other newspapers, about how "Spitfires dive to the attack!" I never once dived to the attack. I was always struggling up trying to make height, as indeed most of us were. Very seldom were we at the proper height, even though we were 25 miles north of London. Other people in different parts of the world experienced things differently. We always climbed into the enemy. No matter where they came from, we always knew where they were going – London, of course – but we seldom intercepted further south than Maidstone and Canterbury.

'We were designed, in the Hurricanes, to intercept bombers. We were supposedly an interceptor aircraft that should have been able to deal with fighters as well, but against a fighter the Hurricane was hopeless. The German fighters could dictate tactics any time they wanted. They were about 50 mph [80 kph] faster than us on the level, and they could climb away or dive away any time they wanted. They didn't have carburettors, they had direct injection, and they had a far better super-charger, a variable-speed super-charger, so in many respects, although the Bf 109 was an unpleasant aircraft to fly, being small you couldn't see out of it – I flew one in 1945 – it had a bigger engine, and certain characteristics that made it superior to anything it fought against in its time.

'We were made operational, deemed fit to take on the enemy, on 2 July, three weeks after I had first flown a Hurricane. On 4 July, the first day we were invited to stay at readiness, later in the afternoon I was scrambled, one of three chaps to intercept a bogey – not a bandit – somewhere out over the North Sea. So I scrambled, one of three – Flying Officer Young, me on the right and a Sergeant Smithson on the left. We took off from Leconfield and flew off the coast, out to sea about 30 miles [48 km] at 12,000 feet [3,658m] up to 14,000 feet [4,267m], and I saw an enemy aircraft. It was Do 17, the 'Flying Pencil'.

'I forgot all about how to work my radio, and I tried to attract this half-wit leading us, Colin Young – he's dead now, so I can speak freely of him – a useless chap, he really was. I tried to tell him, he was much older than me, all of 26, and he wasn't a fighter chap. I was trying to attract his attention and I forgot to put my radio on properly – a TR9D – an HF set which you had to work at. I was beating at the side of my cockpit, shouting, "You halfwit, look!" And he was taking no notice at all.

'I was waggling my wings like mad and suddenly he saw me, recognised that I had seen the enemy, and the enemy saw us at the same time.

'There was about 5/8 cloud and the Dornier saw us. We were slightly above it and we dived to the attack. In order to dive to the attack, according to Fighter Command instructions, you had to go into line astern. He gave the order, "Line astern, line astern – go!" I went into line astern, I was number two, and then he led the attack. I was willing him to get out of the way, because he was right in front of me.

'We dived and I don't know what happened to him but he disappeared, and I had this Dornier 17 in front, just about to disappear into cloud, which it did. We shot into cloud after it, we came out of cloud going – Where is it? Where is it? We couldn't see it. We circled like terriers around a rat-infested haystack and never saw it again.

'So we lost the first aircraft but I didn't really shoot at it. That was the first day of our operations. Intercept one Do 17, almost immediately it dived between our legs and that was that.

'Colin Young disappeared into the mists very shortly afterwards. If people didn't measure up there was no beating their heads saying, "I can't take it." They just disappeared, posted away. That's what happened to Young. I didn't even notice he had gone. He just wasn't around.

'We shot down our first aircraft on 8 July, a few days later. It was my section and it was done by a chap called Sergeant Main, who was killed shortly afterwards. We shot down a Junkers 88 off Flamborough Head. We had shot it down and it landed in Yorkshire somewhere. We got bits of the aircraft in order to adorn the dispersal hut – a swastika up on a wall – and then we went to the cinema in the evening, and the commentator said, "And this is the Junkers 88 shot down by a Spitfire!"

'We were sitting in the stalls, screaming with frustration. It was not shot down by a Spitfire, it was shot down by a Hurricane! We found out that 41 Squadron at Catterick, north of us, flying Spitfires, had intercepted the Dornier over Berwick, on the doors of Scotland, and had attacked it but hadn't shot it down. One of the chaps had been hit and they had to leave it.

'This Junkers 88 was on its way back down to the North Sea when we got it. But it was credited to Spitfires. Sergeant Main, directly afterwards, had an engine failure in his Hurricane and was killed at Duxford.'

'We were then day and night squadrons, despite the fact that I had done only two hours flying at night. I was supposed to be defending England in a Hurricane, and of course you couldn't see a damn thing at night. The only thing you could see if you saw anything was if you got behind him and saw the two exhaust stumps.

'There was one ghastly trip I made in a Hurricane. Despite the fact that I was so young, still 19 at the time, despite the fact that I knew nothing about anything, I was deemed one of the experienced members of the squadron because I had been the first to join it, and I had to do night flying. On this particular night at Church Fenton – we had pulled back there at this stage – we were operating at night, defending Sheffield.

'My flight was brought to readiness one night. It was as black as the inside of a cat, and the enemy came over. We could hear the surging *whoommm whoommm* above us; 73 Squadron was also sharing Church Fenton with us, and they were doing practice night flying.

'When you flew at night in England, you flew with only a small number of gloom lamps. There were no runway lead-in lights, no lead-out, there were no lights anywhere, and of course Britain was blacked out entirely. So you were very much on your own unless you were in touch by radio.

'I found I was number five in line to take off. The flight commander, Bruce Barden, took off first and disappeared into the night. Then a delightful chap called Mika took off. Meanwhile, 73 Squadron were doing circuits and bumps, practicing. So then the flare path was cut off just as Mika was taking off, he took off in total blackness, hit the taxi post on his way into the air, took away half his undercarriage and a bit of his propeller as well, and floated around and said rather plaintively that he was going to have to come back because he really was badly damaged.

'They switched on a few of the gloom lamps and he landed, wheels up, safe. The next chap to take off was Sergeant Maynard – delightful chap, lived in Dundee, had a big black moustache – he took off, and then as we all watched in this absolute blackness of the night, the bombs began to fall. They were incendiary bombs, two or three miles away. I was ordered off. I ran to my aircraft, climbed in, my first night-time operational trip, and suddenly I had white things flying past me.

'The sergeant shouted out of the darkness, "I think you've got a glycol leak, sir!"

'I had to run across, dangling my parachute and bits and pieces, climb into another Hurricane – totally different from mine and it was a couple of years old. It had a metal propeller, my own aircraft had a Rotol propeller, a DH propeller. I raced around the airfield. They switched off the lights as soon as I got there.

'"Christ," I thought, "What do I do now?"

'I pointed myself into space, opened up and took off with no lights at all. I climbed, and selected "up" on the undercarriage, and the aircraft would not go any faster. Why was my aircraft, at full climbing power, not going faster? I didn't know, everything was in blackness in the cockpit. There were no cockpit lights.

'In those days, they monkeyed around with the lights on the undercarriage. If they were down, they were green; if they were unlocked, you lost the lights; and if they were locked up, they were red. They then changed them so if they were down, it was green; if you were unlocked, it was red; and when it was locked up there were no lights. I didn't know whether my wheels were up or down because I had no lights of any kind in the cockpit.

'I had heard that in some aircraft you had to select "up", and you fished around the cockpit trying to find another lever which you pressed down to activate the hydraulics. There must be another lever down here somewhere. So I selected "up" and I found another lever which I pressed, and lo, the wheels came up.

'I climbed to 20,000 feet [6,100m] and it was absolute blackness, I couldn't see a damned thing. It was a black night, no moon, but I remember climbing through cloud. Control kept vectoring me here and vectoring me there, and the voices got quieter and quieter, until there were no voices at all. I didn't have a radio!

'I didn't know where I was. I was somewhere over the Yorkshire coast, could have been out to sea, might not have been, I just didn't know. I flew around – forget about the Germans at this stage, I just wanted to get home – it

Three 'Vics' of three Hurricanes fly over the new Hurricane 1, the RAF's first modern monoplane fighter, delivered to 111 Squadron, 1938. The 'Vics' were the cause of dozens of RAF deaths as pilots' eyes were on maintaining the formation instead of looking out for the enemy.

Bob Stanford Tuck, DSO, DFC & 2 bars, AFC – 'Lucky Tuck' – ended the war as a POW in Germany and Poland. He was credited with 27 kills, two shared and six probables.

Billy Drake, DSO, DFC & bar, flew with 1 Squadron RAF in the Battle of France, scoring 4 kills before being shot down and wounded. He went on later in the war to amass 24 kills.

Famous photo of a staged scramble by Number 1 Hurricane Squadron RAF in France during the Phony War. Left to right: Billy Drake, 'Boy' Mould, Prosser Hanks and LR Clisby.

Peter Ayerst, DFC 73 Squadron, fought in the Battle of France, friend of first WWII Ace 'Cobber' Kane, used as RAF pin-up boy. Went on to score 9 kills and 2 probables in the war.

A Mark I Hurricane (note the 2-blade propeller), of 73 Squadron, landing in France during Phony War 1939–40.

Ground crew servicing and re-arming a Mark II Hurricane. The rapid and easy access to servicing was a feature of Sydney Camm's designs.

Peter Hairs, MBE (Mil). After 30 hours on Hurricanes he was then flung in to fight with 501 Squadron in the Blitzkreig in May, 1940.

An apprehensive Bob Doe, DSO, DFC, third-highest-scoring pilot in the Battle of Britain, mainly on Spitfires, ending as CO of 238 Hurricane Squadron RAF.

Bob Foster DFC, scored 2 ½ kills on Hurricanes against the Germans in 1940, and 5 kills in 1943 against the Japanese on Spitfires. He was later Chairman of the Battle of Britain Fighter Association.

John Ellacombe, DFC & bar, went into his first combat in the Battle of Britain after just 25 hours on Hurricanes with 151 Squadron. A career RAF officer, he retired with the rank of Air Commodore.

Survivors, a group of fighting Group Captains with the medals to prove it, all Battle of Britain veterans including John Ellacombe.

Graham Leggatt (left) with his friend Bob Matthews, both 249 Hurricane
Squadron pilots at Tucali in Malta, 1941. Matthews was killed the day after
the photo was taken.

Ready to fight, with four 20mm cannon (which Douglas Bader opposed strongly),
a Hurricane IIC.

Tom Neil, who won a DFC & bar as a 20 year old fighter pilot with 249 Hurricane Squadron in September and October, 1940. He was a great friend of the only Fighter Command VC, Eric Nicolson. Neil later survived the hardest months' fighting in Malta in 1941.

Douglas Bader, the legless fighter leader, champion of the since-discredited 'Big Wing' tactics, claimed 22 ½ kills before becoming a POW.

remained pitch black and I had no radio. I became almost demented with fear.

'I thought, "My mum and dad, I am never going to see them again, they're never going to see me. I cannot bale out. I might have to bale out but was I over the sea or not?"

'Then I thought, why is my radio not working? Radios, on the whole, did not stop working, except for a reason. They didn't just die away. Possibly it might not be charging? How do you find out what's charging the battery on a strange aircraft? On my own dear aircraft, there were three switches on the left of the cockpit, and the transformer was always "ON". You never touched it. I thought, "Somewhere I have got to find this switch and see if it is wired 'ON'". I tooted around in the blackness until I found switches, all of which I switched to the opposition, so I must have switched on the transformer.

'I gradually began to get lights in the cockpit, and also the radio came on. By this time I had been airborne for an hour and 30 minutes. A Hurricane would only stay up for an hour and 45 minutes. Control gave me a vector to bring me home. I had reached my fuel limits, when, by the grace of God, they switched on the gloom lights and I saw the airfield and landed. I was stunned into silence.

'John Grandy, who had been down in the Ops Room – he was my commanding officer – came to see me. He and I were not very friendly to start with - he regarded me as a young undisciplined yob - and he said, "Ah, Ginger, we thought you had gone for good."

'I said, "Why did you think that?"

'"Well," he said, "you were over Norfolk, and you were supposed to be in Yorkshire."

'That was an absolutely terrifying experience, and brings to light the difference in the aeroplanes that we flew. Some were modified, some were not, some were modern, some were less than modern, and you tried to fly the most modern one you possibly could.'

'July came and went. We were at Church Fenton, now in 12 Group, flying day and night, doing absolutely nothing in the way of interceptions, because nothing was happening in our neck of the woods in Yorkshire. Then, suddenly, we were flying from Sheldon-in-Ellwood, just south of York, and on 14 Aug we flew down to Boscombe Down. I had no idea where Boscombe was, because there was a dotted line between the Humber and the Mersey, and I had never been south of that line except when I was lost over Norfolk.

'I set off to follow my leader, number two to the CO, John Grandy. We were going to the real war, in the south.'

Chapter Nine

FIGHTING FOR SURVIVAL

On 4 September Hitler addressed an excited crowd in Berlin and was carried away with fury. By all the logic of history, Britain should have rolled over and capitulated. It still would not do so. Hitler threatened to wipe the British out, claiming that Germany would never falter. 'Never! Never!' the crowd shouted with ecstasy.

The strategy change targeting London was intended to panic British civilians into surrender. Hitler phrased it as, 'eight million people going mad'. In the next two years, more than 43,000 people in Britain were killed in the German raids.

On 7 September the *Blitz* began, with German bombers heading for London and other cities, a process set to horrify Londoners over 57 consecutive nights. It was probably the single silliest thing Hitler did at that part of the war.

Tom Neil:

'On 1 September, 249 Squadron replaced 56 Squadron, which had been beaten to pieces, at North Weald. We found we couldn't operate because we had TR9-D HF frequency radios, and 11 Group used VHF. What do we do? We couldn't change all the radios in 36 aircraft, so the station commander, Victor Beamish said, "Right, change the aeroplanes!" Suddenly we were flying 56 Squadron Hurricanes and they took ours back to Boscombe.

'I had virtually a new Hurricane which had just arrived, it was V-7313 (if you go to North Weald today, a replica of 7313 is guarding the gate.) I flew that aircraft 61 times against the enemy between 1 Sept and 17 October, until it was shot down by Adolf Galland on the 17th – not with me in it, strangely enough.

'On 3 September I flew three times. This was the day that North Weald was attacked. It had been attacked on 24 August, heavily bombed, and then it was bombed again on 3 September. It is worth mentioning, because it shows how we operated. We were scrambled very early in the morning, a lovely broad summer's day. We took off and climbed and climbed, looking for the enemy. No enemy. We were then ordered to come back and land, which we did.

'As soon as we got our feet on the ground we were told to take off immediately. Half of us were re-fuelled, half of us not, but we took off again, the second flight that day. I was John Grandy's number two, high up in the front of these jaunts, and we climbed as fast as we could. For the first time I saw the enemy *en masse*. It was a frightening thing. There were just 12 of us, and you could see 30, 40, 50 bombers coming at you, all in close formation.

'Behind them, an infinite number of fighters, hundreds, the sky was black with aircraft moving. Crikey, where do we start with this mob? We were climbing up underneath, trying to get height. We didn't know quite where we were except it was somewhere in Essex. Suddenly we heard a voice from below: "Gaynor Leader! We've been hit," said the voice, "but we're all right."

'I looked over the side and I was over North Weald, and it had disappeared. Thirty bombers had dropped sixty 500lb [227kg] bombs on it, the whole place reduced to rubble and there were masses of large ant hills – or so it seemed from 15,000 feet [4,572m] – and we didn't intercept!

'I was thinking, "Why are we not intercepting?"

'We flew around in circles, trying to form up, just 12 aircraft, and we were ordered to pancake [land]! Why were we doing this? We ought to be fighting. We came down and looked at the airfield, and there were holes everywhere, on the airfield, on the hangars, fires, the whole lot. So where do we land? There's nothing in King's Regulations to tell you not to land your aircraft if the airfield has been bombed, and we just made do and did what we liked. We landed between the bombs, screwing like a dirt-track rider between the holes, ended up and began to re-fuel.

'The order came through, "Scramble again."

'I was right up front, still Grandy's number two. I had never seen London before, I had never seen the Thames before, and when I flew over East London and looked down, there was this amazing smoke haze that was London. People forget that London was covered in balloons, thousands of balloons all over, all at various heights, usually related to the height of the clouds.

'We went up to 20,000 feet [6,100m] and we were over Dover and then some 109s flew across the top of us. I had never seen 109s that close before. They were delightful little chaps with yellow noses and black crosses, and I was fascinated, rather like watching a spectacle in which I was not really involved. In fact, they could have come down and shot us to pieces. They didn't do anything, except circle. They didn't attack us. We flew around, went back to the centre of Kent, flew around again, and in the end we didn't see any other aircraft. That was my first real day of operations.'

The bulk of the fighting was done by Keith Park's 11 Group, and he could request – not demand – help from the two adjoining Group commanders. Brand, at 10 Group, co-operated, while there was often argument from Leigh-Mallory in 12 Group, increasingly convinced that Park's tactics were wrong. While Fighter Command overall had Hurricanes and Spitfires in the proportion 29-to-19, in 11 Group the proportions were 70/30, Hurricane/Spitfire.

Tom Neil:
'On 6 September my logbook reads: "My first flight of the day, nearly died of shock. North Weald heavily bombed, did not fly. Up against dragon-nosed Messerschmitt Bf 110s. Very fierce. Later, there were two engagements with the enemy. Didn't ever fight, was chased all around by 109s."

'This was the aircraft I shot down – "Vicinity, Maidstone, 18,000 [5,486m], got him in the glycol and finally made him jump out."

'I don't remember him jumping out. That was a destroyed, obviously, in a single-seater fighter when the pilot jumps out, but I don't remember all the detail, so many things happened.'

Last Witness Bob Foster, flying Hurricanes with 605 Squadron, moved down from 13 Group on 7 September, still committed to the 'simply suicidal' Fighter Squadron Attack formations which had been discredited since the Battle of France:

'We landed at Croydon, having flown in from Scotland and re-fuelled at Abingdon, and we saw London burning. That was our first sight of the real war.

'I remember Bunny Curran say, "Oh God, we're really in for it now, if this is what it's like."

'I didn't fly for a couple of days. We had a full squadron, that is, 20-odd pilots and 12 Hurricanes in operation at any one time. We had our first casualties then, a chap called Jack Fleming was shot down in flames. He got out but was burnt badly, finished up in Archie McIndoe's for 18 months. He was weaving behind the squadron – we flew in tight formations still, with weavers at the back – and old Jack was a weaver. He saw some 109s and was alerting the squadron. He didn't see the other 109s behind him.

'The weavers often got caught, and as a tactic, it was no good at all, left over from pre-war thinking. With hindsight, I think we stuck to our tight formations for far too long. Despite all the casualties, we still flew in these nice tight vics of three, four sections of three to make a squadron. Sometimes it was three sections and one at the back and two weavers. These were not effective because you lose your weaver sometimes and then who is looking after your back?

'The tactic for going into bombers was probably all right, line astern, each of us having a go. But it ignored the fact that we were probably being jumped by 109s at the same time. The theory of the tactic was great. Before the war there was an Air Ministry publication showing you how to attack enemy bombers. It was a series of little drawings where the bombers were flying along. The first drawing you had a section of three aircraft going in the other direction, then they all turned around and all lined up behind the bombers – and when your flight commander said "Open fire" you opened fire. And in the pictures, all three bombers are shot down.

'It never happened like that but that was the official way of attacking bombers.'

Last Witness Tom Neil:

'The first swastika in my logbook was a really naughty thing. We had attacked some bombers, and there was a fracas in which there were fighters present. It was a Whirling Dervish meeting, then suddenly an aircraft flew past me at roughly the same height, and on its own. One thing you never did was fly on your own, whether you were enemy or friendly, you had to fly with accomplices otherwise you ran the risk of being shot down.

'I remember being behind him, thinking, ah, this is not going to be very sportsmanlike. I am going to fly up behind him and he hasn't seen me. That is precisely what happened. It was a 109, I hit him once or twice.

'I know it was fair and square, but at that stage of the war we weren't fighting, we were flying a very strenuous game of rugby, in which the penalty was not a broken leg, it was a death. But this was the way we regarded it. Nobody thought in terms of the Germans invading. We did not really think about it. It was a hard-pressed fight and there I was, taking advantage of a chap who didn't see me, and he was in front of me. I shouldn't really have been doing it. I should have let him go, but I didn't.

'He caught fire. We were at 15,000 feet [4,572m]. You can't hang around waiting for him to crash into the ground. He could have gone 30 miles. So I had to leave him. You then say, later, to the Intelligence Officer, "I think I destroyed him", because if you hit him in the plumbing system, he would then spew glycol and you knew that the aircraft would not go more than five minutes. You could reasonably say, this is a "destroyed"if you hit him badly in the glycol system. I thought I saw him in flames, but then again there was smoke and mostly you didn't see him in flames, so you can claimed a "damaged".

'Then you speak to your Intelligence Officer – this is another thing that is so often mistaken – we would report on what we did and what we saw, and he would then interpret it. Later in the war there was an Intelligence Officer called the Earl of Gisborough – Lord Gisborough – he was in 41 Squadron when I finally commanded it. He wouldn't give you a "destroyed" unless you dragged in the body. You could say what you like but he wouldn't do it.'

On 7 September, Hitler postponed the date for 'Sealion' from 15 September to 21 September. Goering, given that time to finish the job, took charge personally. He believed anyway that he was achieving air superiority, and that the RAF was down to its last few dozen fighters. There had been lots of airfields to hit, and the RAF could scamper from one to another, but there was only one London. No one could scamper there. The RAF had to fight, and that meant that German fighters could engage them.

Tom Neil:
'On 7 September we attacked a whole formation of Dornier 17s. John Grandy was leading us. He was behind a German bomber, firing, he was hit immediately, set on fire, pulled out of the fight and tried to get out of the aircraft quickly, because he didn't want to be burnt. He didn't think he was on fire, but he could smell smoke, black and various other colours were coming around.

'So he made to get out but he pulled his parachute too quickly, and it deployed while he was still in the cockpit. He was plucked out of the aircraft, upside down, with his feet in the air. He came down upside down with his legs entangled in the shroud lines.

'He got down to the ground and fell on his head – very unhappy for one reason or another – wounded in the leg – and he saw a local oik who was so scared at what had happened around him, and wouldn't come near him. The oik was so stunned by the whole thing that he kept circling Grandy, and John Grandy was screaming at him, "Come here you stupid bastard, come and get me out of this parachute!"

'Eventually, Grandy got the oik to help and other people came up and Grandy was taken to hospital. John never flew again after that, he limped around for months.'

The Duxford Wing, led by Douglas Bader, claimed 22 victories on 7 September. From German records, Stephen Bungay reckoned they accounted for three Bf 110s, and shared in two others. They may have got two Bf 109s.

Mike Croskell:
'You did not think a fat lot about losses. It sounds unpleasant. I don't think we were that well-connected with other people in the squadron at the time, socially, to worry too much. The only one I remember was a Sergeant Norris, and I remember him because he had a car. My own car I shared with

Butterfield, and mine was taken over by the bus manager in whose house I roomed, while the officers stayed in a good hotel.

'When 213 Squadron moved from Exeter to 11 Group's Tangmere on 7 September, the bus manager took it away and flogged it for about five bob. I never went back again.'

Tom Neil:

'We lost half 249 Squadron that day. Boost Fleming, killed. The admirable Sergeant Smithson went past holding his hand up covered in blood, half his arm shot off. He disappeared, and we didn't see him for the best part of a year later. We lost a lot of people ...

'Rolls was killed coming back, Smithson, Grandy were shot down. I was very scared. Robert Fleming was very young, about 18, he had been at Oxford or Cambridge, I can't remember where, as an undergraduate. Delightful boy. He always used to fly at full throttle so we called him Boost. He was shot down in flames. Apparently he crash-landed somewhere in Kent. He got out of his aircraft and was rushing around beating off the flames, which were on his backside. The sight of someone running around the field with his backside on fire was fatally funny. We thought that was terribly funny.

'Of course, he died from shock and burns and heavens know what, so we lost him.'

'Grandy was shot down, and the other chap who was shot down was a very close friend of mine called Crossy. His fate was even funnier. He was in position behind a Dornier, shooting at him and he was hit from behind, except he wasn't hit in the tanks, he was hit in the side of the head. There was a heck of a bang, suddenly there was a blow on the side of his face and he felt blood going everywhere.

'He thought, "Oh, God, I'm dead, I'm dead!"

'So he had to get out of the fight, which he did, fell away from it, not knowing quite where the enemy aircraft was hiding. He hoped it wasn't still with him, and praying that he would do a forced landing on the nearest place he could safely find, and hoped he would remain conscious while he did that. He had this terrible feeling he was going to die all the way down to the ground.

'He crash-landed somewhere in Kent, in the cockpit thinking, "Am I going to die or not?" They took him out of the cockpit, took him down to the local hospital and wiped him clean.

'Then they told him, you're not really wounded at all. All the Perspex had come out and it had broken all the veins in the side of his head and, of course, he had bled profusely.

'So when he got back we all said, "What are you doing here, Crossy? We thought you had died!"'

It was not just Goering, but *Luftwaffe* group commanders who believed the exaggerated claims of the *Luftwaffe* pilots, and erroneously thought the RAF to be on the verge of collapse. The switch from attacking RAF airfields to an all-out assault on London released Fighter Command from the vice-like pressure of constant attack and it was able to recuperate. The bombers' new target was at the absolute limit of endurance for the escorting Bf 109s, and the 110 in particular was proving to be a liability against the more nimble British fighters.

Bob Foster:
'After 9 Sept, I started on the two and a half kills I made during the battle. The first one was half a kill, when Bunny Curran and myself shot down a Ju 88 which was a bit of an easy one. The German was on his own. Bunny went in first and got the rear gunner. When I went in there was no return fire at all. He went down somewhere in Kent.

'We were elated about the kill. We were fighting a war against an enemy. You shot down an aeroplane, I don't think human feelings came into it at all. Some chaps had it, some didn't. Bob Doe, I am sure, had it. I never had feelings of hatred against the Germans. My parents lived in Battersea, by Clapham Junction, they were bombed, perhaps, but not regularly. The house was damaged, my mother was not injured but she was blown across the room. You had not got a lot of sympathy for people who were doing this to you.

'Going into battle, flying out of Croydon, I had confidence in the aeroplane. I think for the first few occasions you don't really know what is going on half the time. I fired at quite a lot of stuff but didn't register anything that I know of, because, you didn't hang around in the danger zone. If you did, it was the last thing you would do. Everything was over so quickly.

'In the whole of the battle, which for me was September and October, I was very lucky, and did not get hit at all. Many Hurricanes with the squadron would come back pretty shot up. A lot of the early Hurricanes were canvas, which was a good thing, they could just stick the canvas back on again. As far as I know, Spitfires could not take the same punishment. The old Hurricane in which I thought I had been shot down, when the engine blew up, it still performed perfectly well, the wheels came down and I had lost no control.'

Hawker began supplying RAF squadrons with a new model Hurricane, featuring a two-speed, single-stage supercharged Merlin developing 1,390hp. They came into production as Merlin XX engines were available. The Hurricane II had the same two groups of four machine guns, initially having the same fuselage as a Hurricane I, but later models having a strengthened fuselage capable of accepting a modified wing with later armament options. It was not until 1941 that the four-cannon option was introduced.

Peter Hairs:

'We were stationed at Kenley after 10 September and we used Hawkinge as an advanced base. On this particular day we had flown to Hawkinge and while we were there, we had gone on one or two patrols. Whether there was a combat I don't know because I was never very accurate in recording things in my logbook. I had already lost one logbook, as well as all my luggage in France, when the boat carrying it was sunk.

'We must have been flying back to Kenley, and we took off in the evening to reach base and have our evening meal. We were flying around as a section, and Control came on the blower and said that bandits were in the vicinity. They gave us a height and a vector and we set off to get there.

'Control soon said, "You should be in sight of the enemy now."

'We couldn't see anything, but we were flying above a layer of stratus.

We came down below this stratus and as we broke cloud we found ourselves right in the middle of gaggles of 109s, all around us. I had no idea how many, there was no time to count. I saw one of them in front of me and fired one or two bursts. What annoyed me more than anything, the tracer bullets, where as normally in daylight they left a stream of smoke, being fairly dark by now they showed a stream of glowing light like a firework display.

'I was quite enjoying this and then suddenly there was a thump at the back, and looked in my rear-view mirror. The 109 behind me, he fired a shell and caught my tail unit, so it looked a bit of a mess, actually in tatters.

'I thought it was time to get out of his way. I tested the controls, they were basically all right, and the engine kept going, too. I flew back to Kenley and landed, and gratefully went into the mess for a tankard and a nice meal. I have no idea whether I got that 109. It all happens within seconds. I don't know if we shot any of the 109s down but I don't think we lost anyone either.

'I was glad I didn't have to bale out because I had been looking forward to my evening meal.'

Tom Neil:

'On 11 September I shot down an He 111. The fight started over London docks, and the enemy aircraft crashed by a railway station 30 miles south of London. I have no idea where it was, but I followed him down. People got out, the German crew.

'Do you know, they didn't even wave!

'They may have been shocked, of course.'

With the Germans going for London, this allowed more time for the RAF to position fighters in the right place and, most importantly, at a favourable altitude. As many as four or five squadrons of British fighters could now meet the enemy and deliver heavy, concentrated attacks against the bombers.

Tom Neil:
'The Germans hated their fighters coming across to Britain, because of their fuel situation. They only had an hour and 15 minutes endurance, and they took off a long time after the bombers. Sometimes the bombers were circling around for an hour – you could see them on radar circling over France, sorting themselves out – and they would have to engineer a meeting with the fighters who were very hard pressed for fuel. They would form up, sometimes they missed, sometimes we had the bombers without the fighters, other times we had the fighters without the bombers.

'Mostly they organised themselves, but the fighters never came further than the south end of London. Many times they went home – in a Messerschmitt 109 when you ran short of fuel you had a red light in the cockpit which came on – all the time they were flying back over the Channel with the red light on.

'Many times we shot at people, we may have shot down 20 or 30. Little did we know that another 20 fell in the "oggin", having run out of fuel.'

On 14 September Hitler called a meeting to review tactics, and concluded that air superiority had not been established. He wanted to review the situation again on 17 September, with a view to invasion on 27 September or 8 October – tides governed the best time for the Germans to land.

Tom Neil:
'Every day was pretty similar, up and down, usually one sortie in the morning, one in the afternoon and one in the early evening. Sometimes you saw an enemy aircraft, other times you didn't.

'When the bombers came over, we were the chaps who would be fighting the bombers, in the Hurricanes. But head-on attacks were hopeless. You didn't have time, and of course, you never really see who you hit, because it's over in a flash. Unless you were a stern attack you did not have a prolonged view of the enemy. If you did, of course, you ran a severe possibility of being shot down, as soon as you stayed behind the enemy. You got clobbered by the rear gunner.'

On 15 September came one of the heaviest days of fighting in the whole battle. It is now recognised as 'Battle of Britain Day'. The most famous NCO pilot of the war, Sergeant 'Ginger' Lacey, shot down three Bf 109s and a

Heinkel 111. Two days earlier he had shot down one of the Heinkel 111s that bombed Buckingham Palace before bailing out of his Hurricane. During the Battle of France and Battle of Britain, Ginger Lacey bailed out or force-landed no less than nine times after combat.

This was the day the Germans began to realise their miscalculations, as their losses climbed back towards what had been their peak on 15 August. In effect, the scales fell from their eyes. Paradoxically, the terminally inefficient 'Big Wing', which actually turned up on time for once, was a key factor in the Germans losing their taste for the fight.

John Ellacombe:

'We knew the "Big Wing" was forming, and I do have strong views on it because the "Big Wing" didn't get to us in 11 Group, and we were bombed at North Weald. The first time, Victor Beamish – one of the great men of the whole war – was so furious. We had about nine or ten men killed and quite a lot of damage on North Weald. I lost all my kit including my cameras and photo albums and clothes. The "Big Wing" never achieved anything, and certainly didn't protect our airfield, as it was supposed to.

'We were in the ops room watching it form up. They said, "It's heading your way, go now to dispersal and we will scramble you, and we will be covered by Duxford Wing." The Wing didn't get there because they took so long to form up their five squadrons for Mr Bader's fancy thing.

'There is an accurate record now of claims and losses, in which individual aircraft can be identified and the combats they fought. The first time that "Big Wing" went into action, they claimed 19 aircraft destroyed. On that day, the Germans lost two aircraft.

'There was a tremendous lot of ill-feeling between 11 and 12 Group. As for Douglas Bader, I have nothing but contempt for him. I am convinced he was shot down by one of his own men from his squadron. I have developed this case simply because so many chaps disliked him because he was so bloody arrogant and rude to everybody. He thought he was the finest pilot there ever was. I am told that one of his pilots was a brilliant aerobatic pilot, and he was forbidden to do these various manoeuvres because Bader couldn't do them.

'Bader was not liked in his own squadron. He was a good pilot ... such a good pilot he lost his bloody legs. He just wasn't a good leader.'

On 15 September, Last Witness Mike Croskell was shot down, though with an unexpected silver lining to a very near-death experience.

Mike Croskell:

'I went out and found a lone Dornier flying towards the docks in London. I didn't get right down into the best position to have a shot at it, and all of a sudden there were three or four loud bangs behind me. These two Bf 109s had put four explosive cannon shells into me. These shells were a deadly weapon – we didn't have anything like that, they were very effective – most of the tail disappeared and down I went, completely out of control.

'I went down and down and down and couldn't get out, couldn't get the hood open because the cannon shells jammed it. Eventually, in desperation, I undid my belt, crouched on the seat with both feet, and pulled with both hands. All of a sudden it came open and I was flung out. I seemed to be only 200 feet [61m] up, and the parachute opened as I hit the ground. A copse of young trees broke my fall. I had not the foggiest idea where I was.

'I just had a good swear, and was found there by some New Zealand anti-aircraft blokes. I was bleeding all over the place, particularly in the left foot. They were determined to cut my shoe off but, being a mean Yorkshireman, I said, "No you're not going to." While I was arguing, they cut the other shoe off. And then I got whipped into hospital, and was there for three or four weeks. I finished up in a military hospital, Halton.

'All these years later I cannot have an MRI scan because there are still too many bits of metal in me. They are small bits, but I also have bits in the back of my knee and my foot and my shoulder. Lethal weapons, those cannon shells. I also cannot have an operation to remove the shrapnel in my head because two of the bits are too near my brain … which probably accounts for a lot.

'But while my mates continued with the Battle of Britain, I chatted up the Nursing Sister, Mollie Davies, married her, and lived happily ever afterwards.'

The same day Mike Croskell 'caught a packet', all Keith Park's fighters were committed again. Park was nervous because he did not trust the 'Big Wing' tactics of Bader and Leigh-Mallory, worried that the huge formation would not turn up on time to stop 11 Group airfields being attacked. He was aware that there were political games being played, but in the heat of the battle he could hardly bring this up.

Mike Croskell:

'Being shot down was a major black because I was flying the CO's aeroplane at the time; mine was being serviced. It did not make him love me much, not that he loved me in the first place.

'Is that poor leadership? I am afraid it was. I know my pal, also a sergeant pilot, thought much the same way about it. Our squadron had a majority of officers when I was in it. In our flight of six, we had two regular sergeant pilots – they got commissioned into another squadron – and the squadron was knocked about a bit so a number of chaps got the chop. They replaced those shot down with sergeant pilots being given commissions.

'On the other hand, this was never really an issue at the time and I gave it no thought, even though the sergeant pilots were rather isolated. You just met the officer pilots in the crew room. We mixed all right there, but we never saw them after that. They went to their mess, we went to ours, it was simple but quite separate. It might have been just our squadron, but I don't think so.'

The win/loss figures returned that evening, with claims that the RAF had destroyed 185 German aircraft – celebrated in the newspapers with banner headlines the following day – made Park livid.

He knew it was not true, though it was one of the rare times when the 'Big Wing' appeared on the scene in enough time to frighten the Germans. Most of the claims came from 12 Group pilots, including Bader's 'Big Wing'. The real total was 56.

Last Witness Tom Neil was involved in an epic air fight:

'That was a very strenuous day, 15 September, significant because that was the day we heard the Germans were going to invade. We know now, the Government knew, because of Ultra interception, that it wasn't going to happen and had been postponed. They didn't tell anybody, Churchill didn't tell his own people and we didn't know either, so we went on fighting tooth and nail, into November, still thinking an invasion was possible. Nobody told us. Naughty chaps.

'We flew four times that day, and I was credited at the end of it with four kills. On the first flight we didn't do very much. On the second flight, a couple of hours later, I found myself behind one Dornier and was firing at it. I pulled back a little bit to fire at it again, and suddenly two chaps in front of me baled out. Two bodies with undeveloped parachutes came hurtling towards me. I ducked in the cockpit, I thought they were going to hit me. They flew at me, missed my propeller and I pulled away and then was hotly engaged by 109s. There was a restless period of 30 seconds, I suppose, when all I did was pull and push and shot at people as they were fleetingly before me.

'Then, it always happens like this in a fight, suddenly there's no aeroplanes around you. You look around and everyone is gone. There are 50 or 100 aircraft around but you don't see them.

'Then I looked up and there was another Dornier flying in front of me, obviously going home. I thought, that's the one to attack, so I flew after it as far as I could and was just catching up to it when a Spitfire appeared on my left. We flew towards the Dornier together and we attacked it, from the quarter. They flew into cloud, they flew out of cloud and they began to lose height. And we attacked it again, and attacked it, and attacked it until we ran out of ammunition.

'By this time it was over the Thames Estuary and flew out to sea, across a convoy. It flew at mast height, and I was flying in formation on it, 50 yards [46m] to its right. I could see all the symbols on the cockpit, and nobody was firing back. The aircraft was a shambles at the back. I thought, we're going to lose it, and then the nose came up and up and suddenly the tail touched down and it sploshed down into the water.

'We circled around him, the Spitfire and I circled around. Nobody appeared, obviously they had been killed. We were about 20 miles [32 km] out to sea, so we flew back, cockahoop, it had been a very successful day.

'I was able to congratulate myself because I had shot down one Dornier, and the other Dornier I had to share with the Spitfire, so I could claim one and a half.

'I didn't know who the Spitfire was and suddenly he waved and left me and I flew back to North Weald. Then, I put in my combat report, and a day or two later a highly-ranked Intelligence Officer arrived, and I saw them speaking to John Grandy.

'They beckoned me over and said, "Were you the chap who engaged the aircraft that was shot down over the sea?"

'I said, "Yes, with a Spitfire."

'The Spitfire pilot turned out to be called Eric Lock, a Shropshire farmer, knee-high to a duck and the top-scoring RAF pilot in the whole battle.

'"Well," they said, "the Spitfire pilot has put in a report. Not only did you help him destroy the Dornier that fell into the sea, but he watched you shoot down two 109s."

'I was then credited with one Dornier over the Thames, two 109s eventually – they never appeared in the books. Apparently the people who fell into the water in the other Dornier – despite the fact that the Spitfire pilot and I had said they had perished – in fact, two of them survived and were picked up by the German Air/Sea Rescue organisation.'

On 16 September, Goering stepped up the *Blitz*, bombing London and other cities relentlessly, despite there being no evidence that eight million people were in fact going mad. Quietly, without making a public pronouncement, on 17 September Hitler called off the invasion. He wanted to start thinking about attacking Russia.

Bob Foster:
'We went into some 110s near Gatwick. They were in a defensive circle. They were either escorting or were due to escort some bombers, and they were stuck over England, about nine or ten of them. They went into a defensive circle like the old wagon train, one behind the other. We joined into the circle, and we could get inside them. They were a couple of hundred yards apart, each one trying to defend the other.

'Then my engine blew up on me. I thought I had been hit. But I went in and trailed this one German I had shot down, at the same time I had this huge bang at the front of the aeroplane, a lot of glycol and oil went up, so I assumed I had been hit. I cut the petrol off and got ready to get out. It wasn't burning, just a lot of glycol, but I couldn't see much. I glided out of action and saw a big field below, and dropped the wheels and landed there. I discovered that I had not been hit but that the engine had just blown up.

'In this big field an airman came up to me.

'I said, "Where am I?"

'He said, "Gatwick, sir!"

'Back then it was just a big field. I claimed the 110, my aircraft was repaired and flying again within 48 hours.'

The gross claims of the Duxford Wing now began to assume a real political importance.

On 18 September, Kesselring sent fighters across to attack specific English targets. Park ignored them, so Kesselring sent bombers and 14 RAF squadrons rose to meet them. These included Bader's Duxford Wing.

Eight German aircraft were shot down, including their commander. The 'Big Wing' claimed 24 destroyed, 4 shared, 3 probables and 1 damaged. Bader's 242 Squadron alone claimed 12, and got the public plaudits. They were being noticed in high places, as was intended.

Tom Neil:

'My personal Hurricane, B7313, the one that was eventually shot down by Adolf Galland with a Frenchman in it, was damaged on 18 September. In return, I damaged a Heinkel 111.

'We had spent all our time over Kent. Maidstone to Canterbury was our patrol line, backwards and forwards at 15,000 feet [4,572m]. Sometimes we saw aircraft, we could see them but we couldn't get at them. On this particular occasion, we were vectored against an incoming raid of He 111s which were coming in over Deal. We were going to stage a head-on attack, which I hated.

'They were no good, dangerous for a start, because you've two aircraft coming together at about 600 mph [965 kmh]. You don't have much of a chance to shoot, and you're crowding each other, elbowing each other out to get a decent shot. The chances of collision were high. That one was particularly bad, because the Heinkels were coming in, formed into a big phalanx.

'We were going in at the same height and they opened their bomb doors and jettisoned their bombs. Now, when they jettisoned their bombs in a He 111, they come out backwards, down the other way, and flip forward. They jettisoned their bombs just as we were going underneath. I have a vision to this day of bombs coming out around my ears. I can see it now, 500lb [227kg] bombs, just flicking past me.

'Then we shot down some. It was a running engagement, but it didn't get as far as London. Eventually, I was credited with a "damaged".

On 18 September Keith Park issued a directive telling his pilots that the first 24 hours of any actual invasion were the most important, and they would be expected to fly six – instead of the normal three – sorties a day. Churchill was impressed with the preparations the Germans had been making, collecting ships in every port, and was daily monitoring the weather forecasts. The pilots waited, still fully tuned for a fight.

John Ellacombe:
'I went into hospital after bailing out of my burning Hurricane and when I was recovering in a ward, there was another chap there. I was delighted to find that it was Frank Czajkowski, the Polish pilot who had gone down in the first sortie.

'He said, "John they've taken all the mirrors out of the room but I've got a little mirror here. Look at your face, it looks very funny."

'They had sprayed tannic acid and that forms a great big scab. The doctor and the nurse were furious with me, that Frank had done that. But he was a great character, and had been wounded in the leg and in the shoulder. He used to go off in his wheelchair and he came back one day and said, "John, there's a German ward about three wards away and they've got a lot of German airmen in there. One of them was from the Heinkel you shot down on 24 August. I've been talking to them.

'Then the young doctor came in and he said, "Look, I speak fluent German. Keep Czajkowski out of my ward. He's telling them we're going to get them better and then interrogate them and shoot them – and they're not getting better."'

'So Frank wasn't allowed to go in there any more. We were moved out of Southend because the place was bombed, and we were taken up to St Luke's Hospital in Bradford. We were there for about six weeks until we were fully recovered and all our burns had recovered, and Frank's bullet wounds. After four weeks' leave we reported back to our squadron.'

Tom Neil:
'27 September was the last day that the Germans came out in force with their bombers. They produced the best part of a thousand bombers. When you think of Kent, sometimes there were almost two thousand aircraft over Kent, all fighting one against the other. There were a lot of people around.

'The first flight we didn't do very much, the second flight we were vectored south to a part of the country we didn't normally go. Normally in 249 Squadron we were over the Thames Estuary or the south of Essex or the north of Kent as far down as Dover. We didn't go south, that would have taken us into the Biggin Hill – Kenley – Tangmere area. This time we were vectored south and suddenly ran into a group of Bf 110s over Reigate. It was an engagement into which we were pitch-forked. We didn't see anything and then suddenly there were aircraft all in front of us.

'You did not want a Bf 110 in front of you, firing at you, because it was heavily armed, with cannons and it didn't do to get hit by those. Yet they were in a defensive circle, which is very strange. It indicated defeat, rather than attack, that they were each covering the other. I remember we were going around the wrong way to the defensive circle, we were going one way, they were going the other. I remember thinking it was a silly bloody thing to do, why didn't we go the right way?

'I reared up in an attack on a 110, and firing at it and seeing it so close it was wobbling. I don't know exactly what happened but it went on fire and it went down and that was it. I began to attack a second 110. This time it decided to dive away from the action. This was still over Reigate, and it went very steeply down to the ground, and lost 15,000 feet [4,572m] until it was just above the villages. Quite a few of them did this in order to escape from us. I followed this bloke down and I found another Hurricane on my left. We were both firing at it, and it was very low on the ground and you couldn't really get below it, which was the safest place to be. He was very low over the hills and the trees.

'The Messerschmitt was badly damaged but the chap in the back kept firing back at us – you could see the bullets coming, they used to come out like a paper stream twisting and flicking over your head. I always ducked. The bloke on my left turned out to be John Beasley, from my own squadron. He suddenly broke away and disappeared. He had been hit in the leg, broke all the bones on his instep. He was in a rather bad way, his foot full of blood, semi-fainting but he landed. He was dragged away to a hospital where he remained for several months.

'I followed this Bf 110 down, and suddenly I had oil everywhere. I was showered in oil and I could not see out of it. But there was this badly damaged German aircraft just in front of me, and I couldn't see it. Anyway, after a time I flew alongside it. I thought, bugger it, I am not going to drop into the sea as a result of lack of oil. So I left it and turned around and went home. It was probably destroyed and went into the sea but I couldn't wait to see that. I was too concerned about my own aircraft.

'I then attempted to fly back to North Weald, but I didn't make it. Halfway across Kent, the oil got so bad I had to land at Detling. I put down there on the grass. I had not been hit, strangely enough, but I had a vicious

oil leak. Something had broken. I got the engine filled up and flew back to
North Weald.

'In the afternoon there was a unique engagement, the bloodiest contact
I had. They were Ju 88s, we hated attacking them because they were so
tough. You could hit them in one engine and they would catch on fire with
enormous bursts of red flames coming from them. But they would still fly on
at exactly the same speed.

'The two aircraft in the morning were 110s. The second flight in the
afternoon were Ju 88s. This was a sad, sad blow to me, because one thing I
learned very quickly was that when you attack bombers, you don't attack
bombers in the middle. You start at the outside and work your way towards
the centre of the formation. If you start in the middle you get all the flak
from left and right. This had happened to me very early on in my career and
I decided I'd never do that one again.

'On this particular occasion, we were flying astern at these Junkers 88s,
and there was a bloke on my left called Brian Wreaker, who had shot down
eight enemy aircraft – a delightful boy. I was shooting at something, and then
suddenly the aircraft was hit by something, either by me or something else.
It could have been hit by anti-aircraft fire. We were right in the middle of
anti-aircraft shells all the time, it never stopped firing just because we were
there. We were clustered all around by anti-aircraft bursts. Suddenly the Ju 88
turned away, turned over, uncontrolled, whether the bloke had been killed I
don't know, it just disappeared.

'Then there was another aircraft in front of me, this one was on fire, and
we followed it, it was a raging roaring furnace on one engine. We tackled it
and we shot the other engine out. It came down and down and crashed into
the sea off Shoreham, on the south coast.

'Having got to the coast a dozen other people joined us, and I dare say
they all went home and claimed it. We claimed it and we were credited with
it, so we got two, but it could have gone either way. We had a squadron score
that day of 22 aircraft. They were littered all around the place, and that was
the last major offensive they had.

'I had a cannon shell ricochet off. My ground crew, young kids, like me
really, 19 years old, they asked me, "You been hit?" They could always see if
you had fired your guns, because of the tapes over gun ports. They were dead
keen to see if you have been hit, when you got a cannon shell burst.'

Goering went after the British aircraft industry. A special, and effective,
group of Bf 110's called *Erbrobungsgruppe* had already made two attacks
on the Supermarine Spitfire works in Southampton, and on 24 September
they had another go. Damage was slight but 41 workers were killed, and 63
injured. Costly raids were made all through 11 Group's area, for a loss of 57

Luftwaffe aircraft and their crews, against 29 RAF losses. This was definitely not contributing to *Luftwaffe* 'control of the air'.

Bob Foster:

'We were flying around at 18,000 feet [5,486m] on a lovely, sunny day, again, in this tight formation, and suddenly someone shouted out "Break, break, break!"

'This meant that the Germans were coming down on us. When you hear that you don't hang around. I broke but my number two was a bit late and last time I saw him was going down in flames – a chap called Charles English – he got out of the aeroplane but got stuck on the tail-plane and was killed.

'I dived down without any argument and when I pulled out, in front of me was a 109 going home. I don't think he saw me. I shot him down near Enfield. I think what had happened was that the 109s had jumped us and he was one of them, and thought, job done, home for breakfast or lunch, and of course, you can't do that.

'I still had speed from my dive, he was going home at low level. He seemed to have relaxed, but once you were in the danger zone, and the whole of England was a danger zone, you didn't sit around, thinking, "I have just shot somebody down – what a good chap I am!" I got him from behind.'

Last Witness Bob Doe, having made his first 13 kills on a Spitfire with 234 Squadron, was one of only three unwounded survivors by early September. He had been fighting continuously for 28 days, when he was sent back with the Squadron remnants to Cornwall to get new pilots and train them.

Bob Doe:

'I was posted to 238 Squadron on 27 September on Hurricanes, where I got three more. I was posted in as a flight commander, but never got the rank. I was a pilot officer, the lowest commissioned rank, and I was actually CO at one time.

'I did two hours flying on Hurricanes before I went back into the battle. Whereas the Spitfire was a musician's aeroplane, a dream, the Hurricane was a very efficient workman's tool. The Hurricane needed brute force. I don't like putting the Hurricane down because I spent most of the war flying Hurricanes, but it did not have the finesse of the Spitfire.

'When I got the Hurricane, I got three Germans, but on the first occasion I got into trouble because there were only six aircraft in 238 Squadron at the time. I was acting CO, leading the six. We found this huge gaggle of German aircraft over the Isle of Wight area. They were going in circles around what I thought were two big aeroplanes at the bottom, plus some Heinkels. I took my chaps right down through the middle because I thought it was the best way to go. I believed in head-on attacks – not everyone's taste.

'At that time there were 12 Spitfires sitting above us. As I turned over
to go down, I saw the Spitfires turning away. Later I accused the squadron
commander of cowardice. I shouldn't have done, I suppose. Unfortunately,
he went to live in Tunbridge Wells after the war, and we met on a number
of occasions. I asked him to his face why he turned away, and he said he was
giving us "top cover". A load of codswallop.'

On 28 September, on a rare occasion for the *Luftwaffe*, they got their own
3-to-1 kill ratio which they had been seeking, and expecting, since the battle
began in July. They sent over a small group of the tough Ju 88s, accompanied
by a lot of Bf 109s, and caught a lot of Fighter Command still climbing.
Twelve RAF fighters were shot down, against a loss of four Germans.

Peter Hairs:

'After we had been in combat the sky seemed to be absolutely clear of aircraft.
I was flying along, and we had arranged that the section commanders – I
happened to be one at that stage – would waggle wings to attract their section
and get the other aircraft to formate. I was doing this and saw something
coming down from my left, and thought it was my number three coming to join
up.

'I then thought, "It's not a Hurricane!"

'It had a big hole in the nose, and the Germans fired their 20mm
cannons through the propeller boss. He was pretty close by then so I thought
I had better do something.

'I pulled my Hurricane around in a very tight left turn, more or less
towards him. At the same time I could see the shell coming out of this hole. It
hit my starboard wing and made a hole there – this was a split-second thing
– and I went into a high-speed stall and spin, possibly accelerated by the force
of the shell in my right wing.

'I recovered from the spin, looked around, and there was nothing in
sight. If I had not made that sudden turn, he might have got me with a
second cannon shell.'

The last day of September saw another serious German effort, with a raid
by 200 aircraft in the morning which only reached Maidstone before being
turned back in sporadic fighting by eight 11 Group squadrons. A hundred
German aircraft further west were also repulsed. In the afternoon, two raids
totalling 200 aircraft reached into Kent and were then involved in individual
combats. That day saw the highest *Luftwaffe* fighter loss of the battle, because
of a miscalculation.

Escorting bombers, which had a much longer range, in a raid on London, the Bf 109s – harried by Hurricane and Spitfire attacks – left it too late to dash for home, and many were forced to ditch. The RAF lost 19 aircraft in the day's fighting; the Germans a total of 43, of which 14 were bombers, one a Bf 110, and 28 were Bf 109s.

Bob Doe:

'My Hurricanes went into the fight on 30 September and I lost one of them, which is why I got so cross with the CO of the Spitfire Squadron. I pulled up underneath a 110 and shot it down, and then headed for home, only five of us left. I wasn't hit on that sortie, but on every other occasion in Hurricanes I was hit.

'The second time was when I went head-on with a bunch of He 111 bombers. We were in the right position, so I did a head-on attack on them. I was a great believer in the head-on attack because the pilot just has glass in front of him, and it frightens them. I damaged one, and then knocked him out. But on that occasion he hit me, a bullet through the propeller blade. They were wood propeller blades on the Hurricane, and he split it from end to end, but it never fell out. It got me back safely.

'The last occasion I was in action with a Hurricane was when I shot the tail off a Ju 88. That time I got 12 bullet holes in my own aircraft so I knew I had been in action then. Ju 88s were tough aircraft.'

Chapter Ten

CHANGING ATTITUDES

I n October the *Luftwaffe* began to switch to night raids against large cities, and day attacks concentrated on hit and run tactics, individual Bf 109s carrying a single 250kg (551lb) bomb, protected by a second Bf 109, both able to act as fighters after the bomb was dropped.

Tom Neil:

'At the beginning of October, the scene became totally different. The Germans didn't send over their massed bombers. Instead, they converted their Bf 109s into bomb-carrying aircraft. They would send 30 or 40 of these over, 20 carrying bombs, the rest as escorts. We came across them day after day after day. You would have fleeting views of them and then they were gone.

'I see in my log for October 6 I have written, "constant stooge patrols, Maidstone patrol line, saw lots of 109s every day." We were the monkey and they knew it. Occasionally they amused themselves by shooting one of us down.

'We lost a lot of aircraft; we lost chaps shot down, usually they were the arse-end Charlies at the back of patrols, mainly killed by Adolf Galland and his roving squadrons. The 109s had complete control of the situations, facing Hurricanes. They could out-dive us, they could out-climb us, they could out-do us on the level. They would attack us from the rear, diving down, going about 150 mph [241 kph] faster than we were, pick up the chaps at the back, and of course, they had cannon.

'They only had to have one or two hits and we were destroyed. Time and again we lost chaps. This went on throughout October.'

Many RAF fighter pilots, despite having eight 0.303 inch Brownings, felt a growing disadvantage taking on Bf 109s because their machine guns did not have the power of a 20mm cannon. Hundreds of bullets seemed to enter a German aircraft, particularly Ju88s, and they carried on flying. Cannon could go through armour, where 0.303 bullets couldn't. Experiments carrying cannon had shown a degree of unreliability, the cannon jamming because they were mounted on their sides, and their reputation was poor.

By the Autumn, and more experiments, a way was found to mount cannon upright, and to cope with the ejection of empty shell cases.

Going into the winter of 1940, Sholto Douglas assembled some of Fighter Command's top pilots to discuss the issue of cannon versus Browning machine gun. The debate included the famous 'Aces' Douglas Bader, Bob Stanford Tuck and 'Sailor' Malan. Bader had been leading 242 Hurricane Squadron, Stanford Tuck had scored many of his victories on Spitfires before taking over 257 Hurricane Squadron, while Malan flew Spitfires from the beginning of the war, and was CO of 74 Squadron.

Bader, older than the others, immediately came down against the cannon, saying no one wanted to change from the Brownings…'no doubts…stick to the Brownings…damn fine guns…served us well….changeover do more harm than good…a proven weapon…can't monkey around with cannon… don't trust them…bloody new…probably full of bugs…let's wait until they have been modified…'

Sholto Douglas turned to 'Sailor' Malan, who took the diametrically opposite view, 'so many German aircraft carry armour plate … over 500 yards [457m] Brownings were useless … everything so fast that a three-second burst was all you had time for … a single cannon shell hit could destroy an aircraft … armour-piercing and incendiary shells were the ideal mixture … nothing revolutionary about using cannon.'

When it came to Stanford Tuck's view, which chimed with Malan's, a blazing row immediately ensued, with Bader and Tuck standing and shouting into each other's faces for 30 seconds. Malan said later that had Bader not been such a bloody-minded man, he would never have overcome the disability of flying with two legs missing. But the cannon argument eventually won.

John Ellacombe would have been just as happy with heavier-calibre machine guns:

'The Hurricane could out-manoeuvre the Bf 109 but it didn't have enough guns, nor the right calibre. We thought afterwards when we saw the first American fighters – especially the P51 Merlin-engined Mustang – with its 0.5 inch machine guns, that was much better. The number of times we fired at Heinkels and Dorniers and saw all our shells exploding (the ammunition we carried was eight guns with 240 rounds apiece, firing at 16 rounds per second) most of them were armour-piercing high-explosive – and you'd see them exploding on the wings but not bursting in the plane.

'It was very frustrating. Later on, when we got 20mm cannon and we saw that exploding, we realised what we had missed. Of course, the Americans with their P51s had the point fives, and when they fought the German fighters, they out-shot them. They had this much better gun.'

As a source of intelligence to back up the radar system, 421 Flight was formed on 8 October 1940, as a detached unit of 66 Squadron, operating from Gravesend. Their task was to patrol the Channel and report on the movement of enemy aircraft.

They were called 'Jim Crow' units, named after a cartoon character, a tough-looking crow with a top hat and a cane. In America, the term 'Jim Crow' was used as a derogatory term for a black person and the 'Jim Crow Law' was to do with racial segregation, but the RAF was clearly unaware or unconcerned about the unsavoury nature of the term. Over the English Channel, a Jim Crow's job was to shadow enemy formations and report by radio direct to the 11 Group operations room. They were supposed to avoid combat, which was easier said than done.

Jim Crow units, equipped with Spitfire IIs and Hurricane IIs, mounted two patrols a day, manned by pilots who had fought through the Battle of Britain. Last Witness Billy Drake, a 1 Squadron Hurricane veteran of the Battle of France, flew as a Jim Crow:

'The reason we were formed into an organisation, 421 Flight, was that a few of the radar stations had been knocked out by the German Air Force and, therefore, 11 Group and Fighter Command were not getting the full picture. What they wanted was to form an organisation that could be scrambled off once they had seen the build-up of forces over France.

'We were sent off as Jim Crows, a pair of aeroplanes, to monitor the build-up and radio back to 11 Group how many aeroplanes we thought there were, what direction they were flying, their height. We were always below them, you couldn't do this by looking down, you had to look up to get the full picture.

'It was a very hairy job. If we were not being jumped by the 109s, we were being jumped by our own fighters. They hadn't got time to verify who we were, they just saw something below them, easy meat, and came down at us. They had no luck, thank God.

'Very few people realised the Jim Crows existed. The Germans certainly had no idea, but we were successful. We were not jumped every time. Depending where we met these formations the RAF was far too busy looking after themselves and looking for the formations that they were detailed to attack. It was always a 50:50 chance. It depended entirely on whether you were over the Channel or over England, but everybody else was busy. They more or less left us alone but one had to be very careful that one wasn't caught.

'I don't think we were secret, *per se*. People realised we existed but I don't think we ever had time to talk to anybody else about what we were up to. The RAF squadrons knew we were a part of the early warning system.

'My first DFC was for the number of aeroplanes I had been involved with in France, and then the job we did during the Battle of Britain. It was three and a half victories in France and one with the Jim Crows. We were not supposed to be shooting down the enemy as Jim Crows, but twice we came across German aeroplanes, and working as a pair, we went for them. The number two always looked after the leader.'

The Jim Crow 421 Flight became 91 'Nigeria' Squadron in January, 1941. The daylight battles gradually petered out as the *Luftwaffe* began to withdraw units in preparation for Operation Barbarossa, the invasion of Russia. Over Britain, the enemy bombers now concentrated mainly on night raids. With no really effective specialist night fighter available – aircraft production had been concentrated on day fighters – Hurricanes were pressed into service in the role. Lacking airborne radar the pilots had to rely on their night vision to intercept their quarry. The Hurricane was difficult to operate in the dark but was considered safer than the Spitfire because of the latter's narrow-track undercarriage. There were also far more Hurricanes around.

Throughout the battle the supply of new or repaired Hurricanes had built up to such an extent that 512 were on strength at the end of October. By comparison, only 285 Spitfires were available. It was a vindication of the view that Hermann Goering was 'arrogant, incompetent, egotistical and divisive,' that the *Luftwaffe* did not really mount a determined attack on aircraft production throughout the battle. Hurricanes were produced by Gloster in Gloucestershire, and some Hurricane X's were shipped from Canada, but most were built by Hawkers at Kingston Upon Thames, and Langley in Buckinghamshire. Both were at the limit of the range for a Bf 109, but could have been targeted by Bf 110s.

Although the intensity of the daylight raids began to diminish, both sides continued to sustain losses in the battle over southern England. Last Witness Bob Doe became one of the Hurricane casualties when he was shot down on 10 October:

'We were scrambled against some 109s flying at altitude, around 20,000 feet [6,100m]. The Hurricanes should not have been used for such a task, we should have used Spitfires, but we were scrambled and told to climb. We went into cloud at about 4,000 feet [1,219m], and stayed in cloud for about 18,000 feet [5,486m].

'It is an odd property of cloud that, when you're looking down into it, you can see what's climbing out of it for the last 500 feet [152m] of its climb. But if you're the one in the cloud you can't see a blind thing until you're totally clear of it. I was hit from behind and in front (how they did that I will never know) before I came out of cloud. I always trained myself that, if I saw anything coming past me from behind – tracer fire, for example – I would hit the stick without thinking. I trained myself to do that, and I did that on this occasion. So I went into a bunt, that's an outside loop, but by then I had had a bullet through my left shoulder, a bullet through my left hand and a cannon shell had exploded under the parachute I was sitting on. A hunk of metal went through my right heel, which cut the Achilles tendon.

'I thought, "I really ought to get out of this thing," and I pulled my Sutton harness to release and of course, nothing happened. I was not thinking clearly enough to realise that it was just my weight holding me in the cockpit. I tried to stand up which released the harness and I fell out. The aircraft had been upside down by then, and the hood had either come off or was shot off. I pulled my parachute release and it opened, and I looked up and it looked like a colander rather than a parachute. It had holes all over it. I was coming down all right but faster than normal.

'I eventually came out of the cloud at 4,000 feet [1,219m] over the most beautiful blue lagoon, and I was drifting towards an island in the centre of this lagoon. It was Poole Harbour, and the island was Brownsea Island, and I landed slap in the middle of the island, where there was a quagmire into which their drains ran. Luckily, this saved my life because of my fast descent. I had no legs to stand on because of this cut Achilles tendon, and I had no movement in my left arm. I was knocked out and I came to my consciousness again to find an Irishman standing over me with a big iron bar, saying, "What are you?"

'In very polite English I told him I was an Englishman. You can imagine how polite I was. He was then wonderful. He carried me down to the jetty where the Navy had sent over a picket boat, and I was taken to the local Cornelia Hospital in Poole.

'I was not out of action for long. The tendon didn't heal for three years, but you could still fly an aeroplane. As for the bullet in the shoulder, they removed the deltoid muscle. All these years later, I have no deltoid muscle at all. I had a bullet that went through the armour plate, through my watch – which annoyed me – and finished up sitting in my hand.

'I was back on operations at the end of November.'

Last Witness Tom Neil also lost his Hurricane, even though he was miles away at the time:

'17 October was the first time I had not flown Hurricane V-7313. I had put it in for servicing to have a 40-hour inspection, and I went on leave. Normally what one liked to do is organise your leave when your aircraft went in for inspection, you had a weekend off, your aircraft was inspected, and you came back and you would immediately expect that no one else had flown your aeroplane.

'I put my aircraft in for inspection, it was taken out and flown by a Frenchman called Peranne, who had just joined the squadron [Peranne survived the war, and went on to become a Deputy in the French Government]. He was shot down immediately by one of Adolf Galland's merry men, and my aircraft was lost.'

It was the English Channel as much as the RAF which, by October, made the Germans despondent. They called it *'Kanalkrankheit'*, Channel Sickness. One German fighter squadron based around Cherburg, Guernsey and Brest was said to have become so nervous that their daily briefings were given while the pilots sat on toilets, so many of them wanted to be in that once-private place at the same time.

Battle-weary pilots on both sides were still losing comrades on a regular basis, despite the height of the battle having passed.

Last Witness Peter Hairs:

'I suppose one did not have time to make real friends in that period, because we were always so busy. I used to spend time in the mess in the evenings but when we were at readiness, we flew in the early morning until about lunchtime.

'Afternoons we were called back to readiness, having already spent a few hours there. I can recollect going back to the mess for lunch, the soup was served, I was just about to eat the first spoonful and the tannoy came on, "501 Squadron get back to readiness." Then it was straight back to dispersal and carry on.

'One expected to have casualties. You're sorry when you knew someone particularly well was killed, but nothing much you could do about it. I didn't hate the Germans, particularly. I didn't like their system of government, but the fact they were flying over England – how dare they!

'Yet there was no real hatred.'

A certain amount of suspicion had grown up in German bomber squadrons about their fighter compatriots. Bf 109s were designed to be flown at height, pounce out of the sun, shoot down an enemy and then climb back up again faster than he could be chased.

When they were tied to escorting bombers and told to stick by and protect them, the only way they could fight was in a dog-fight, and that was initiated by the RAF.

Goering, along with many German bomber pilots, thought their fighter pilot friends were more interested in their own personal scores than protecting the bombers. This was, in any case, a German tradition left over from the Great War; Richtofen, Udet, Boelke, Voss, were all very keen on high individual scores.

Yet the Germans pilots, often low on fuel by the time they met their RAF counterparts, did not, or could not, always take the opportunity to enhance their scores.

Bob Foster:

'I did about 70 sorties in the Battle of Britain, but not more than a dozen combats. It is surprising, looking at the logbook, how often we took off but there was no combat. People seem to think that everything went 100%, but it didn't. You take off to intercept some aircraft coming over Dungeness, and they turn away. We didn't always make contact.'

Graham Leggatt :

'I remember my first scramble resulted in no contact made. There was a lot of cloud around, we didn't see the enemy at all. We were up there, stooging around and then Control came on and said, pancake – land – and that was that, nothing much had happened.

'On the second sortie a fairly large formation of Messerschmitts went over the top of us, 500 feet [152m] above us. Our formation leader told us, "Gun-sights on," and we expected these Messerschmitts to dive down on us at any minute. But we held formation, and they passed over the top and then they came around the other side, and some of them dived at us. I dare say there was the best part of 20 of them. We had a couple of chaps watching our tail, they were called "weavers" – a couple of experienced chaps weaving behind us – and they yelled out "Snappers!" The Germans swept over the top of us and kept going for France. The rest of them stayed up there and went on in the same direction, for France.

'That was my first real encounter with the enemy. They were not very aggressive. That was the extraordinary thing. I think if we had been in their position, nearly always with a height advantage and with a slight speed advantage, I think we would have made a lot more of it. But they didn't.

'They had a few stars in their formation, and the stars were sent down to shoot us up, but the rest of their guys stayed up there. Those that did come down, it got into a circling winding match. I think I did a couple of complete 360 degree turns. Then our formation leader came up and called on us to re-form, which we did. They didn't get any of us. They did on the next trip, though. One of ours caught it and went down in a ball of fire.

'So it went on, a cat and mouse game really. Now and again they would come down to fight.'

Stephen Bungay, in *The Most Dangerous Enemy*, quotes an American study about fighter pilots, winners and losers, published in 1966 by Herbert K. Weiss. Weiss concluded that over 90 per cent of pilots had only a 50:50 chance of getting through their first decisive combat without being shot down. After five decisive encounters his survival chances increased by a factor of 20. Only five per cent of fighters scored five or more victories, thus becoming an 'ace'. These aces scored about 40 per cent of all victories claimed in the air.

This data remains consistent across all campaigns Weiss analysed in both world wars, and in Korea. 'There are,' concluded Bungay 'two types of pilot, a small group of hunter-killers, and a large group of the hunted.'

On 25 October, four days after he first went into battle, Graham Leggatt started his own personal quest to survive and become a hunter-killer by destroying his first Bf 109, though it was years before it was actually confirmed:

'We were over the south coast, 12 of us, hotly engaged by 109s out to sea around Hastings. We were separated out, four of us in two pairs, Thompson on my right, Ozzy Cross on my left and Sergeant Davis was behind. We were flying parallel to the coast just behind Hastings, in battle formation, fairly close, and suddenly white things began to fly by my left ear. I thought, "That's odd." There's an element of amusement in these things.

'The chap on my right, P/O Thompson, had never seen an enemy aircraft. Suddenly he was confronted by one which shot at him. This was a little frightening. He was told to follow me, do nothing but follow me.

'I had this 109 right in front of me in a very precarious position. What does it do? It shoves its nose down, the pilot is almost shot out through the top of the cockpit but of course he is strapped in. He can do that because he has a direct-injection engine, his engine doesn't splutter. I cannot do that, I have to follow as best I can. I don't even do that, yards of black smoke coming from the engine. We try to follow him and he's getting away from us, but all the time I am shooting at him. We are up to 380, 400 miles an hour [644 kph], going straight down and then he disappears into cloud.

'Have I shot him down? I really have no idea. We whisk through the cloud, the 109 had gone. We fly around and then go home, jolly thankful for being spared.

'Years later I was told that a German aircraft crashed at the place when I shot at him. The pilot, I heard, had baled out, he had been burnt but he was alive. His aircraft had crashed near Nestling, which is reclaimed land, and when you hit the ground there you go 30 or 40 feet [12m] under, because it's sand.

'Forty years later I got a telephone call from someone who said, "Look, we're trying to do a television broadcast, would you be prepared to come down to talk about the aircraft that you shot at on 25 October 1940?" The German was an NCO pilot. He had apparently been tended to by a 17-year-old nurse, locally, who had been very supportive. She tended to his burns, he was badly shocked.

'The local populace turned up and wanted to lynch him! Everybody is of the opinion, having seen *The Darling Buds of May* with David Jason, that the East Enders are delightful people, Pearly Kings and everything else, cracking jokes – believe you me they weren't. They were vicious buggers. They had had all their houses knocked down in the East End of London, and they didn't like Germans at all, and they dealt with them very roughly from time to time. Some Germans were very soundly beaten. They had to be protected by the military.

'On this particular occasion, these people collected and were going to lynch this chap, but the 17-year-old young lady bravely stood in front of him and protected him. He was taken by the military and locked up in jail, and later sent to Canada for the rest of the war. For years and years afterwards he kept in touch with this nurse, but the broadcast never came to fruition because this German pilot died before it happened. They had invited him across to take part in the broadcast but he had died before he could do so.'

Peter Hairs, like many other pilots, had an instinct for survival and a deep desire to return to home comforts that far outshone any ambitions he may have had about becoming an ace:

'I think I had a guardian angel. I was lucky. I was a reasonably good pilot – the mark in my logbook was that I was an above-average pilot – with flying, you increase your skills as you do more hours on any one particular type.

'What I remember, having landed and been in combat, the Intelligence Officer – IO – used to be among us with his book, wanting us to tell him what had happened. Rather than talking to him, I was more interested in getting back to dispersal and having a cup of tea. I suppose I was a bit naughty, really. I enjoyed my comfort, I would rather have a cup of tea than sit down with the IO and tell him stories.

'I really don't have any recollection of doing a lot of damage. I think I may have frightened one or two of the Germans, but that was about it. My wife did say when the fighting slackened, that, when she saw me, I was exhausted, absolutely drained.

'There were very few pilots who could claim to have shot down more than half a dozen of the enemy. We got by.'

Stephen Bungay also highlighted original research done long after the Second World War into the Hurricane's one great advantage over its friendly rival, the Spitfire, and its deadly rival, the Bf 109, its ability to turn tighter than them in a fight. It is something that the Last Witnesses comment on time after time.

In *Aerospace Internal report 9701*, credited to Ackroyd and Lamont, the turning radii for the three aircraft under achievable combat conditions were found to be:

Bf 109	854 feet
Spitfire	684 feet
Hurricane	663 feet.

That tight turning circle worked to the advantage of Graham Leggatt:

'I got my first confirmed kill on October 29, 1940, two days before the official end of the Battle of Britain, though of course we did not know that then.

'About six 109s came down, and we all went into 360 turns. I levelled off to look around. Straight in front of me was a yellow-nosed Messerschmitt coming in my direction. My dear old friend Charles Ambrose, long since gone, he was on this chap's tail. For some reason the Messerschmitt, instead of coming at me and firing, just pulled up into a really steep turn, up to his port. I had plenty of speed on, pushed the throttle forward and went after him. Ambrose was a bit further behind so I got in first. The Messerschmitt continued on his steep climbing turn, and I got straight on to his tail, fairly close, and pressed the button and fired.

'I looked up in my mirror and there was another one of them, right on my tail, so I pulled away to port. I looked over my shoulder to see where he had gone and he had disappeared somewhere.

'We milled around for a bit, little by little the squadron got together, and headed home, there was nothing else to be done. I don't know what happened to Ambrose. One by one we landed and taxied in. As always, they had given me the longest walk out from dispersal to the parking place. I got to the squadron hut, and they were standing in a group, chattering away.

'As I approached, one of them said, "Who fired at the one who was climbing, then?"

'My ears pricked up. I waited for a few moments, and then I said, "What happened?"

'They all looked at me. "Well, he bailed out," they said.

'At that point the Intelligence Officer came along with his pad. That was the first bit of fun. I did not know what the drill was about claiming. I didn't even know you had to claim, or if you did, how you went about it.'

Peter Hairs does not recall the differences between the Hurricane and Spitfire being quite as pronounced as some might think:

'I know I enjoyed flying a Hurricane. I did a number of hours on Spitfires later in the war. A Spitfire was rather a nippy thing to fly, but apart from its increased speed and ability to fly higher, there wasn't really a lot of difference. The Germans never admitted to being shot down by a Hurricane, it was always a "Schpitfeur". It's the name, for one thing, and also the fact that it's a rather beautiful looking aeroplane. It has those lovely lines and it has a small and slender build.'

Graham Leggatt firmly believes that the Hurricane squadrons were what kept the Germans at bay:

'The Hurricane was a good aeroplane. We would have lost the war if we had not had them. I don't think there's any doubt about that. Hitler made the fundamental mistake of switching from his attack on airfields, primarily Hurricane airfields. He switched his attack to London and the battle was lost and won over those few days. We just about held things together, long enough to get the airfields working again, because the damage to the airfields was very considerable.

  'The aeroplane proved itself good. You could take a Hurricane out and blast it full of holes and then the lads come along with their strips of fabric and a can of red dope, paint over the holes and say, "Okay, off you go – that won't do you any harm." A Spitfire, of course, much more highly bred, modern construction techniques, required more intensive backing than the good old happy-go-lucky Hurricane. Good aeroplane. Good aeroplane. That's as good an epitaph as any.'

Tom Neil of 249 Squadron got a DFC on 8 October. When he won a bar to his DFC seven week later, the propaganda and the politics were starting to flourish as the realisation dawned that the Germans were not about to invade Britain.

Tom Neil:
'You don't get a DFC immediately. It comes days and weeks afterwards. That was the month we were on the BBC, me and my Spitfire friend. Erik Lock, a very distinguished fighter pilot with 41 Squadron. We turned up at the BBC at lunchtime. Lock, credited as the highest-scoring pilot in the Battle of Britain, was the Spitfire pilot who had confirmed two of my victories on 15 September.

  'I had borrowed a car in order to get to London, and we parked it roughly outside the Ministry of Defence in London. We went into the BBC, rehearsed all afternoon – that was how the BBC worked then. We didn't do it very well, because we were down in the bowels somewhere. There was a very attractive woman doing the announcing.

  'Finally the producer said, "Look, you chaps have really got to ham it up, because we don't want a broadcast as though you're reading the fat stock prices. Could you not be a little more animated about it?"

'Poor old Lock, as brave a fighter pilot who ever trod foot on this earth, he went into shock immediately when he saw the microphone in front of him. He could not get a word out.

'Eventually we went on the six o'clock news – or whatever it was – my parents were listening to it in Lancashire, but no one else I knew listened to it as far as I know. After we had broadcast, they said, "Would you like to stay and broadcast for the Overseas Service? You'll have to stay on until very late?"

'We did the broadcast for the Overseas Service, got out about 12 o'clock, went outside and found that somebody had pinched the car. It had gone! We were stuck in the middle of bloody London at night with no car.

'Finally we went down to Scotland Yard and said, "Somebody's pinched our car!"

'They said, "Yes, we know, we've got it."

'It was two o'clock in the morning before I was allowed to take my car back.'

On 17 October 1940, certain they had won the Battle of Britain, Hugh Dowding and Keith Park came face to face with the political consequences of refusing to use the 'Big Wing' in the way Leigh-Mallory and Sholto Douglas wanted.

A meeting was called by Sir Charles Portal, nine years younger than Dowding, but who been promoted over his head to become RAF Chief of Air Staff. Among others there were Sir Quentin Brand, heading 10 Group, and Richard Saul, leading 13 Group.

Without notice, Leigh-Mallory brought a relatively junior officer, Squadron Leader Douglas Bader, the well-known advocate of the 'Big Wing'.

As soon as Park saw Bader, he knew he was being stitched up.

He had not been given the opportunity to bring his own young champion 'Sailor' Malan, who would have spoken strongly against the 'Big Wing'.

Tom Neil was too junior an officer to have been asked his opinion at the time, nevertheless:

'All we saw of 12 Group's contribution to engagements was a vast formation of Hurricanes in the (discredited) neat vics of three, streaming comfortably over our heads in pursuit of an enemy who had long since disappeared in the direction of France.'

Park had been seething with Leigh-Mallory ever since the gross RAF claims on 15 September, claims led by Bader and 12 Group. Instead of getting mad in return, Leigh-Mallory got even.

The alleged purpose of the meeting was:

To work out how to out-number the enemy.

How to ensure German bombers were attacked while their guarding Bf 109's were held off.

How to ensure that interceptions should be with the advantage of height.

In fact, it was a meeting to shaft Park and Dowding. The 'Big Wing', now seen as useless, was not seen as such then. The Air Ministry was in favour of it. Bader, with his unstinting support for the 'Big Wing', was the weapon used by Leigh Mallory against Park.

Keith Park produced a document showing he had called on Bader's Duxford Wing on every possible occasion during the last part of October. In ten sorties, Park showed, they had intercepted the Germans once, and had shot down just one enemy aircraft down.

No one cared.

With Dowding, they got him on not having any night fighters, despite the fact that he had been stretched to the limit on day fighters. Coventry had just been destroyed by night bombing, and Dowding had no night fighters. He had not paid enough attention to this new subject in the middle of the daytime fighting, and it was deemed that he should have. Day fighter Hurricanes were drafted in to do the night fighter job, with little success.

Leigh-Mallory's reward was to get Keith Park's job the following month, and Sholto-Douglas took Dowding's. Until he was shot down in August 1941, their catspaw, Douglas Bader, led the Tangmere Wing, amid claims to have introduced the 'finger 4' tactic the Germans had been using since the beginning of the war, and Malan had introduced to 74 Squadron in June 1940.

Dowding was considered, at 58 years of age (just one year younger than Tony Blair in 2010), to be too old to remain as head of Fighter Command. He was seven years younger than Churchill. Perhaps a role could be found sending him to America to talk to the Yanks?

If any Fighter Command leader ever deserved the title of Marshal of the Royal Air Force, Dowding did. Even that was refused him.

But Keith Park was to get a well-deserved second chance.

Chapter Eleven

ERIC NICOLSON, VC

In the whole of the Second World War, of more than 150,000 RAF and Royal Navy flyers, only 32 aircrew won the highest of all awards for bravery, the Victoria Cross. Most were from Bomber Command.

Only one was awarded to a Fighter Command pilot, Flight Lieutenant James Brindley Nicolson, on his first sortie with 249 Hurricane Squadron in the Battle of Britain. Nicolson was born in the middle of the 'war to end all wars', on 29 April 1917, in Hampstead, North London. His family moved to Shoreham-on-Sea, and he attended Tonbridge School, which he left aged 18 to begin work as an engineer. In 1936, he joined the RAF and was posted to 72 Squadron in 1937, flying Gloster Gladiators. He joined 249 Hurricane Squadron in 1940.

A VC is given 'For Valour' in the face of the enemy. It takes precedence over all other orders, decorations and medals. Since the first presentation by Queen Victoria on 26 June 1857, only 1,356 have been awarded (although she gave out 62 that first day, allegedly without getting off her horse).

Three men have won bars to their VCs, two of them doctors. No woman has yet won one. They have also become more difficult to come by. Many of the early VCs might qualify nowadays only for a mention in dispatches. Originally, they were never given posthumously; that changed in 1900. Nowadays, it is almost impossible for a live warrior to win one.

Nicolson was badly wounded during the action that led to his VC. Last Witness Tom Neil could easily have been on that flight that day, and suffered a similar fate. He knew Nicolson well:

> 'He had come down to us from 72 Squadron. He was tall, as I am, 6ft 3inches [1.9m], an ex-public schoolboy with hair like a black mop. His uniform always looked as though he had slept in it. And he was a raconteur the like of which you have never come across. He used to tell stories, and fibs, from morning to night, and was an expert on everything. There was no subject in the world he could not talk on.
>
> 'He used to lecture us (he was a Flying Officer, I was a Pilot Officer – that's like being a First Lieutenant and a Second Lieutenant) on what we

would do if we intercepted the enemy. He had never seen an enemy aeroplane in his life, but he knew everything about it!

'Eventually he became flight commander, but I was his buddy and I knew him probably better than anybody else.'

'On 14 Aug, we flew down from Yorkshire to Boscombe Down, which is just north of Salisbury in the south of England. It was a satellite station to Middle Wallop in 10 Group. On 249 Squadron, we hadn't seen anything of the Germans in Yorkshire.

'I was flying my dearly beloved Hurricane, P3617. It happened that your own Hurricane becomes like a household dog. Nobody else flew it if you were sufficiently senior in the squadron. I was young in terms of years, just 20, but I was the first pilot to join the squadron, and people tended to look up to me, despite me being just a Pilot Officer, the lowest commissioned rank. So I always had my own aircraft, GMO 3617.

'The following night, 15/16 August, I was on night duty as Operations Officer, which meant I had to man the single telephone we had. I remember I had a long conversation with a very pleasant lady. That was the extent of my involvement that night, so I was not worn out. On 16 August I came out to my aircraft thinking, "Whacko! I am going to be on the first ops!" We were all frightfully keen to get into the action. The other flight of 249 Squadron had been in action the previous day and had intercepted a series of German aircraft around Southampton, and they had shot down two or three. There was a great amount of excitement about.

'I turned up at eight o'clock, rubbing my hands and saying to Nicolson, "Right, I'm your number two – you're my flight commander."

You can imagine my feelings when he said, "You're not flying. You have been on duty all night. You are not up to it." I said: "I am."

He kept saying I was not flying, and I kept saying: "I am" with great deliberation.

He said: "No, you're not. You have been on duty all night, you are not up to it."

I said: "I am young, I am strong, I want to fly!"'

There was nothing I could do about it.

He said, "I am going to give your aircraft to Squadron Leader King."

I said, "Treat it gently..."

'So, in high dudgeon, I walked around, very cross. I saw them take off and they all disappeared. This was about lunchtime. I thought, "Bugger them all," and I went to the Mess for lunch.

'While I was there, news came through that they had intercepted the enemy. I rushed back and the aircraft came back in dribs and drabs, in the usual way after a fight. What had happened?'

On 16 August Flight Lieutanant James Nicolson of 249 Squadron took off at about 1.05 pm at the head of a flight of three Hurricanes. Whilst climbing with the sun behind them they were bounced and all three aircraft were hit. Squadron Leader King, flying as one of Nicolson's wing men, sustained major damage and turned for home. The third member of the flight, confusingly also called King, was in trouble when his Hurricane caught fire. He bailed out, but his parachute was shot full of holes by the Home Guard, who mistook him for a German, and he fell to his death.

Nicolson's aircraft was also in flames and he was about to bale out when a Bf 110 shot past him. He stayed in the cockpit and opened fire at about 200 yards (182m) until he could bear the heat and flames no more and took to his parachute. His ordeal was not over, however, for just as he was landing, as he laconically noted in his combat report, he was shot in the buttocks by an over-zealous Home Guard. Badly burned, Nicolson was taken to hospital.

Tom Neil:

'We had lost Nicolson, and we had lost King. Squadron Leader King was a "supernumery", and he came back with his aircraft – my aircraft! – in tatters.

'We discussed our first major casualties, and my beautiful aircraft, and it was all a bit of a joke, because Nicolson was shot down, the chap telling us how to do everything and shot down on his first do! To us, this was the funniest thing that ever happened.

'The fact that he appeared to be mortally wounded didn't mean anything to us. It doesn't when you're 19. All we then heard was that he had been forced down and he had been badly burned and was taken to hospital. We got a letter the following day addressed to John Grandy, the squadron commander. It was a four-line letter, saying: "I was shot down by a Messerschmitt, I did this, I didn't do that, and I am badly burnt and I am not at all happy"... something like that. No dramatics at all. It was written by his nurse, because he couldn't write as his hands were so burnt.

'The Adjutant, Lomar, went to see Nicolson in hospital, and came back and told us how nastily he had been burnt. He was also shot in the arm and the leg. As he got slightly better the stories got slightly more enlarged. Nicolson was hideously burnt all around his head and his face and his hands.

'In a Hurricane there were three petrol tanks. It held 97 gallons, each tank had roughly 30 gallons [113.5 litres], that is, 30 in the front tank and 33 gallons [125 litres] in each of two wing tanks either side of the cockpit. They were aluminium tanks, not self-sealing at the time, though later they were. If you were shot from behind, the first place you got hit was your tanks in the wing, left and right, not the tank in front of you. It had been thought that the gravity tank would be the first to get hit; it never was. It used to be shielded by the pilot's armour plate behind. But it was the wing tanks which caught fire with 20mm cannon shell, which were explosive. The flames used to come up through the wing-roots, straight up behind the cockpit and into the pilot's face.

'We used to have silly little jokes about the cockpit belt which would drop down, and what happened to all the instruments, did they melt? At this stage, in August, we were flying in our shirt sleeves. Immediately after what happened to Nicolson we flew with everything on, our goggles on – most of us didn't fly with goggles, we saw better without them – but at that time, because it was summer, we used to fly with our bare hands.

'The Hurricane was very, very bad for burns. Eighty per cent of the people who were burnt in the Battle of Britain were flying Hurricanes, and it was all because of those wing tanks. The order of the day was to attack the bombers, which we used to do from the side or come up the back end. Of course, the German fighters would be sitting behind us, and you'd get hit from behind.

'But there was something riotously funny about some of the events that happened. Those of us who didn't get shot down used to discuss what happened to our mates. And because we were 19 years old, it all became funny if it happened 50 miles [80 km] away. You'd see your buddies bleeding, or burnt, or whatever it was – see what happened to Charlie! – and he wouldn't be sleeping in the next bed tonight, and it was seen as fun.

'Then, of course, Nicolson got his VC.'

John Grandy, 249's CO, put Nicolson up for a DFC, and this citation went into the machinery that decided decorations. During this period, 249 Squadron was moved from Boscombe Down, a 10 Group station, to North Weald, an 11 Group station. This meant the sign-off for the DFC was done by North Weald's station commander, Wing Commander Victor Beamish, on Grandy's recommendation. Beamish had never had Nicolson as a serving officer on his station. He made a mistake with the spelling of Nicolson's name, spelling it Nicholson, and the same spelling mistake was to be repeated higher up the ranks. This was on 26 October, 11 weeks after Nicolson was shot down, almost as if catching up with the paperwork after the white heat of battle.

Two days later, on 28 October, with that recommendation in front of him at 11 Group HQ in Bentley Priory, Keith Park, AOC 11 Group, made an exceptional decision among the flow of award recommendations that tumbled in front of him daily:

'Flight Lieutenant Nicolson showed exceptional courage and disregard for the safety of his own life by continuing to engage the enemy after he had been wounded and his aircraft was burning.

'For this outstanding act of gallantry and magnificent display of fighting spirit, I recommend this officer for the immediate award of a Victoria Cross.'

Six days after that, on 3 November 1940, Park's recommendation went in front of Dowding, AOC Fighter Command, who wrote:

'I consider this to be an outstanding case of gallantry and endorse the recommendation for the award of the Victoria Cross.

It was gazetted on 15 November 1940:

'*ROYAL AIR FORCE.*
'The KING has been graciously pleased to confer the Victoria Cross on the undermentioned officer in recognition of most conspicuous bravery : —
Flight Lieutenant James Brindley NICOLSON (39329) — No. 249 Squadron.
    During an engagement with the enemy near Southampton on 16th August, 1940, Flight Lieutenant Nicolson's aircraft was hit by four cannon shells, two of which wounded him whilst another set fire to the gravity tank. When about to abandon his aircraft owing to flames in the cockpit he sighted an enemy fighter. This he attacked and shot down, although as a result of staying in his burning aircraft he sustained serious burns to his hands, face, neck and legs. Flight Lieutenant Nicolson has always displayed great enthusiasm for air fighting and this incident shows that he possesses courage and determination of a high order. By continuing to engage the enemy after he had been wounded and his aircraft set on fire, he displayed exceptional gallantry and disregard for the safety of his own life.'

Except for the last line, this is virtually a replica of the citation for the DFC. In his own account that he gave in a BBC Radio broadcast later in the year, Nicolson describes flying one of three Hurricanes which drove a number of Ju 88s into the range of a squadron of Spitfires. As he climbed to rejoin his flight, his aircraft took four hits from a Bf 109:

'The first shell drove through the hood of the cockpit, sending splinters into my left eye, and one splinter, I discovered later, almost severed my eyelid. I couldn't see through the eye for blood. The second shell hit the spare petrol tank, setting it on fire, whilst the third shell crashed into my cockpit and tore off my right trouser leg.'

One account has it that Nicolson had climbed halfway out of the aircraft to bail out, when the Bf 110 flashed in front of him, and he climbed back into the burning cockpit to shoot at it. In his account – possibly not scripted by him, but by Ministry of Information minders – he said he chased a German aircraft:
    'I remember shouting at him when I first saw him, "I'll teach you some

manners, you Hun!" and I shouted other things as well. I knew that I was scoring hits on him all the time I was firing, and by this time it was pretty hot in the cockpit from the effects of the burst petrol tank. I couldn't see much flame, but I knew that it was there all right. I remember once looking at my left hand which was keeping the throttle open. It seemed to be on fire itself and I could see the skin peeling off it – yet I could feel little pain.'

He made three attempts to leave the burning Hurricane, succeeding on the third try, and pulled the rip-cord, playing dead to avoid being shot at by other German aircraft.

'The burns on my left hand left the knuckle showing through and for the first time I discovered that my left foot was wounded – blood was oozing out of the lace holes. My right hand was pretty badly burned too … then after a bit more of this dangling down business I began to ache all over, and my arms and legs began to hurt a lot.'

He told BBC Radio that he was cheered to hear that the Bf 110 he had been firing at had fallen into the sea … so it hadn't been such a bad day after all!

Nicolson's wounds were so severe that one doctor gave him only 24 hours to live. He had extensive third-degree burns and cannon shell wounds and splinters of Perspex all over his body. He had been three months convalescing in Torquay when the news of the VC came through.

He is reported to have said, 'Now I'll have to earn it.'

He sent a telegram to his wife Muriel: 'Darling just got VC. Don't know why. Letter follows. All my love. Nick'.

Tom Neil:
'The story we heard was that King George VI and his entourage were going around the southern counties, and the King turned to his PA and said, "Why is it that nobody in Fighter Command has got the Victoria Cross? They were giving Victoria Crosses by the dozen (a gross exaggeration) to Bomber Command, why nothing for Fighter Command pilots?"

'"Well, the answer is, sir, in order to get the Victoria Cross you have to have witnesses. If you're flying a single-engined aircraft, nobody is a witness and, therefore, we can't give them."

'The King said, "Well, I think we ought to have a Victoria Cross given to a fighter pilot."

'This was – allegedly – how it started and this was how it worked up.'

The Secretary of State for Air, Archibald Sinclair, wrote that he wanted to honour the recent exploits of the RAF by finding a suitable candidate for the Victoria Cross. Dowding passed this note on to his Group Commanders at about the time that Victor Beamish recommended Nicolson for a DFC. Park changed it to the VC 'for this outstanding act of gallantry and magnificent display of fighting spirit.' Dowding concurred and, after some discussion, the RAF's Personnel Services agreed to pass the recommendation on to the RAF Awards Committee.

Many considered that a number of other pilots were also worthy of such an honour, but the general view had evolved since the First World War that the purpose of a fighter pilot was to shoot down the enemy, and if he does so, he is only doing his normal job. Also, as a fighter pilot is alone, there is only his word, usually, of any heroism. There were high-scoring pilots already in the Battle of Britain – Sailor Malan, Stanford Tuck, Douglas Bader, Bob Doe – and while they won medals, none were VCs.

Last Witness Eric Brown:
'I know a lot of pilots feel that Nicholson's VC was "the bottom of the range". He could have felt that same way. I gather he was embarrassed by the whole business.'

It is not unusual for a winner of the VC to show embarrassment at winning that medal. Eric Brown cited a famous case of the sort of sacrifice made in the Battle of Britain that would probably have won a VC recommendation in the Great War, where a furious young Hurricane pilot, out of ammunition, rammed a German bomber to bring it down.

On 15 September, a seminal day in the Battle of Britain, Oberleutnant Robert Zehbe was a pilot with a crew of four, flying a Do 17 in an attack on central London. German pilots had been told they were winning the battle and that the RAF was down to its last few fighters. But that day they were assaulted by large groups of Hurricanes and Spitfires. Two of Zehbe's crew were killed, and he told the two others to bale out, which they did successfully. He then set his autopilot, and bailed out himself. He landed in Kennington, near the Oval and, dangling from power cables, was set upon by an angry mob, including a number of women with bread knives and pokers. Soldiers rescued him but he died of his wounds the following day.

His aircraft continued on its way, empty except for two dead bodies, heading for Buckingham Palace and pursued by five fighters from three RAF squadrons. It was then sighted by Sergeant Ray Holmes of 504 Squadron, who dived to attack. When he tried to fire his guns, he discovered he was out of ammunition. His blood up – 'the machine looked so flimsy!' – Holmes rammed the German aircraft.

Its tail came away and it went into a spin, both wings broke off, and it fell to the ground, scattering its bombs around Buckingham Palace. Holmes'

Hurricane went into a vertical spin and he bailed out, his aircraft crashing into a block of flats right next to Victoria Railway Station. According to Stephen Bungay, Holmes' 'parachute caught in some guttering and he hung with his feet resting on top of an empty dustbin. Cutting himself free, he kissed two girls who appeared in the next-door garden and, having inspected the nearby wreck of his kill, went to Chelsea Barracks to have a celebratory drink in the mess.'

In all, nine RAF pilots, including Holmes, claimed to have destroyed Zehbe's Dornier. The young sergeant pilot's reward? Not even a DFM – Distinguished Flying Medal – the rare gong occasionally presented to NCOs.

Ramming was not unknown as a way of attacking the Germans. On 7 October 1940, Belfast-born Ken Mackenzie, flying with 501 Hurricane Squadron, had shared in the destruction of a Bf 109 over the London docks. He chased another, scoring a number of hits before running out of ammunition. As the 109 turned for France and dived away, Mackenzie closed on it. Determined not to let it escape, he positioned his Hurricane on the enemy's port side with his starboard wing over its tailplane.

He then slammed his wing tip on the 109's tail. It snapped off, sending the German fighter diving into the sea. This violent manoeuvre immediately removed the outer part of Mackenzie's wing, but it was a clean break and he retained some control. Although pursued by two more 109s and with his engine damaged by enemy fire, he managed to clear the cliffs near Folkestone and belly-land his Hurricane in a field. The force of the impact threw him against the gun sight and he lost four teeth. He won a DFC, but it might so easily have been a VC.

It took 13 months, to September 1941, for Nicolson to make a recovery, and then more months struggling to be returned to flying duties. He was said to have been aware of the unease in the RAF about his VC, and keen to make amends.

In 1942 he was posted to India. Between August 1943 and August 1944 he was a Squadron Leader and CO of 27 Squadron, flying Bristol Beaufighters over Burma, chiefly on ground attack. He was never engaged in aerial combat again, though he was awarded the DFC.

He was killed in May 1945 while a passenger on a B24 Liberator which crashed into the Bay of Bengal.

Eric Nicolson's VC and DFC were sold in 1983 by his widow, Muriel. They were expected to fetch a respectable £25,000, with the rarity of being the only Battle of Britain, Fighter Command, Hurricane VC – but they went for a then-record £105,000.

They are on display in the RAF Museum in Hendon.

Some VCs now sell for £400,000.

Chapter Twelve

POLITICS, LESSONS AND THE DEATH OF THE 'GOLDEN BOYS'

Although there is doubt about RAF over-claiming kills (by a factor of 1.5-to-1) Fighter Command claimed 2,741 kills in the Battle of Britain.

The 34 Hurricane squadrons claimed 1,560 kills, or 55 per cent.

The 19 Spitfire squadrons claimed 1,189 kills, 43 per cent.

The average Hurricane squadron claimed 35 German aircraft for the loss of eight pilots,

Spitfire squadrons claimed 63 kills for 8.4 pilots, a rate 30 per cent better.

269 Hurricane pilots lost their lives, and 160 Spitfire pilots.

The *Blitz* brought an end to the Battle. There are various estimates on the numbers of pilots who fought in the Battle – they differ by about two dozen and don't always add up. The standard figure is 2,927, but Stephen Bungay estimates that 2,946 pilots made at least one operational flight during the July-October 1940 period – a figure confirmed by Group Captain Patrick Tootal of the Battle of Britain Association – of whom 537 were killed.

There were 2,353 Fighter Command pilots from Great Britain and 574 from overseas, who took part in the battle. It should also be noted – it is often forgotten – that 718 *Bomber Command* crew members, more men than Fighter Command lost, and 280 men from Coastal Command were killed fighting during the Battle of Britain. On 6 July 1940, Fighter Command could call on 1,259 active fighter pilots but such was the rate at which Britain was producing pilots, that after the battle was over, on 2 November, Fighter Command had 1,796 pilots, that is 40 per cent more.

Fighter Command lost 1,023 aircraft, against the *Luftwaffe's* 1,887 aircraft.

But Bomber Command lost 378 aircraft attacking German bases and barges in France and Germany, and Coastal Command lost 148 aircraft, so

British losses were 1,547 against 1,887. The *Luftwaffe* lost only 20 per cent more than the RAF.

In air fighting, the actual ratio of RAF kills to *Luftwaffe* kills was 1.8-to-1. The Germans were looking for a kill ratio of 5-to-1. It was never remotely on that year, and only reached that figure during relatively benign conditions – for the *Luftwaffe* – in 1941.

The Germans started the Battle of Britain with greater fighting experience than the RAF, and better tactics in Molders' *schwarme*. As the RAF gave up its 'Fighting Area Tactics' and achieved greater production of British aircraft and pilots, the balance changed. The Bf 109E's margin of superiority over the Hurricane was slight, and the Germans became obsessed with Spitfires.

The top 10 per cent of pilots made 55 per cent of the claims. Some pilots were great Hun-killers – including Last Witnesses Bob Doe, Billy Drake and Tom Neil – and some were there, like Bill Green, to be shot down and hopefully survive.

Tom Neil:
'The Hurricane ceased to be an effective fighter after the Battle of Britain. After that, on Hurricanes, we always found we were flying an inferior aircraft, even when we had Hurricane IIs, which was the old aircraft, just a little better. I always felt that I was fighting with a disadvantage from then on. I don't think the Hurricane was able to take more punishment than a Spitfire, and anyway, who wants to take punishment? I did not want to be hit.

'Another of its disadvantages was that it was an aircraft with an inline engine which was water-cooled. It got better later on, and you can argue that people flying P51s – the North American Mustangs – one of the most successful aircraft of the war, also had a water-cooled engine.

'You always felt that in a Hurricane, or indeed in any of our aircraft, flying over enemy territory with the inline engine, we were running the gauntlet.'

Before the war ended in 1945, a further 791 Battle of Britain fighter pilots were to lose their lives, an estimated 190 of them (along with hundreds of fresh and inexperienced pilots) in 1941 when Leigh Mallory finally got the means to try to show the world how wrong Keith Park had been in his tactics.

None of that was known by pilots at the time, who cared little for political wrangling, but would really have appreciated a little recognition.

Tom Neil:
'During the Battle of Britain I flew 141 times, fighting operationally, between 10 June and 31 October. I did not see my first German aircraft before 10

July. The Battle of Britain, so-called, was between 10 July and 31 October. This period of time was only arrived at in the autumn of 1943, when it was decided to give us a clasp, which we were going to wear on the medal ribbon that we didn't have.

'It was going to be an exotic little thing, in silver gilt. It turned out to be a little bit of bent tin, for which the Government must have paid nothing more than sixpence for the whole ruddy lot.'

Mike Croskell:
'After the end of the battle, and my time in hospital when I was shot down on 15 September, I returned to 213 Squadron, still flying Hurricanes. We were based up in Yorkshire and then the north of Scotland, and we never got into any combat at all after that. I had pretty well finished my operational tour when I married Mollie Davies, who nursed me back to health, and I became a flying instructor, and an officer. I didn't have to bother after that about being shot at, because I was teaching. My son was born in 1942.

'I served for 15 months as a Sergeant pilot, from the winter of 1939 to the Spring of 1941, for those four kills in the Battle of Britain. Medals for NCOs were a bit thin on the ground. I am not being jealous, but in my opinion NCOs did not get quite the recognition they ought to have done. My friend Reg Llewellen, shot down in the same fight as me, finished up in the same hospital as I did. He had been in the squadron just as long as I had. He was a sergeant as well and he got nothing at all. If you look at the various manuals, very few sergeant pilots in those days got a medal.'

In the whole of the RAF through the Second World War, 20,354 DFCs were awarded, along with 1,592 bars to DFCs. The overwhelming majority went to Bomber Command, which lost about 15 times as many aircrew as Fighter Command. Just over 6,000 DFMs were awarded, the equivalent medal for non-commissioned officers, though 40 per cent of RAF pilots were NCOs.

Hurricane development did not end as winter came on, and nor did the fighting. That winter the Hurricane IIA was introduced with a slightly lengthened fuselage, and the Merlin XX engine installed. The next variant, the Hurricane IIB, incorporated a newly-designed wing which carried 12 0.303 inch calibre machine guns and was able to carry two 500lb (227kg) bombs.

This was eventually superseded by the Hurricane IIC which had the eight Browning 0.303 inch machine guns replaced by four Hispano 20mm cannon. A redesigned wing was incorporated in the Mk IID with two 40mm cannon installed, along with two 0.303 inch calibre machine guns used as aiming or 'spotting' weapons.

The final production variant was the Hurricane Mk IV, equipped with the Merlin 27 engine of 1,650 hp. It was the most powerful of the lineage, the ultimate evolution from the 990 hp prototype of 1935.

As for the fighting, in November 1940 no one knew that the Battle of Britain had actually ended on 31 October, and there were still epic daily fights. On 11 November, the Italian Air Force raided Britain, in what became known as the 'Great Italian Turkey Shoot'. Last Witness Graham Leggatt is characteristically modest about his role in it:

'The Italian attack was a big story in my excursion into fighter operations in South East England. We were in North Weald. The morning came and went, and nothing happened. We got into the air for a convoy patrol, formed into a formation, all 12 of us, and set off for the North Sea where there were some ships wanting protection. We got out there and had been going up and down for over an hour, getting a bit bored, and then the controller said, "Twelve plus bandits, angels twelve, engage."

'We all tightened ourselves up. There was something around but they couldn't tell us what it was, except there were 12 aircraft.

'After a few minutes a voice piped up, "They're bloody Eyeties!"

'So we all pulled ourselves together, and there, sure enough, was a formation of largish twin-engine aircraft, which I knew at once was an Italian BR20. We went full bore to try and catch up with these chaps, by which time 257 Squadron from Martlesham Heath were beginning to get involved. By the time we got there, two of these Italians were falling out of their formation. Everybody was milling around firing at anything in sight. One of these chaps, a Fiat BR 20, flew straight across in front of me. And I fired.

'At the same moment a door in the fuselage flew open. There he was, miles out over the North Sea, no chance of being picked up, and he still thought it worth while to jump out. The others stayed on board and disappeared down to starboard.

'I pulled back and started to climb up again, at which point a bomb, a big yellow bomb, went past my wing-tip. I looked up and there was one of these BR 20s letting his bombs go. I didn't know whether he thought he might hit me or was just letting the bombs go, which he didn't like having on board. One of them just missed my wing.

'I looked around for something to have a go at, and all around people were having dog-fights. Then I saw, almost by himself, one of these Italian bombers. I went after him. No one seemed to be paying much attention. I got into a firing position, squirted at him, I was too far away, I did a quick flip around, came back for another go, and I did that twice more.

'He was a tough customer. I did not expect him to last as long as he did.

He did start to lose height. I latched on to this chap as he flew inland over Orfordness, gradually losing height. I went in for a final go at him but I was out of ammunition. It was all gone. I sat on his starboard quarter, no one else around. He flew inland, losing height steadily all the time, down to about 6,000 feet [1,828m].

'Then he turned, 90 degrees port, heading for Ipswich, and kept losing height. He turned 90 port again and headed for a fairly large field with a conifer plantation down one side of it. He headed for this field.

'I was still sitting up there beside him, watching him heading for the field. He ran across it, wheels up of course, came to the end of the field where it turned into a conifer forest, and he ploughed into it, bits flying off as he did so, and came to a standstill.

'I reckoned I had done a useful job of work. I had a look at my fuel state, which was really low. I had been going full bore the whole time, so my fuel was really short. I went into Martlesham Heath, where Stanford Tuck had his 257 Squadron.

'I stayed at Martlesham Heath, as there was fog at North Weald. I did not see the Intelligence Officer until mid-morning. He called me and I told him my story. They credited me with a third of the kill.

'I was not very happy because I regarded that as my kill. It was mine, and although I didn't make a song and dance about it, in my own mind, that was my aeroplane. But in the official record they booked it as a third. The Italian gunner in the upper turret was killed, but there are newspaper clippings from the day, and a couple of the Italians, the pilot and the navigator being marched out by the military police.

Tom Neil, whose 249 Hurricane Squadron was based at North Weald alongside Leggatt's 46 Squadron, was also involved in the 'turkey shoot':

'249 Squadron destroyed the back-up to the Italians, a Ju 86, and a sea plane, a Heinkel 59 – they shot both of them down – which was claimed to be a dastardly thing to do, because they both had red cross markings. Red cross or not, we were ordered to shoot them down. We had a lot of them in Malta later and shot them down, too, because there was no quarter asked, or given.'

Neil himself missed that fight with the Italians following a mid-air collision four days earlier after which Neil had to pretend to his parents that the limp he was disguising was nothing serious:

'In the beginning of November, we were scrambled, expecting the usual patrol over Maidstone. We were down at the entrance to the Thames Estuary, and every day now we had to climb up through cloud. This had a great impact on the formations we flew, because in order to be able to go through cloud, particularly if it is dense cloud, you have to fly very close in, the closer in the safer you are.

'We climbed up through a lot of cloud to get to about 16,000 feet [4,876m], and Control at North Weald was saying, "You should be seeing them!"

'"Well, we're not!" I snapped. "We're at 16,000 feet and we can't see a thing!"

'And, of course, the Germans were down at 2,000 feet [610m]. Down we went through this massive cloud, and there, something I had never seen before, Ju 87s – Stukas! There was a whole cloud of them dive-bombing the outbound convoy from the Thames. There were little green spots where their bombs had dropped.

'I was doing 200 mph [321 kph] faster than the German in front of me. It looked like they were going backwards. I passed them about 20 yards [18m] away, all three of us – they had a pilot and rear gunner – gawping at each other. I was virtually putting the wheel brakes on trying to slow down.

'Then I was suddenly confronted by another Stuka. I shot at that, it was hit and curved away and dived towards the sea. I thought that was a goner, and then I was immediately attacked myself by four 109s.

'The thing to do when you're attacked like that is to go crazy and attack them. They thought they were flying against a poor defenceless Hurricane – they did not expect to come across a madman who was going to fly direct at them and attack. We had a brief melee at the fringes of the cloud. Apparently there were 30 109s and there were 30 Ju 87s. I only saw about three or four. I shot after the 109s, firing at them, and someone was obviously calling for them to re-form.

'I flew as far as Margate and beyond, out into the North Sea, before I turned back home. I read later that the chap I had shot down, which I thought I had destroyed, I didn't. The chap was badly wounded but he managed to creep back home. But apparently we had very considerable success.'

'That was just about lunchtime, 7 November 1940. In the afternoon we were scrambled again. We were over Maidstone, we had been flying all day and fighting, and we were getting a bit tired. We were at 16,000 feet [4,876m], lots of cloud, pearly and thick. I remember climbing through 5,000 feet [1,524m] of cloud. I was thinking how much teatime would be welcome, a cuppa and a wad.

'We were flying in fours. I was leading the second four, and the bloke in front of me was Victor Beamish. He was a Wing Commander, but he never led. He always flew as part of the squadron, which meant that he could come and go as he pleased, which he did. Beamish disappeared. There was action somewhere else in Kent and that is why Beamish disappeared, but we were told to stay where we were, which we did.

'I moved up slightly to fill the hole left by Beamish. I was sitting there saying nothing to nobody and suddenly felt a hell of a bang at the back! The stick was torn from my grasp, and the Hurricane just stood on its tail and went upwards into a vertical climb. I remember thinking, "This is really rather silly. What do I do?"

'The aircraft turned over and began to spin, upside down. The natural instinct of any pilot in that situation is to try to correct the spin. I went through all the motions to correct the spin but it didn't seem to do any good. Again, if you're a pilot and your engine is going, you are very reluctant to leave the aircraft. Then somebody way up there said, "I think Ginger has had it."

'At that moment, at 6,000 feet [1,828m], I disappeared into cloud – this is where God comes in. He says, "Ginger, me lad, this cloud is a thousand feet thick and you've gone in at 6,000 feet. Coming out at 5,000 feet you haven't got much time to do anything."

'I came out at 5,000 feet [1,524m] and it was at that time I thought I would get out. I could not control the aircraft, which was spinning around like mad. I decided to go over the side. I managed to get to my feet, I had my helmet on, and I was flung out forward, over the front of the cockpit towards the propeller. My head was not far away from the propeller, whirling around like mad, and my toes were wrapped around the windscreen. They were being held in position by a long piece of "elastic", in fact my oxygen tube, which stretched from 4 feet [1.2m] to 8 feet [2.4m]. Either it snapped or – I don't know – I just felt a hell of a clump on my head. I fell off the side of the aeroplane, hit the wing and slithered off.

'Then there was silence. I thought, have I opened my parachute or not? I looked up and I couldn't see it there. Then your training comes into it. I remember being told, if you ever have to pull your parachute and you don't really know what's going on, go from a place of importance, like your tie, and work your way down, your buttons, your Mae West, until you come to your parachute rip-cord. If it's there, you pull it, and if it's not there you don't. So I felt my way down and thought, blow me, it's still in its housing, so I pulled it and the parachute opened with a jerk.

'It was not an unpleasant jerk. I was pretty close to the ground then, about 1,000 feet [305m]. I saw I was going to fall into a wood, just north of Maidstone. I thought, I don't want to fall into this wood, because I could fall out of the trees and damage myself. But I had no control over it and I did fall into the wood. I fell into a tree and then I fell out of the tree, and I damaged myself and lost consciousness, briefly.

'I came around to hear voices, and four people came towards me and surrounded me, four pairs of feet. I heard them through a haze, saying, "Is he one of ours or is he one of theirs?"

'No one on the ground seemed to be able to recognise airmen of either side – we looked pretty well the same – and had I been a German I think things would have gone hard for me.

"I had landed at a place called Walderslade. I came round and they saw I was young and sweet-looking, and that I must be one of theirs. They tried to get me to my feet but I couldn't stand because my legs had been damaged. Then some army people turned up and took me to their mess.

'I was given a tea at the army mess and asked if I wanted to go and see my aircraft. I said, "No, I don't. I am not in the least bit interested in my aircraft."

'The thing was, earlier that day I had been taxiing out with my own aircraft and I fell down a hole. It turned the aircraft upside down. This was eight o'clock in the morning. I had broken the propeller, ruined the reduction gear. I climbed down from being stuck up in the air, and John Grandy rang up and shouted, "Ginger, what the hell have you been doing?"

'I had to use his aircraft ... and it was his aircraft I had baled out of.

'I could not get through to North Weald – they thought I had bought it and were on the verge of packing my kit – until nine o'clock at night (from four o'clock in the afternoon) to say, "I'm alive!" I was taken into the billiard room where they had covered one of the tables, and put on the table while the doctor looked me over.

'I was sent home on leave but I didn't want to tell my parents why I had bailed out and damaged myself, so I never said a word. They would have worried. I had to spend three or four days at home, repairing my limp.'

There were a number of 'damaged' entries in Graham Leggatt's logbook covering this period, but an excess of modesty made him reluctant to claim any kills:

'Patrolling over Rochford at the end of November, we were over a big cloud layer. We had had a bit of a milling around with some 109s. As always, after a milling around, everything disappears. One minute Germans are all over the place, darting this, that and the other way; there are aeroplanes everywhere. Then you get into a bit of a turning match with somebody. You come out of it, look around and there's not an aeroplane in sight. Everything has disappeared.

'Still over the cloud layer, suddenly I spotted, way, way down below, a 109. I dived down close and fired at him and there was a flash. It seemed to come from his starboard wing. He dived into the cloud. I went down through it, hoping he would pop out underneath. I could only assume that I had hit him and he got down, but I didn't see any more of him. I thought he was a goner, I thought I could justify a claim, but then again, I did not make an official claim.'

After the destruction of Coventry on 14 November in a night raid by 449 German bombers, John Ellacombe's 151 Squadron was removed from North Weald and sent to Wittering, flying Hurricanes at night. After the Coventry raid, the mood of war grew darker.

John Ellacombe:

'At Wittering we had a strange man called Stephens who came to join us. He had been an experienced pilot pre-war, and he absolutely hated Germans. His wife and children had been killed in a bombing raid. He shot down about eight or nine aeroplanes with us at night. The first one he shot down he got so close that on his starboard wing were all the blood and guts of the German rear gunner. When he landed he wouldn't let the ground-crew clear it off. He wanted that left there as a souvenir.

'On another occasion, when he had shot down a Heinkel, I drove him out in a tiny van that we had. We found this Heinkel with the army looking after it. The rear gunner had had his gun stuffed through his guts. Steve said, "Hold his shoulders and I'll pull the gun out."

'He did that, there was a disgusting smell and I went and puked. He took the gun down to the river and washed it and he kept that as a souvenir.

'He hated bloody Germans. He was a very nice chap to talk to, and to drink with, but his hatred was just unbelievable. As for the rest of us, we didn't like them at all. We were quite determined to kill them if we could. I don't think we would have shot one down in a parachute if we saw one, but we were told, don't bale out if you think there are German fighters around because they will shoot you down. The hatred was great.'

The attempt at trying to cope with the nightly *Luftwaffe Blitz* by using Hurricanes – without radar or other aides – as night fighters, nearly did for Last Witness Bob Doe at the end of 1940:

'In early December we had a signal from Group asking for volunteers to go up at night. It was a full moon. The idea was that they would try and vector us into the German bomber stream coming in. This was 3 January, so it was pretty cold. Though I was still 20 years old, I was acting as CO – a pilot officer acting as CO – I went off with a bloke called Jacky Irwin-Mann, the other flight commander. We took off from Middle Wallop, the only airfield locally with any night flying facilities. I had been married in December, and my new wife was invited down to watch the fun.

'We climbed up through a thin layer of cloud at about 3,000 feet [914m] and above that the sky was absolutely clear, with a beautiful big moon. We got up to 16,000 feet [4,876m], which I thought was the height the bombers would be coming in at, when I noticed odd things happening to my instruments. My oil pressure remained constant but the oil temperature was shooting off the clock. I called up Middle Wallop and told them what was happening, and they said, "You'd better come back. We'll alert Warmwell, an airfield on the coast, to be ready for you."

'I started going back and eventually a whole load of sparks came up and the engine stopped dead. I was left cruising down through this lovely night, following the course they had given me to steer. I lost contact with them after a while, and I came over this thin layer of cloud, slap over the middle of Warmwell, which I had seen before but I had never landed there.

'I knew that one end had hangars and at the other end was woods. I reckoned if I kept my speed up to about 160 knots I could put a Hurricane down wheels up at that speed quite safely.

'I kept my speed up and came in over the hangars, towards the woods. But since I had last seen the place, it had been bombed, and they had brought in a whole load of rocks to fill in the bomb craters. I went straight into the rocks, which threw me forward.

'My nose got knocked off, my right eye-socket was smashed and my upper jaw was separated from my skull. My left arm was broken. I put my right hand up to my head to feel what had happened. I found my nose stuck on the top of my head. "That's funny," I thought. "It shouldn't be there."

'A couple of blokes turned up. (I had a letter from one later.) They were scared – they thought I was dead. They managed to get me out. One of the blokes had to scramble down between my legs and undo my feet which were tangled around the rudder bars. They laid me down on the grass. In those days they had a nursing sister in the sick quarters, and the nursing sister came up in the ambulance, with this lovely motherly voice. I took hold of her hand, and it apparently took about twenty minutes to get her hand out of my grip.

'They took me to sick quarters and rang the local hospital, Bovingdon Hospital, which had operating facilities but no surgeon. They called in surgeons from the local division and one of the surgeons stitched everything back where he thought the bits ought to go. I woke up the next morning. A little VAD was sitting there, trying to stop me swallowing my tongue. Her only topic of conversation was that Lawrence of Arabia had died in the very bed I was lying in. This did not make me too happy.

'I was moved from there to an army hospital where I stayed for a week. Then they sent me to a lunatic asylum, Park Prewitt Hospital near Basingstoke, where I underwent 22 operations by pioneering NZ plastic surgeon, Sir Harold Gillies.

'Gillies rebuilt my face. He stitched the jaw back on to my upper face, and stitched my eye in place. There are still wires in the upper part of my face. My nose had been torn right off, but a small bit was still attached, so the skin was alive. This he stitched down. He took a little bone out of my hip and dovetailed it into my forehead. It's not dovetailed there now because I walked into a door shortly afterwards, but the nose he put on is still there.

'I was back on operations in May, as a flight commander of 66 Squadron. I did look a bit battered, but I was still alive. I had a very pretty wife at that time but that didn't last. It was a typical wartime marriage. She disappeared when I was in Burma.'

There were big changes in Fighter Command following the formal removal, on 18 December 1940, of the two men most responsible for winning the Battle of Britain, Dowding and Park.

Dowding had been the strategist, but Keith Park was the daily general. However right Dowding was in May 1940 to stop Churchill throwing away all Fighter Command's Hurricane squadrons to placate the French, Churchill didn't stop the behind-the-scenes political moves to get rid of him. Dowding was sent to the USA and retired in 1942, given a barony in 1943.

Keith Park was sent to 23 Group as AOC Flying Training Command. There he discovered it was still on peacetime schedules and continued to use the now highly discredited 'Fighting Area Tactics'! He shook it up before being sent back to an active Command in the Middle East in 1942, in which he was equally brilliant and successful. Understandably, he remained bitter for the rest of his life about his treatment.

In the 21st century, Stephen Bungay believes Keith Park to be one of Britain's greatest warriors:

'What Keith Park achieved in the Battle of Britain is in itself enough to place him among the great commanders of history. He is the greatest fighter commander in the short history of air warfare.'

Thanks not least to such influential opinions, and the financial muscle of City banker Terry Smith, a permanent site in 2010 in London features a statue commemorating Park's achievements.

One of the reasons for Leigh-Mallory's appointment to command 11 Group was that he was seen as an offensively-minded leader in the Trenchard mould. Winston Churchill was always attracted to those who trumpeted and snorted and demanded 'attack, always attack!' Leigh-Mallory 'talked the talk' and wanted to be given the chance to 'walk the walk.'

Tom Neil:
'The Machiavellian Leigh-Mallory and his cabal of underlings got rid of Dowding and Keith Park. They wanted to get rid of him earlier, but they

couldn't, because he was the chap who knew most about the aircraft we were fighting with – and against – and he knew all about the defence system. He knew about radar, which nobody else did. He was the kingpin so they couldn't get rid of him.

'Leigh-Mallory was an entirely different chap to Park. Keith Park was a New Zealander, and very much a hands-on sort of chap, tall, rangy and he flew in a Hurricane every day to see individual squadrons. Nice chap. I got on very well with him.

'But I got on very well with Leigh-Mallory also. He came down to lead 11 Group, where all the action was. And it was there he called for all the squadrons to meet him at Hornchurch, which had Spitfires on it, on Christmas Day. What a day to ask anything! The Germans let it be known they were not going to fly against us on Christmas Day, but we were never told this.

'Leigh-Mallory was the chap who came to North Weald when I was flight commander, and addressed me by my Christian name – which I thought was rather nice – and he used to say, "Now look here, Ginger, I want your opinion. We are thinking," he said, "of changing the camouflage on our aircraft, now that we're thinking about invading the continent. We're thinking of changing the spinners."

'I said, "Whatever you do, sir, don't change the spinners on our aircraft! Our spinners are painted black, and it is most important you don't touch that because when I'm in extremis and I look around over my head, if I see a coloured spinner behind me, I get out of the way. I know it's a German. Colour our spinners and I won't be able to recognise our own side."

'"Right!" he said. "That's a good point."

'He went back and immediately all our colours were changed and we had duck-egg blue spinners from then on. Obviously somebody else had made a different point. He tended to listen to the last person who talked to him. And, of course, prior to that as AOC 12 Group, he was partially under the influence of Douglas Bader.

'Bader was the world's most gutsy man, but to all the rest of us, he was a menace. He caused more people's deaths by doing the wrong thing at the wrong time than anyone else of that rank I can think of. When we did our first "rhubarbs", going in under the protection of clouds in order to attack silly sorts of targets in northern France, we ran into scads of German fighters. We should not have been there. Bader's own squadrons had already done a morning raid. We each had a day to do this particular thing and this was our day to do it. Bader's squadrons had been doing it since dawn. He had produced a hornet's nest amongst all sorts of the enemy, so they were waiting for us when it was our turn later in the day.

'He always did that sort of thing.'

Last Witness Bob Foster:

'The "rhubarbs" in 1941 are down to Sholto-Douglas, Leigh Mallory and Douglas Bader. We had left 11 Group, thank God, by then, but it is now coming out from history that there was a terrible waste of lives. I remember Sholto-Douglas having us together when we were at Martlesham and saying, "We have to take this to the enemy now. We can't let things just lie down."

'We would have accepted it had we been ordered into the thing, obviously. I think we lost more pilots during that period – 1941 – than we did during the Battle of Britain, and all for nothing. Just to bring the *Luftwaffe* into the air, and shoot us down.'

Once appointed, Leigh-Mallory soon introduced wing-sized fighter sweeps into France, known as 'rodeos.' When accompanied by bombers to provoke enemy fighters, these were known as 'circus' operations. The pilots called them 'rhubarbs', and young survivors of the first full year of the war were soon involved in the new tactics.

Tom Neil:

'On 10 January 1941, we were going into attack on the first offensive sortie into northern France. Six Blenheims were going to attack the Forêt de Guîne, just behind Bordeaux. They were to drop bombs, and they were going to be escorted by 108 fighters, 249 Squadron with Hurricanes, and 56 Squadron were going to be close escorts. We were also going to be below the level of the bombers in order to prevent the Germans climbing up underneath them. The place you never want to be is below the bombers!

'The bombers were briefed to go in at 7,000 feet [2,133m], which meant that we were going in at 5,000 feet [1,524m]. Nobody in his right mind would fly over enemy territory at 5,000 feet! Our people stacked up to 15,000 feet [4,572m], all the Spitfires there at the top, romping around and waving the flag. We poor suckers in Hurricanes, we were down the bottom end, receiving everything. We crossed the coast with Bader, who had come from 12 Group in Duxford. He came to lead us.

'I remember looking down as we went over the coast, and there were the German fighter bases around Calais-Mark, and thinking, "Crikey, we're going to be hit very shortly." But we were so much of a surprise that no one shot at us. There was snow everywhere, very cold, and Bader thought, this is not easy enough for the enemy so he took us lower.

'Eventually I found myself 20 or so miles into France at 2,000 feet [610m]. Then the balls and the flak began to come up, whistling around my ears. Red balls, every conceivable kind of flak, and I think this lunatic, what is he doing to us?

'Eventually I got down to 800 feet [244m], still over France, crossing the coast and going back out to sea, saying, "Thank God for that." I was low over the water, thanking God that I was in one piece, three miles out to sea.

'There was a bloke just in front of me on the right. I considered it was another Hurricane. The red balls were going between me and him, and suddenly he was hit. It was really terrible as he went down. We sugared around over the Channel for a bit and then made it back to England, crossed over Kent, and went back to North Weald.

'I reported to the Intelligence Officer that it was a pretty useless trip, and everyone else was pretty incensed about the whole thing. I then said, "We lost a chap. Does anyone know who it is?"

'We were two chaps short. One was Mazajowski, one of our Poles, the other chap was O'Connell. "No," I said, "there must be another one, because I saw a chap destroyed."

'I was absolutely insistent but to this day I am told we didn't lose a third aircraft. O'Connell flew into the cliffs at Dover, and Mazajowski force-landed at Manston.

'But who was the person who was destroyed right in front of my eyes? Is it really likely I would be flying 20 yards from a German?"

'As for Bader, he was totally irresponsible. He had a philosophy well-described by an NCO of my squadron. This was, he said, "Me first, I'm next, and anything left, I'll have."

'This was made abundantly clear when he was captured in 1942, and locked up in a PoW camp. There's a film made about Bader (*Reach for the Sky*), and all the PoWs are lined up and Bader is taken away to Colditz, and all the PoWs were clapping, saying "splendid chap". The PoWs were clapping because they were so glad to see the bugger go!

'At Colditz he didn't behave very well. He had a chap who looked after his legs, his batman. The batman was given permission to go home early because of his medical condition. Bader refused to let him go. That was the sort of man he was.

'In "rhubarbs" we behaved stupidly. You were supposed to take advantage of the cloud but sometimes we were forced to do them without the cloud. We lost so many golden people being hit by flak. Flak does not discriminate. In a fighter versus fighter contest, you can hold your own, no matter what you're flying. But you can't cope with flak at low level if you're hit, particularly with a water-cooled engine. If you're hit in the plumbing you're a goner, and that's it. So many people were lost going like that, golden people, Battle of Britain people, and it was a shame that we continued to do it, day after day, week after week. It was ridiculous the way we persisted in doing such stupid things.'

Another view of Bader came from Last Witness Billy Drake, at this time working as an instructor passing on his experience from the Battle of France:

> 'Bader was such a character within his own rights that one just admired him being able to do what he did do without any legs. He was a very forceful chap, but he was respected by everybody concerned. That doesn't mean that he was liked.
>
> 'No one denies you had to get a large number of aeroplanes on a certain spot in the quickest time possible. But the "Big Wing" concept was completely wrong. By the time you had got 24 or 48 aeroplanes together, the enemy had disappeared. It was as simple as that.'

Last Witness Eric Brown, at ease in German and French as well as English, whom others regard as the greatest of all test pilots, had this judgement on the new tactics:

> 'The greatest aerial tactician of the war was the German, Werner Molders. He dictated the tactics which still work today. The "finger four" was Molders' idea, and he projected that in the Spanish Civil War, which was highly successful.
>
> 'Goering had made Molders General of Fighters, and Adolf Galland only took that role once Molders died. Goering always had a higher regard for Molders than he did for Galland, because Molders was a brilliant tactician and highly intelligent.
>
> 'I think the practice of sending large wings of fighters in formation to sweep through France in 1941 – favoured by Bader, those "rhubarbs" – was a serious tactical error. I know Bader's views were very much in favour of the large wing, and there's a lot of revision now about his role.'

The whole recruitment of new pilots gathered pace in 1941, the Empire Air Training Scheme producing 50,000 aircrew a year from schools in Canada, Australia, New Zealand, South Africa, Rhodesia and the United States. Trained pilots from German-occupied Europe were also at a premium, and snapped up. They did not always fit in.

Tom Neil:
'In 1941, February, we had an influx of Poles into 249 Squadron. We always had about three or four Poles. They varied from the good but difficult to put up with, to the totally inefficient.

'We also had a series of French people. Francois Labouchiere looked like Charles Boyer. He was so handsome, he dated all the girls. The other Frenchman was Phail, the son of an admiral or general.

'Skolski, a Pole, was about 40, a nice chap, brilliant. He was new to the

squadron and we sent him on a sector reconnaissance. This was meant
to be a bit of a joy ride in which he flew a Hurricane around the sector
to familiarise himself with the area. We sent him off in the middle of the
afternoon, broad daylight, and told him where to go, all around Essex. I went
back to the officer's mess, my room there, in order to shave and make myself
presentable for dinner.

'Whilst in the act of shaving, all the lights went out. I had this terrible
thought. Skolski! Sure enough, Skolski had flown through the high tension
cables at Chelmsford and taken them all down, and the whole of East Essex
had been plunged into darkness. He had been flying at about 20 feet [6m].
He arrived back at North Weald at 11 o'clock at night, covered in bandages,
because he had been through the front of the aircraft.

'He admitted he had been flying "a bit low" and then he said, "I took out
a map to see where I was …" A map at 20 feet! That was Skolski.

'I sent him away on leave to recuperate. He was away the best part of a
month, by which time we were joined by the two Frenchmen, Labouchere
and Phail. I brought one of the two new Frenchman, Labouchere, plus a
another, Decidevoie, and Skolski together.

'"I want you three to take Hurricanes and do a little formation practice."
I said. "Skolski will be a leader, and after a period of time you will be taken
over by Labouchere, who will also be leader. Then Decidevoie will take over
as leader, one at a time. Do this on hand signals."

'The three started up their engines, took off, and disappeared. An
hour passed. Suddenly there was a terrible wail of an aircraft returning, a
Hurricane largely without a propeller, making more than 4,000 revs but
just about staying in the air. Skolski's circuit was like a crippled duck but he
landed with his wheels and flaps down. We tumbled out of dispersal and ran
to where Skolski was. As we approached, the aircraft sank to its knees.

'The aircraft was a wreck. The propeller, which is supposed to have an arc
of 11 feet 6 inches [3.5m], was about 2ft 6 inches [76 cm] in diameter. The oil
tank in the front of the wing was gone. The whole aircraft was covered in goo.

'Skolski couldn't give a coherent explanation. Apparently, he had been
leading the formation and he gave what he considered to be a hand signal,
which meant he was going to relinquish the leadership and someone else
was going to take over. Both Frenchman decided to take over the leadership
together. All three met in a hideous jumble of aircraft.

'Labouchere found his aircraft completely uncontrollable and fell out of
the sky but managed to bale out at 800 feet [244m] and hit the ground at the
first swing of his parachute. Decidevoie could not control his aircraft and
ploughed through about four different fields, shedding bits in each field.

'Skolski tottered back. It was so easy to lose three Hurricanes without
even trying.'

On 22 June 1941 there was a step-change in the war when Britain ceased to be alone. As the CO of 257 Squadron, Robert Stanford Tuck, was recovering from his celebrations the day after downing three Bf 109s in his Hurricane II, Germany invaded the Soviet Union in Operation Barbarossa. The *Luftwaffe* did to the Soviets what they had wanted to do to the British, and in lightning *Blitzkreig* raids destroyed 1,800 Soviet aircraft in one day, mostly on the ground. The Germans lost just 35 aircraft.

When it became clear that the Hurricane was becoming outclassed as a pure fighter, other duties were assigned to it. In October 1941 the 'Hurribomber' fighter-bomber came into being, carrying either two 113kg (250lb) or two 226kg (500lb) bombs under its wings. The Hurricane Mk IID of 1942 was fitted with two 40mm cannon for tank busting and two machine guns, operating mainly in North Africa against Rommel's desert forces and in Burma against the Japanese. Other Hurricanes carried rocket projectiles as alternative ground attack weapons.

Trafford Leigh-Mallory was appointed air commander for the Dieppe Raid which took place on 19 August 1942, during which Fighter Command operated 50 squadrons in close cover and six in close support. Losses during the ill-fated raid were heavy, partly because of the superiority of the new German fighter, the FW 190, over Spitfire Mark Vs.

Leigh-Mallory used multiple wing formations – the 'Big Wing' again. His Command lost 97 aircraft in action, but claimed 96 destroyed, 39 probables and 145 damaged.

In fact, the *Luftwaffe* lost just 48 aircraft, and only 13 pilots. The RAF lost 47 pilots killed, and a further 17, including John Ellacombe's wing man, were made PoWs. It is not difficult to sympathise with Ellacombe's vituperative view of these operations when one considers that he went into the fight in a cannon-firing Hurricane IIC, which could hardly live in the same air as a FW 190.

John Ellacombe:
'Leigh-Mallory was a most unpleasant man, from my own experience of him at Dieppe in 1942.

'Briefing us on how we would cover the Dieppe Raid on 19 August, Leigh-Mallory said, "We are going to attack Dieppe. The army are going to land. They're a brigade of troops. They're going to walk into the town and show the Germans how we can invade when the time comes.

'"There are a lot of guns placed around. I have told the light bombers from Bomber Command that I don't want them. I want to take out all the defences with my Hurricanes and my Hurricane fighter-bombers. I don't mind losing 50 per cent of them."

'This was us he was talking about!

'"I don't want Bomber Command," said Leigh-Mallory. "This is going to be a Fighter Command operation."

'This was not taken very well by the squadron and flight commanders. We were supposed to brief our chaps, but we didn't tell them that. We went down to Friston, just on the hill above Eastbourne, and my squadron was there, 253, where I was then a flight commander. On the dawn of the day of the raid, it was just getting light, and as we went over the French coast we were attacked with a tremendous lot of tracer bullets. My number two on my left, a boy called Flying Officer Seal, he was hit, and he went down and burst into flames. I thought he was dead but he wasn't. He was actually thrown out of the aeroplane and landed in a haystack, so apart from being badly bruised he was actually all right, though he became a PoW.

'We didn't find anything to shoot at, it wasn't really light. We made two sorties and then saw the boats were being withdrawn. Going in on a third sortie we were bounced by Focke Wulf 190s and we broke and my number two stuck with me. He was flying a 12-gun Hurricane – a IIC. We then went inland and I found a gun battery, I think they were 88mm in a field, and I attacked them.

'As I broke away, I had seen my cannon shells exploding on the guns and on the men, I was suddenly hit. I was at full throttle and that was shot away. I turned immediately and went out to sea.

'My number two took a perfect picture of me flying through, as he had to dive underneath me. He came back to Friston with a bit of high tension cable which he had flown through.

'I managed to reach the French coast when the engine stopped. I had flown about four miles with glycol pouring out of the engine, which was obviously going to stop as it overheated. I managed to pull up to 600 feet [182m] and bale out. As I jumped, I thought the parachute was on fire, because when I looked up all the tracer bullets were going through it. I landed in the sea, but the German machine guns kept firing at me. I was not far from the coast and it was pretty terrifying. I kicked my boots off, undid the parachute and started swimming to Newhaven.

'It was 60 miles away, but I wasn't going back to France where people were machine gunning me. I was swimming away quite happily, thinking I had made quite a lot of distance, when a little assault landing craft came and picked me up. They pulled me in. I had hardly swum anywhere ...

'There were four Petty Officers and a Sub-Lieutenant, and they had been there all day, bombed and shot at, and they were absolutely punch drunk. They were just beyond any more fear.

'We were making four knots and being shelled, so it wasn't very pleasant, until the Navy sent a big steam gunboat. They threw us a rope and towed us to the main convoy.

'When I got out at Newhaven, an army officer said, you haven't got any boots on. We've got a lot of dead men here who died on the way back. Can I get you a pair of their boots? I got a pair.

'It was a pretty exhausting and horrifying day as I went back to Friston. Having been shot down at Dieppe after a very long tour – 13 months – I was told I must take a rest.'

The Dieppe disaster did not affect Trafford Leigh-Mallory's career, which went from strength to strength. He became C-in-C Fighter Command in late 1942 in time to plan the D-Day landings. Hurricanes were still sent out to fight in Western European operations, but their main theatres of war became the Western Desert, Greece and Malta, while thousands of other Hurricanes fought in Russia and the Far East.

The range of the 'Hurribomber', as they were unofficially known, was not greatly affected by the extra weight of their bomb load and operations against enemy-held northern France began in October 1941. Spitfires accompanied these sweeps; escorts often out-numbered their charges 3-to-1 in an attempt to draw the enemy fighters into combat.

Targets included airfields, railways and shipping. These operations proved the fighter-bomber concept, because the Hurricane, once free of its bombs, was restored to a useful fighter, manoeuvrable enough for enemy pilots not to want to tangle with it, even if still relatively slow compared to the Bf 109G. The light bombers used in 1941, on the other hand, Blenheims, were a liability to the escorting fighters to and from the target.

At the end of 1941, the whole game changed again when the Japanese attacked Pearl Harbour in Hawaii on 7 December. The following day, the USA declared war on Japan and, crucially (given a choice, would the USA really have wanted to take on two powerful enemies at the same time?), Germany declared war on the USA.

Hurribomber operations were also conducted at night. All-black Hurricanes known as Night Intruders bombed and strafed targets by moonlight and using flares. The first such mission took place on 27 January 1942 when shipping off Ostend was attacked by five bomb-carrying Mk IIBs. These raids by day and night were little more than a nuisance but they ensured that the *Luftwaffe* maintained a strong fighter presence in the west when they could have been deployed on other fronts.

Sydney Camm at Hawkers considered a Mk III Hurricane using the Packard-built Merlin engine that the Americans claimed was better than the original Rolls Royce Merlin. The Mk III never came to fruition. By the middle of 1942, the Hurricane Mk II was rapidly approaching obsolescence as a fighter in the 'big boy's war' in Europe, which is why work began on a specialised ground attack version to be known as the Mk IV.

By March 1943 a modified Mk II was flown as the prototype IV. Powered by a Merlin 24 engine producing 1650hp, the new version was externally very similar to the Mark II. Differences included a heavily-armoured radiator bath, which had an angular appearance. An additional, 350lb (159kg) of steel plate had been added to cope with the accurate and lethal flak now appearing on all fronts. The Mk IV wing could accept 20mm cannon, 40mm anti tank guns, drop tanks, bombs and the three-inch rocket projectile.

The operational debut of the Mk IV took place on the 2 September that year when No 137 Squadron attacked lock gates on the Zuid Beveland canal in the Dutch Islands. This was a hair-raising attack and low-flying Hurricanes trailed back carrying pieces of telegraph wire and branches, along with extensive flak damage. One aircraft snared a duck in its leading edge, which was handed to the ground crew for dinner! Sadly, four aircraft were lost in the operation. The escort was provided by Hawker Typhoons, which gradually replaced the Hurricane in the ground attack role.

By 1944, the Hurricane Mk IV was withdrawn completely from the European theatre, but continued to give excellent service in the Far East where six squadrons were so equipped. In any case, the next generation of Hawker-designed fighters were proving far more capable in every role previously fulfilled by Hurricanes.

Chapter Thirteen
HURRICANES IN MALTA

After the Italian declaration of war on 10 June 1940, the air defence of Malta initially depended on six Gloster Gladiators. When these were reduced to three, they were dubbed 'Faith, Hope and Charity'. On 21 June, eight Hurricanes reached the island that was to assume a pivotal role in the Mediterranean theatre of war.

The Hurricane was superior to the Italian fighters it came up against in 1940, and more than capable of dealing with the SM 79 bomber. By August the Italians had been forced to abandon daylight raids over Malta. Things changed at the start of 1941. With the Italians facing the very real threat of being expelled from North Africa, Adolf Hitler was forced to send help to his ally, Benito Mussolini.

In February and March the *Luftwaffe* mounted frequent raids against Malta. Hurricanes could cope with their Italian opponents, and with the German bombers, but the Bf 109Es were a more serious danger. Luckily for Malta, and the desperate band of RAF defenders, German involvement was short-lived at this point, because German resources were required in the east ahead of the invasion of Russia in June that year.

In May, 1941, the irrepressible Last Witness Tom Neil, a young fighting veteran with two DFC's, flew into Malta in terrific fashion in a clapped-out old Hurricane I, to catch the tail end of *Luftwaffe* power:

'It's 1941, I am a 20-year-old flight commander with 249 Squadron, and Butch Barton is our Squadron Leader. He was a Canadian, splendid, could not have looked less like a hero. He was another pilot, like Eric Lock, who was knee-high to a duck. He bit his nails, smoked ghastly *Gauloises* cigarettes, had a uniform which looked as if it had been left out at night, he didn't have good teeth – he looked a wreck. He was one of the best fighter pilots that ever happened. Shot down about 16 aircraft. Absolutely brave as a lion, and utterly able as a leader. I was delighted to fly behind him.

'I was second in command at that stage, and we were bellyaching about getting Hurricane IIs. The Hurricane I was now totally outclassed. During the

Battle of Britain we could have done twice as well as we did, if we had had better aircraft. We did well, but we were fighting over our own territory.

'The point is, statistically, if you had two air forces roughly comparable in terms of types of aircraft, if they fly over your territory, they will lose two to your one. If you fly over their territory, you will lose two to their one. If you look at the statistics, that's exactly how it worked. During the Battle of Britain, they lost two to our one, but a lot of our "ones" were saved because we were able to bale out over our own country.

'When they lost their bombers, they lost four people at a time, either killed or captured. Dare I say it, we didn't win the Battle of Britain … but we didn't lose it. We prevented them doing what they wanted to do. The same people we had fought against, literally the same people, we went to Malta and they dusted the floor with us!

'This was because they had better aircraft. In February 1941 we were re-equipped with Hurricane IIs. They had a different super-charger to the Hurricane I, a two-speed supercharger that enabled you to go a bit higher, and a bit faster, more boost, slightly better self-sealing tanks, otherwise it was more or less the same aeroplane. Even the Hurricane II was woefully inferior to the 109F and the 109E was still 30 mph [48 kph] faster than the Hurricane II.

'In April 1941, we were told to go to the Middle East. I was partially responsible. We had had a rather disastrous trip escorting bombers over Dunkirk, and we lost a couple of people, which we need not have lost. I was fed up with being out-stripped all the time by Bf 109s. I remember landing at North Weald, and running into Victor Beamish

'I said, "We're just sitting ducks. I wish I could fly over some piece of land instead of being over the Channel all the time. Once you fall in the Channel, you are gone. In the winter time you haven't got a hope, because you're dead within 40 minutes."

'Victor Beamish said to me, "Do you really want to go to the Middle East, Ginger?"

'"I am happy to go anywhere," I said.

'Apparently, a month or two later, he let it be known that 249 Squadron wanted to go to the Middle East. Before you could say Jehosaphat, we were told we were going to the Middle East on board an aircraft carrier.

'Big chaps came out and said, "Now, this is very secret – you're going to the Middle East. You're probably going to get there by aircraft carrier. You're going to fly off. You're going to be back on Hurricane Is again."

'We said, "What!? Hurricane Mk I! But they're hopeless! The implication was that they had 6,000 Hurricane Is they were going to get rid of, and they were going to use them or lose them, come what may.

'"Why don't we have Spitfires?" we shouted.

An American Hurricane pilot 'Scrambles' to his waiting plane, with ground crew preparing the aircraft for engine start in the background, March 1941.

Six Sea Hurricanes of 885 Squadron, Fleet Air Arm, wait on the deck of HMS Victorious with engines running, ready for take-off, 22 August 1942. In a non-stop two day battle to get supplies through to the island of Malta, FAA pilots claimed 39 kills for the loss of eight. Victorious was sunk by U-Boat soon after the photo was taken.

Mark IIC, bought by 'United Provinces Cawnpore' flown by S/L Dennis Smallwood – later Air Chief Marshall – CO of 87 Squadron, 10 Group, based at Charmy Down in Somerset. Hurricane LK-A later fought in the Far East.

Hurricane Mark IIB of No. 134 Squadron RAF taxies out past Russian sentries at Vaenga airfield near Murmansk in Russia. No. 151 Wing RAF, known as 'Force Benedict', provided defence against German aerial attacks on Allied Convoys, and escorted Soviet bombers on raids. The Wing's pilots then trained and converted Soviet pilots on to the Hurricanes, before handing their aircraft over to the Red Air Force and finally returning to Britain at the end of November 1941.

Three Soviet pilots in September, 1942, posing in front of one of the 2,952 Hurricanes sent to the Soviet Union between 1941 and 1944 from British and Canadian production. Stalin had hundreds of Hurricanes thrown down mines after the war, ashamed of letting his subjects know he used British-built fighter aircraft.

Bill Swan flew with 33 Squadron in the Western Desert in 1942, he was nearly killed by 'friendly fire' and went on to become a test pilot.

Terence Kelly, survivor of Hurricane squadron fighting in Singapore and the Dutch East Indies, he suffered nearly four years as a Japanese Prisoner of War and was just 35 miles from the Hiroshima atom bomb blast, August, 1945.

Graham Skellum flew up to three ground attack – 'bomb and strafe' – sorties a day in Burma in 1944–5, on Hurricane IIC's. He saw only one Japanese fighter.

Colin Ellis flew photo-recconnaissance Hurricane IIC's in Burma. He was one of just 10 pilots, of a total of 176, who survived being shot down behind Japanese lines in the jungle.

Tom Adams instructed on all Marks of Hurricanes in the US, and flew 30 bomb and strafe operations in the Far East at the very end of the war between June and August 1945.

Tom Adams and a 'clapped-out-Hurricane' fulfilling a common pilot ambition, flying under an intact bridge over the Irrawaddy River in Burma.

After a very neat operation by Hurricane fighter-bombers, the same Irrawaddy bridge out of action.

Hurricane IIDs of 6 Squadron RAF, carrying two 40mm cannon, and two sighting machine-guns, lined up for take-off at Gabes in Tunisia on 6 April 1943, intent on a tank-busting sortie.

Burma, 1943, ground crew service cannon-firing Hurricane II's – Hurribombers – on a forward airstrip, ignored by a local in a bullock cart.

January 1943 Ground crew, including a WAAF, refuel a Hawker Hurricane IID 'Tank-Buster' at Milfield, Northumberland. Armourers have removed the fairings from the two Vickers 40mm anti-tank guns beneath the wings in order to re-arm them; a warning notice to that effect hangs from the barrel of the gun under the port wing.

The survivor, one of the two Hawker Hurricanes flying with the Battle of Britain Memorial Flight.

'"Ah, well," they said, "Spitfires are not really tough enough or strong enough to cope with conditions in the desert."

'In due course, in the month of May, all our Hurricane IIs were taken away and we had Hurricane Is and they said, "Now would you like to try to lean out the engines? We're going to fit them with two 44 gallon [200 litre] tanks which will give you an extra range. It will give you 1,020 miles [1,641 km] total range.

'"This is a theoretical estimate, it's not practical, and if you fly at low revs and not more than 160 mph [257 kph], you'll be able to get that range."

'"The only thing is," they said, "these are not fighting fuel tanks. You can't get rid of them. So if you are caught by the enemy, your number is up. With or without fuel in the extra tanks, they are still highly inflammable. If you're hit in the tank, even though it's empty, you'll go up like a bomb.

'"You will go by aircraft carrier, but your ground crew, 180 men of 249 Squadron, NCOs and others, will go by ship around the Cape of Good Hope. You will meet your airmen somewhere in Egypt when they get there, if they get there."

'Of course, what happened was that they disappeared to the south and we never saw our baggage or them ever again. We got on board a carrier called HMS *Furious*. This was a 1918 ex-battle cruiser, but halfway through its construction it was made into a flat top. There wasn't really accommodation. There were going to be, apart from the normal complement of crew, about a thousand men. There were going to be three squadrons of Hurricanes, three times 18 aircraft, at least for a period. Everything was going to be overcrowded. All our chaps – even officers – had to sleep in hammocks. I was one of the only chaps, being a flight commander, who rated a cabin.

'The aircraft arrived at HMS *Furious* by Pickford's van, and the carrier had a lift which could accommodate the wingspan of a Hurricane; our Hurricanes did not have folding wings. They were brought on to the *Furious*, if necessary assembled on the *Furious*, with their wings, and brought up through the lift, because the lifts were sufficiently big. We were destined originally to go on the *Ark Royal* but it was initially thought that we couldn't use the *Ark Royal* because the lifts on it were not big enough

'I will not attempt to describe the trip except it was ghastly. The next ten days getting to Gibraltar were horrible. Then we really did transfer to the *Ark Royal*, a lovely big carrier. We were going to fly off the carrier, and we were heading for the Middle East with a thumping great squadron of ships, three carriers, two battleships, half a dozen Sheffield-class cruisers, about 25 ships. We were going through at dead of night.

'The system was, to fool German observers, if you were going eastward into the Mediterranean, you took off into the Atlantic. If you were going the other way, you did it the opposite way around. The Germans knew exactly what we were doing. Just two miles away from Gibraltar there was the German consulate, and with a pair of binoculars he could see exactly what we were doing. He knew flipping well that if we headed west into the Atlantic with carriers at the dead of night, we were actually going to head east.

'We took this enormous force through the Straits of Gibraltar on 21 May 1941, intending to take off at dawn. At dawn 23 of our aircraft were on the deck of the *Ark Royal*. We were going off in two flights, 12 and 11, and I was the second leader in the flight of 11. Butch Barton was leading the first 12, because he was physically that much closer to the sharp end of the ship.

'We had no hooks, no means of stopping if we had to land on again. All we knew was that we had a full complement of fuel – 97 gallons plus 88 gallons – and the thing was, we didn't know if it was going to work or not. Down in the basement where they were assembling these things, they said each of these tanks has an electric motor inside. There are no gauges or anything like that, so what you did was empty the fuel tanks into the main part of the aircraft, and then pump the fuel in from the wing tanks. You had to do this by dribs and drabs, all the time keeping the main tank full. But you didn't know whether or not it would work. All you knew was that if the wing tanks were empty, there would be nothing left but the fuel in the main tank.

'"Please make absolutely sure that the electric motors are working," they said.

'We sat down below with our ears to the wing tanks, trying to hear the pumps working, and the noise level of a ship going at half speed was incredible. We could not know for sure whether the electric motors were working. Some of the chaps spent hours listening and still could not be sure.

'At this stage I was in a thoroughly truculent mood. They said, you will take off at dawn. I said, why do we have to take off at dawn just because Errol Bloody Flynn took off at dawn in 'Dawn Patrol'? Why don't we have a decent breakfast? This was an indication of my mood.

'On the morning in question we got up at four o'clock, had breakfast, and climbed into our cockpits. It was dark, raining, cloudbase was at about 800 feet [244m]. It was 895 miles [1,440 km] to Malta. We had to land there, refuel in one of three airfields – Takali, Hal Far or Luqa – I was going to land at Luqa – take off again and fly another 810 miles [1,303 km], all across the sea at 100 feet [30m] to Mersa Matruh.

'We took off. For me, it was a disaster. We had no means of carrying our clothes, we were allowed to take 30lbs [13.6kg] of equipment, which we carried in our ammunition tanks. We had no ammunition, but carried towels, shoes, personal things, shorts. We had nowhere to put things in the cockpit, towels and things left and right but nowhere to put maps. There was a small map case in the Hurricane on the left hand side but it was full of this and that, and I had put my series of course instructions – all the things I was supposed to do as leader – down a crease just behind the windscreen.

'I had just got off the *Ark Royal* when there was a hell of a bang. As soon as my wheels came off the flight deck, there was a bang, and I didn't know what had happened. I thought I had lost a tank. I dived over the side of the aircraft carrier, thinking I was going in the water! I looked to the left and saw that a big flap that covered the guns had flown up to 45 degrees and it had stuck there. So I had three ailerons, one fully extended to one side, and the two normal ailerons. On a Hurricane I there was no bias on the rudder control, I couldn't trim out the bias, so my foot was fully extended on the rudder, trying to keep the aircraft out of the water.'

Tom Neil avoided ditching in the sea and, as he built up a little speed, managed to climb high enough to circle the Ark Royal. He knew that, overloaded with fuel and without proper control, he did not have the luxury of being able to land back aboard the carrier. He had to carry on.

'All my other chaps took off and began to formate on me. I was the leader, but we were going to be guided to Malta by a Royal Navy Fulmar, which had a navigator in the back. He was going to be able to lead us to the island.

'We formed up behind the Fulmar with my foot still right over, with the control column right over, trying to steer a straight line, reduced the revs down to about 1,800, reduced the speed to about 160 mph [257 kph], and we set off into the darkness, the rain, the cloud, with my aircraft in that condition.

'We had been told before we left that we had to maintain total R/T silence, no talking on the radio. We mustn't say a word or the Germans would know where the fleet was. So I just flew on. We took a course parallel to the unseen coast of North Africa, for an hour.

'I prayed, I honestly prayed. I did not know if I had the strength and luck to hang on until we reached Malta. We were scheduled to reach Malta in three or four hours at the speed we were flying. Then the Fulmar, flying in front, suddenly began to put on speed, and 50 to 60 mph [80 to 96 kph] and left us immediately, stood on its tail, went straight into the cloud and left us completely.

'I thought, "Christ Almighty, what do I do now?" I didn't have any maps, which had been blown out of my aircraft when I had gone virtually sideways in order to stop myself falling into the water. No maps, no course, no anything, left in the middle of the Mediterranean – and it was raining – not knowing where Malta was.

'I did not know what to do, I was just 20 years old. I flew around in a circle, with ten aircraft formating on me still, in the middle of the sea, not saying a word to anybody, while I worked out what to do. We had been airborne for about an hour, and I reckoned we had 800 miles [1,287 km] to get back to Gibraltar, plus an hour's flight, so just under 1,000 miles [1,609 km] to get back to Gilbraltar.

'So that's the way I set off. I had this curious feeling of satisfaction that had become almost humorous. All right, I didn't know what we were doing but we were bloody well going to make it. I flew for the best part of an hour, all my chaps flying behind me, like lemmings. No one said a word.

'Suddenly I saw, in the water, a wake – of the fleet! When a fleet goes through it leaves a stain that lasts six or seven hours. We followed up the wake and then suddenly we saw the fleet in the distance, 25 fighting ships, and they saw us. Naturally, they thought they were being attacked by torpedo bombers. They were off like greyhounds in all directions, ships heeling over in order to get out of the way. Afterwards, we laughed about it.

'We got back to the carrier, circled the carrier and saw that the deck was full of aircraft of one sort or another. We flew round in circles and they got rid of all the aircraft down various lifts. Then they found another Fulmar which took off.

'There is a God in Heaven. He pulls the string and enables you to do things you could not otherwise do. The Fulmar headed for Malta, this time 580 miles [933 km] away, and I led my cohorts along behind him, still at 100 feet [30m] above the water.

'We followed a course between a number of islands held by the Italians – Pantelleria, Linosa, Lampedusa – having been warned to keep a strict look-out passing by Pantelleria because it had lots of Bf 110s. We had no guns, our aircraft were totally incapable of fighting. From time to time enemy aircraft flew across the top of us – Dorniers, various types – and we could do nothing about it.

'I had briefed my chaps before this whole event began, with all the authority of a 20-year-old, that on no account was anybody to lag when we went past Pantelleria. As we approached Pantelleria, the other ten aircraft in my flight scudded past me, joining the Fulmar, until I was the last in formation.

'We went on and on, the weather got worse and worse, the fuel went down and down. We were in the air for almost six hours. After 5 hours and 35 minutes, I said to the Fulmar, "Bugger the R/T silence. If we are not down in five minutes we are all in the water."

'Divine providence intervened. The clouds lifted, and there was Malta level with my shoulder. We were supposed to circle a little island south of Malta to identify ourselves. I said, "Forget it, we were going in immediately." I was going to Luqa, some of our chaps were going to Takali, others to Hal Far. My airfield was in the middle.

'All this time I had been flying with one leg jammed against the rudder, and I was totally numb. I remember crossing the cliffs and I saw jagged streaks of black flame coming up. I thought, "They're firing at someone. Why on earth are they firing?"

'I didn't pay any attention, I was so dead keen to land because I had no fuel at all. We later found six gallons in my tank. I could see Luqa below me. Suddenly the whole of the airfield erupted with bombs. Two aircraft in front of me – a Blenheim and a Wimpy[1] – burst into flames as about 50 or 60 bombs burst around the airfield. I looked up and the sky was black with German aircraft. I had been looking in every direction except upwards.

'The only thing to do was to go to the little island, which was a rendezvous point in the event that something like this happened. I set off there to get out of the way of the bombers, then thought, "What is the point of going out to sea if my engine is going to stop and I am in the water? Sod it!"

'I turned around. By this time the whole airfield was under a pall of black smoke. I chose to land in the black smoke, between the bomb holes, and got down. I arrived at the end of the runway, which was comparatively clear, strangely enough. The raid had gone, I didn't know which way to taxi, and it was hot, by God it was hot, somewhere in the nineties. I stopped the aircraft, but I couldn't get out. I was crippled with the effort of having held the rudder over for nearly six hours. I felt they had to get me a crane to get me out. But one way or another I levered myself out and I stumbled and fell to the ground. I was grabbed by the arms and rushed down to the black hole of an air-raid shelter. "

In the shelter Neil met one of the pilots he knew who had flown out with 'Butch' Barton's flight of 12 Hurricanes.

'He said, "Have you heard? We're not going on to the Middle East, we're staying here." What we were going to do, he explained, was that our aircraft were going on to the Middle East, but we are going to take over the remains of 261 Squadron, which had been beaten into a pulp by the Germans.

'We were told we had to move to Takali, three miles that way. We got into an ancient bus, much like the buses that took the French to the line of the Battle of the Marne to save Paris in 1914, only this seemed older than that. It had a lunatic driver, around a narrow road, I thought we would never get there.

'When we got to Takali we found the remains of 261 Squadron which had six aircraft, all Hurricane Is, all in various states of disrepair. Some had their tail wheel tyres stuffed with straw. These were the aircraft we were going to defend Malta with. There was no accommodation except the Takali mess. I remember sleeping in the corridor. The mosquitoes were just unbelievable. I was just bitten to pieces, because we had no mosquito nets.

'That was the first night.'

Graham Leggatt made the flight to Malta in a second wave on 29 June 1941. Like Tom Neil, he was taken some of the way into the Mediterranean on

---

1 *Service personnel referred to the twin-engined Vickers Wellington bomber as the Wimpy, naming it after the character J Wellington Wimpy in the* Popeye *cartoons.*

HMS *Ark Royal,* which had picked up 24 Hurricanes in Gibraltar. They sailed into the Mediterranean, halfway to Malta, and then set off to fly the rest of the way there.

Graham Leggatt:

'We landed at Takali on Malta, after four-and-a-quarter hours flying, non-stop, using non-droppable long range tanks. On our particular trip we did it without loss. The next one they lost one, if not more. I think on every Malta reinforcement trip they all had some losses, mostly engines failed before they managed to get to the island.

'We lost the *Ark Royal* some little while later.

'I arrived with a whole batch of guys from North Weald, 249 Squadron and 46 Squadron, these two squadrons had been resident at North Weald. When they reinforced Malta they decided to do it with two complete squadrons. They were both good squadrons, but for some reason or another 46 Squadron was phased out as a name.

'My unit, 46 Squadron, had been reformed around two surviving pilots after the debacle of HMS *Glorious*. Despite this disaster, the squadron was operational again by the end of June, once again at Digby. August 1940 saw a brief spell at RAF Duxford, but the real return to combat came at the start of September, when the squadron moved south to Stapleford Tawney to take part in the later stages of the Battle of Britain.

'The squadron briefly returned to the north early in 1941, before in May it began a move to the Middle East, which would not be completed for an entire year. While the ground crews arrived in the Middle East on schedule, the pilots were diverted to Malta, where they took part in the defence of the island. On 22 July 1941 the remaining pilots were absorbed by No 261 Squadron.

'The Messerschmitt Bf 109E, which is what we grappled with during the Battle of Britain, was on a par with the Hurricane. The pair of us were pretty well matched together. The Hurricane I was more manoeuvrable than the 109, but on the other hand the 109 was a little bit faster. It was certainly extremely fast in a steep dive.

'In Malta, some of the Hurricanes we got were clapped out, but there were Hurricane IIs in my reinforcement flight when we took two whole squadrons, a total of 24 aircraft. On the island, already, there were 8 or 10 Hurricanes.'

Tom Neil:

'Malta was a period I did not enjoy, although strangely enough, we were not really hard-pressed when the Italians were there. Their heart really wasn't in the war. In some respects their equipment was worse than ours. The prisoners our armies captured, Italian prisoners, were in their tens of thousands.

'We used to say their tanks had five gears, four backward and one forward. But they made beautiful engines.'

Graham Leggatt:

'The autumn of 1941 in Malta was rather a nice little war. It had started more or less in June when we arrived off the carrier. On that day it was rather pleasant. Here we were in this Mediterranean seaside resort, all the amenities a chap could ask for, including girlfriends from the rather posh families who lived up in Medina who used to entertain us.

'They were Maltese families, big families, and the Politchinas were the most famous. They had six daughters, but of course in strict 1940s style, these very attractive young ladies were always under the eagle eye of the mothers. There was a lot of very good-humoured friendship.

'We were not fighting the Germans at that time. The Germans had been in Sicily, in some strength, and HMS *Illustrious* was one of the constant targets. They bombed our airfields, but bombing the airfields is a bit unproductive, because we go and fill in the holes next day.

'So from the day we arrived, we had a lot of fun with these young ladies and life was very pleasant. We had enough pilots to do two complete shifts. A shift came on in the morning, went off at lunchtime, and another shift could take over as of tea-time, and then we'd break up for the night. It was very agreeable.

'As for actual fighting, in the Hurricane squadrons we were not aggressive very often. Now and again we would be given a little job to do. We would go and drop some of these little 20lb [9kg] bombs on their airfields. It was a fun thing really. We would go in the Hurricanes, and they would push up the little Macchis they had. They would never stop and fight for very long, the Italians. They would have a go and then dive for home.

Tom Neil:

'On the first day we were able to muster a total of eight aircraft, and there were 26 pilots. We had to divide the squadron into two. Butch Barton was going to command half the squadron, I was going to command the other half. We would co-operate with shifts. He was going to do the first stint at Takali. He came on duty with the eight Hurricanes – absolute wrecks, I can tell you – no markings, no this, no that, all Hurricane Is, and he went on duty at 5.00 am.

'Then at one o'clock with my motley horde of chaps. I just chose an aircraft and picked up a parachute. My aircraft looked like one of the original Hurricanes ever built. But we were there to defend Malta, so we put our chaps in the various aircraft. Our total accommodation was two tents, each of them to hold about 12 people. One was the tent, the sides rolled up, in which the pilots lived, the other was for the NCOs of 261 Squadron.

'From our tent there was a single wind-up telephone connected to

Control somewhere in Valetta, six miles away. I arranged my mob and waited for the enemy.

'It was breathtakingly hot and we were sweating cobs, and bitten by mosquitoes. After half an hour, the air raid siren went. I immediately rang Control and said, "The air raid siren is going, what's happening?"

'"Oh, nothing, old chap, nothing to concern yourself about."

'We were all sitting in our cockpits, on stand-by, me included. I had been sitting there five minutes and then the air raid sirens went off again! I jumped out of my aircraft, ran into the tent and told the airman of the watch, "Get me Control immediately!"

'Just at that moment the enemy appeared, 109s, ten feet high. There was a terrible crackle of cannon and gunfire, bullet holes appeared in the top of the tent. The poor chaps sitting in the aircraft, they were sitting ducks. We lost five Hurricanes, two on fire, the other three were put out of commission. Chaps were wounded as they sat in the cockpit, chaps had miraculous escapes, chaps with cannon shells through the parachutes they were sitting on. One chap had dark glasses at the end of his nose knocked off by a bullet.

'Another chap, Pat Wells, was shot in his foot. It was his third wounding; he had been shot twice in the Battle of Britain. He was in and out of the hospital like a fiddler's elbow.

'I remember going to see him. Two columns of smoke, two aircraft on fire and Pat was hopping around on one leg. I ran towards him, held his arm.

'He said, "I am sorry, I am really sorry old chap ..." He was in shock. "Don't bloody well hit me again! Why don't they shoot at somebody else?"

'Then we had three aircraft left. I took to the skies a little later on that day, bravely to defend Malta with three aircraft. That was our first full day on Malta.'

Graham Leggatt:

'My logbook for 14 July reads, "Ammunition exploded and caught fire in starboard wing, broke away from formation, and landed!" By this time I was a full Flying Officer, my year was up as a Pilot Officer, the lowest of the officer ranks. One was elevated once you became a Flying Officer, you got a thick stripe instead of a thin one.

'We were on our way out towards Sicily, it was a scramble, I don't think we made contact, I was Red Two. What I do know is we were flying south-westerly in formation, all 12 of us, a nice enough day, at our usual height, 12,000 feet [3,567m]. Everything was quiet, there was no nattering going on.

'Then a voice said, "Red Two, you have a glycol leak."

'A glycol leak is one thing that Merlin engine pilots do hate, because in no time at all your aeroplane can be burning furiously, and you've got to get out quick. I looked at my starboard wing and there were flames and smoke pouring out of the upper surface. I didn't care too much for that.

'On the other hand, we were over the ocean and I didn't care for a swim that day. The fire, clearly, was in the ammunition bay, where all the belted machine gun ammunition was stored when the aircraft was in the air. There were flames and smoke, white and black smoke, pouring out of this hole in the wing. Any moment now the fuel tank could blow up.

'I decided to go into a side-slip to port in the hope that the flames would be carried away from the fire, and that is just what happened. The flames slid away to starboard, and if anything, they were decreasing. I thought I'd see what happened if I kept up this side-slip and little by little the flames went down. By this time I was quite close to Takali. I thought, "I can land here." I went down quick, plonked the Hurricane on the ground and staggered across to the squadron hard standing.

'People came running out carrying fire extinguishers and all sorts of things. I was undoing my gear and Butch Barton came over.

'"You're a fool," he said. "You go milling around, over our airfield, over us. Any minute you could be on fire and fall out of the sky, and clobber the lot of us."

'Well, I had got his aircraft on the ground in one piece, and then he told me off for doing it. I didn't think that was very charitable.'

Tom Neil:
I was in Malta eight months. It got worse and worse. We had terrible aircraft. Some had Vokes filters, because the air intake on a Hurricane and Spitfire is underneath the wheels. It collects all the dirt, and Malta was a terribly dusty place. When you took off a cloud of sand rose to 1,000 feet and stayed there for half an hour. Most of it went up the air intakes and stopped the engines. We had terrible engine problems. I had five engine failures in eight weeks.

'I survived by luck. Usually the failures happened just after I had taken my wheels off the ground. You opened the throttle, and instead of getting nine pounds boost, you went through a vast taxiing experience to the far end of the airfield.

'Malta is full of fields, 50 yards [45m] square, with brick or stone surrounding walls. The only place to land in Malta is on an airfield, if you can make it. The alternative is to land in the sea, but land in the sea and you are drowned. An outlanding wrecked you, and you burst into flames. We had terrible, terrible trouble.

'Fortunately, after that initial flurry of action from the Germans on 21 May, they left to go to Poland and attack Russia. We didn't know. All we knew was, no Germans! Where have they gone to? Nobody knew, nobody told us. Somebody must have known, but at the sharp end you are never told.

Graham Leggatt:
'On 17 July 1941 we had a scramble on Malta. At this time the Italians had been sending over big formations of these Macchis, 20 or 25 of them at a

time. They sent over one of the BR 20s, the same aircraft with which we had such fun over Orfordness some months ago in the "Great Italian Turkey Shoot". They would have one of these bombers and a big escort. They would come over and take photographs. Sometimes they would drop a bomb or two, but I don't think they hit anything.

'Anyway, we got scrambled, and up we went. There was this bomber surrounded by all these Macchis, quite a splendid sight in fact. They saw us and all turned for home.

'"Butch" Barton was leading, and for some reason he kept it quiet. We could easily have attacked before they were halfway back to Sicily. For some reason Butch decided to stay with them, which we did. We sat up a little bit above and behind, maintaining quite a close formation, stooging along, watching these Macchi 200s.

'Just as we were crossing the coast into Sicily, the Italians broke their formation. Immediately, Butch led the whole squadron down to attack them, milling about all over the place. The Italians had a really quaint idea about carrying out a dog-fight. Their idea was that one chap would go and get another chap and chase him all over the sky. They could put up quite a reasonable little show, but they weren't terribly good shots. However, this one chap, he decided he was going to outshine the others in his squadron, so he dived away. I followed him down. He pulled out of a very steep dive. I immediately added a little bit of extra speed and power, and got on to his tail straight away, and then fired.

'He just toppled over. There was no smoke or flames, I didn't see anything come out, no bits coming off. He just toppled over on his starboard wing and that brought me up level with him. I could see him in his cockpit, slumped up against the canopy, so I was sure I had knocked him out. The aircraft went into a steep dive, and it kept on going down into the sea.

'Butch got one, much on the same basis as I did. One or two others claimed probables or damaged. Butch and I were the ones who got the score that day. That was a good day.'

Tom Neil:
'During that period, May to December, I did about 80 operations. Describing it now, it was not too bad, strangely enough. We were mostly up against the Italians. They had Macchi 200s which had a lesser performance than even our Hurricanes. Our Hurricanes were our main problem. You couldn't keep the engines going, people were baling out, we had coolant trouble, it was terribly difficult to keep the aircraft in service.

'We began to get a few Hurricane IIs which made it better for us. We could cope with the Macchi 200s – they had air-cooled radial engines of lesser power than the Merlins – and the Savoia 79s, the three-engined bombers and the twin-engined Fiat BR 20s which we met at night.

'We quite enjoyed ourselves at night, because we knew exactly where the enemy was going and that was Valetta. All we had to do was wait, and catch the search-lights. We had radar, not in the Hurricanes obviously, but you didn't even need radar, you knew they wanted to hit Valetta or us. The island was only fifteen miles by six [24 km by 10 km]. We would see them coming by radar as they passed Sicily 66 miles [106 km] away. We had some success at night. I fired at one but I missed.

'I did shoot down what I thought was a Bf 109 but it turned out to be a Macchi 200. Then, about August, they were equipped with Macchi 202s, which were exactly the same as 109s. They had the same engines as 109s and they left us standing. They were the best Italian fighter of the war, and only the later marks of Spitfire and the Mustangs could cope with them.

'Our AOC, Hugh Pughe-Lloyd, had been briefed to use Malta as a base from which to attack the Afrika Corps, using the Blenheims and all the naval aircraft. The Wimpys were attacking everything in sight but were suffering terrible casualties. The submarines were there, Force K was there, and terrible damage was done to Malta.

'We did nothing! All we did was protect the base, so far as we could. The famous Blenheim pilot Ivor Broom – he became an air marshal and was knighted – was a sergeant back then, and he went from sergeant to Wing Commander in no time flat. Their casualties were horrendous. Every time they took off they had losses.

'We also lost quite a few. I survived because God is good. Poor old Butch Barton had an engine failure on takeoff, except that he got off the ground, not like me. He crashed straight ahead through a couple of fields, and was wrecked. He was horribly burnt because the batteries came loose and doused him with acid.

'If your engine failed, you baled out. Hopefully, if you baled out over the sea, the air/sea rescue found you.'

Graham Leggatt bailed out over Malta on 21 December 1941, four days before Christmas:

'We got a scramble, early morning. We were operating from Luqa, because our own airfield Takali was under flood water. It was extremely wet and boggy. While we were re-fuelling we were given a scramble. There was panic stations all round, getting these aircraft into the air. There were ten of us, we got together and we were climbing away. I had been given a shagged-out old Hurricane, and no sooner had we taken off than I was beginning to lag behind the rest of them.

'We got up to about 12,000 feet [3,657m], heading due north, strung out. You could hardly call it a formation, we had not really got together. Then we were given a new heading, and I glanced down to the starboard side. And there, to my amazement were three Junkers 88s in close formation, heading towards Malta. The trouble with my aeroplane, apart from the fact that it was tired-out, was that it had no oxygen, so if the squadron continued to climb I was going to have to leave them to it, and it also had a broken radio.

'I yelled at my microphone, "Three bandits below!" and no one took the slightest bit of notice. I thought I'd better have a go. I went into a steep turn to starboard and headed for these three Junkers. As I got close, I could see they had an escort. There were, in fact, six Bf 109s milling around these bombers. The fighters saw me coming down and pulled away from their close escorting duties and came up to meet me. That immediately put me into a scrap with all these chaps.

'We were going around and around in circles and they were shooting at me. All of a sudden there was a tremendous flash and a bang down by my left leg, and everything was covered in thick, black, hot oil. It smeared the entire cockpit. It got in my face and my eyes. I couldn't see anything at all.

'I decided I had got to get home if I could. By this time I was down to about 2,000 feet [609m] and was crossing in over the coast. There was just a chance, I thought, that I could land the thing at Luqa. I selected the lever for the undercarriage. You could see through two tiny windows in the floor of the Hurricane whether or not the undercarriage came down. I could see the undercarriage wheels, but they were flaming, seriously on fire. I decided this was no place for me, and dived out of the aircraft, over the side.

'I looked up just in time to see the parachute opening. I looked down the other way and the ground was coming up very fast. It took about five seconds at most before I hit the ground. I sat and thought things over, and an army truck showed up. The driver was a captain in the Hampshire Regiment with whom, the very night before, a total stranger, I had had a couple of drinks. Out of all the people on the island, he turned up.

'I said, "Better go and have that drink we missed." I didn't go in for parachute jumps after that.'

Tom Neil:
'The instruction from the AOC was to do long-range patrols of three hours with our long-range tanks in Hurricanes. With dodgy engines this really wasn't fun. We would fly all the way down to Pantelleria, Linosa, Lampedusa, all the way down to North Africa, looking for aircraft on low-level flights, reinforcing the Germans. Sometimes we found them. We got quite a few victories one way or another.

'Then we were ordered to bomb Sicily with 20lb [9kg] bombs. We used to fly over Sicily trying to drop … crackers, silly bloody business. It meant a 60-mile [96 km] journey each way, over the sea, very inhospitable, and, of course, running the gauntlet of the Italian Air Force when you arrived.

'Then, in November, the Germans came back. How they slaughtered us, 249 Squadron.'

Graham Leggatt:

'The real fighting started in Malta when the Spitfires arrived, and the reason was, numbers. The whole operation in Malta was geared up when they came. In the glorious summer of 1941, we just lounged around. In 1942 the whole operation in the Middle East was geared up.

'The key to the whole thing, of course, was Rommel in North Africa. He had to be supplied if he was to do his job and he needed a vast input of everything under the sun. To do that they had to use ships, lots of them, carrying everything across the sea to Rommel.

'The Royal Navy committed as many submarines as they could spare to cutting this lifeline to Rommel, and squadrons of Blenheims were stepped up, anti-shipping. There were three or four squadrons at Luqa at any one time, coming and going, all the time clobbering these ships. They sank a tremendous tonnage of shipping, but the Blenheim squadrons took the most terrible hammering.

'They always flew in sixes, tight formation, and they always flew at nought feet, straight over the masts of the ship they were attacking. Out of the formation of six, four or five might come back. Sometimes it was only three. Unfortunately, they were operating beyond our range in Hurricanes, so we couldn't go anywhere with them.'

Tom Neil:

'Hugh Pughe-Lloyd, the AOC, was a Bomber Command man, but he had bombers and fighters. I used to say to him time and time again, "Sir, we must have different aeroplanes. We can't cope with Hurricanes. If the Germans come back, we have had it. In fact, we can't even cope with the Italians after they were equipped with the Macchi 202s."

'On one particular occasion, I think we may have lost a chap, we came back and we landed at Takali, and got down dishevelled and hot and really very unhappy with ourselves, and Hugh Pughe-Lloyd came to see us. He drove up in his car and shouted, "Hello there, Neil! How're you doing?"

'I said, "We're not doing very well. We simply can't cope."

'"Hugh Pughe" had a horrible method of impressing one. He tried to emulate Cromwell – he had blue eyes – and he would push his face right into yours, about a foot away in a curious way and stare into your eyes and talk to you in brief sentences.

'He growled, "You know, Neil. It isn't the aircraft. It's the men!"

'I thought, "I am going to hit this bugger!"'

'He saw my intention, because he took a step back, as indeed did some other people around me. He had no understanding.

'We used to say. "We have got to have Spitfires!" There were Spitfires coming out of our ears in Britain at the time. We couldn't get them. They had so many Hurricanes to get rid of, didn't they? The poor sods in North Africa, they also got stuck with Hurricanes.

'Eventually, when we were down to acting as targets for others, they brought in Spitfires off the carriers in March 1942. The situation changed almost overnight. They were Spitfire Vs, not the most up-to-date, but even so even Spitfire Vs could cope.

'A couple of days before Christmas in 1941, I was ordered home. Butch Barton and I were going to be sent home. I was to command something. Most of our other people were being sent further east. I was going to be relieved by a Flight Lieutenant Brandt, a nice little chap. Three or four days before Christmas, I was still at the stage of leading my flight, and we heard that Flight Lieutenant Brandt … "who is going to lead you, is coming towards Malta in a Wimpy, which at this very moment is being attacked by aircraft from Pantelleria. Get out there and save him!"

'I thought we'd better save this chap, because I was not staying there any longer! I rushed out with my group of pilots and we headed for Pantelleria. Of the three Wimpys we went out to protect, two were shot down, but the one that Brandt was in got through. Brandt had been manning a machine gun through a hole in the middle of the aeroplane.

'Brandt said to me, almost immediately, "When do I take over?"

'I said, "You just have!"

'"Oh, no, no, no, I can't do that," he said, and he asked me to help him until he could find out what the hell was going on, which he did after a couple of days.

'He went on for about four days and was killed.'

'In my view we had six thousand too many Hurricanes, and they had to use them up. People in command do not really understand unless they have done it themselves at the sharp end. A lot of people making decisions in the Air Ministry in London had not done the sharp-end bit themselves. They just had a lot of equipment that they had to dispose of.

'Hugh Pughe-Lloyd did not fight for Spitfires to be sent to Malta. Spitfires were thought to be unsuitable for the Middle East because they had spindly undercarriages. On the contrary, they could stand up wonderfully well.

'Spitfires were the savours of the Middle East – it was really touch and go. In another month in Malta, the Germans would have invaded. The only reason they didn't invade is that they had such a severe beating in Crete. They lost thousands of people, and their Generals were not keen to try that again, but they were on the verge of doing it. If they had parachuted in, I didn't even know where my gun was.

'We had situations in Malta where it looked as though we might be invaded by the Italians, and we got up in the middle of the night, saying, "Where's my gun? It's somewhere around the bed." We were expecting parachutists by the dozen to land.'

249 Squadron remained a part of Malta's air defences from 21 May 1941 throughout the fiercest Axis onslaught against the island, re-equipping with Spitfires in February 1942. As delivery aboard a convoy was out of the question, the only option remained to fly the Spitfires off an aircraft carrier. This method of delivery was already well established.

From November of that year, 249 Squadron moved over to the offensive, with attacks against targets in Sicily. The squadron left Malta for Italy in October 1943 and began operations over the Balkans.

But Last Witness Tom Neil left earlier, a day after Christmas, on 26 December 1941, just as the *Luftwaffe* returned with a vengeance and the Me109F. The Hurricane IIs defending Malta were now totally outclassed. Though they could still out-turn their German opponents, but they had virtually no chance at all of choosing when to engage in a fight. Ten RAF pilots were killed in December alone, including Neil's replacement.

Tom Neil had fought in Malta for seven months, in the thick of the battle, and won no decorations at all. Hugh Pughe-Lloyd got his knighthood that winter. Neil returned to England in early March 1942, via the Middle East, South Africa, West Africa and Canada, having survived watching a torpedo crash into the side of the ship below his feet, and not explode.

'The ship was carrying a thousand refugees from the Japanese victory in Singapore. They were kids and wives and things – it was great fun – and eventually we got caught up in a storm in the middle of the Atlantic. We were in a single-funnel and single-propeller ship with 1,000 people on board, and we just sat in the middle of the Atlantic, hove-to, pointing into the wind.

'These mountainous waves hit us, took away three-quarters of our lifeboats. We were all in Mae Wests or equivalent, until eventually we went to Canada – and didn't land in Canada. We went to Greenland and to Iceland and finally got back to Liverpool, having been on board that ship for three months.

'I never went back on Hurricanes. I was posted to command 41 Squadron on Spitfires. Later in the war I fought with the Americans, flying Mustangs and P-47 Thunderbolts. The difference between them and Hurricanes was as chalk and cheese. The Americans selected a number of RAF fighter "heroes" to go and teach them. We usually went in threes, an operational pilot – me – an Intelligence Officer, and also an Equipment Officer. I stayed with the 100th Fighter Wing of the 9th Air Force from January, 1944, until January 1945.'

It took a new CO of 249 Squadron, Squadron Leader Stan Turner, another Battle of Britain ace, to convince the newly-knighted Sir Hugh (Pughe) Lloyd that the Hurricanes had to be replaced with Spitfires.

'Either, sir, we get the Spitfires here within days, not weeks, or we're done. That's it.'

It wasn't until March 1942, faced with overwhelming attacks – 300 German and Italian sorties a day – that 15 Spitfires flew in to Malta off the carrier HMS *Eagle* to join Hurricanes already stationed there. Many of the new aircraft were almost immediately lost on the ground and the island's defences reverted back to the battered Hurricane.

Outnumbered 12-to-1, and facing the new Me109F, the Hurricanes daily punched their way through German fighter escorts to get at the Ju 87 Stukas and the tough Ju 88s bombing the island. The situation grew desperate, with a shortage of everything – food, fuel, ammunition, spare parts and aircraft. Aircraft wrecks were routinely cannibalised to make one single serviceable fighter.

In the fighting on 23 March 1942, to protect an incoming convoy, 14 Spitfires and 11 Hurricanes, all the fighters Malta had, sailed into a fight against 520 *Luftwaffe* aircraft, and 300 Italians. The island, which won a George Cross that year, was kept alive by a series of desperate convoys, and those convoys were defended by carrier-born Sea Hurricanes of the Fleet Air Arm.

In July, Sir Hugh Lloyd was replaced by the victor of the Battle of Britain, Keith Park, who arrived along with a big supply of Spitfires, all short of fuel. In August, just five merchantmen out of 14 that set off from Gibraltar reached Malta, but the convoy included the deeply crippled SS *Ohio* with a big supply of aviation gasoline. There were now five Spitfire fighter squadrons on the island, and with Keith Park matching his wits against his Battle of Britain opponent, Kesselring, he took the fight to the Germans, virtually eliminating further daylight bombing. Malta went on to play a crucial role in the air defence of the Mediterranean, and the invasion of Italy.

In 1941 a total of 300 Hurricanes had been delivered to Malta, most of which were destroyed in the heavy fighting that followed the return of the Germans in December after the invasion of Russia. The process of getting Spitfire replacements had been completed by 9 May 1942, when 64 Spitfires from HMS *Eagle* and USS *Wasp* reached the island.

The previous day saw the last Hurricane victory over Malta.

Chapter Fourteen

GREECE, THE WESTERN DESERT AND THE HURRIBOMBER

W hen Italy entered the war on 10 June 1940, the RAF had three fighter squadrons in North Africa, all equipped with Gloster Gladiator biplanes. There was only one Hurricane in the region, and that was unarmed. It had been undergoing service trials in Khartoum with an air filter fitted ahead of the carburettor air intake.

The Vokes filter was designed to prevent airborne sand at low level destroying the engine. Once at altitude, the pilot was able to open a shutter within the filter to allow clean air to feed the engine. The Vokes and its fairing became a common sight on Hurricanes used abroad in all theatres, though it lowered the Hurricane's maximum speed.

The lone Hurricane now played a bluffing role, as Air Commodore Raymond Collishaw convinced Italian reconnaissance flights that many more Hurricanes were available by moving it from base to base. The Italians spoke of the coming campaign against the outnumbered British in Egypt as if it was a walkover but it took three months, until September 1940, for Italian forces under General Grazziani to march from Libya into western Egypt.

British forces under General Sir Archibald Wavell pulled back to their main base at Mersa Matruh, ceding the Italians the air base at Sidi Barrani. By December 1940, Wavell had counter-attacked, destroying most of the Italian invaders as a fighting force and taking more than 100,000 prisoners. The RAF deployed 60 fighter aircraft, of which half were Hurricanes. The much larger Italian Air Force in North Africa was forced onto the back foot.

The Hurricanes were welcome but they were not always suitable for taking on the Italian CR42 biplane fighters. In one dogfight Hurricanes and CR42s circled each other without much happening until six Gladiators appeared. They shot down eight of the Fiat CR 42s.

The Hurricane was the most advanced British fighter aircraft in the region from June 1940 until the arrival of the first Spitfires in March 1942. At first the Hurricane could just about hold its own against the Messerschmitt Bf 109E when the Germans appeared. The Bf 109F, however, was a much superior aircraft, possibly the best version of the German fighter. Once it appeared, Hurricanes struggled.

Meanwhile, the Italians had also invaded Greece on 28 October 1940, and the air war there was initially fought between British and Greeks on one side, and Italians on the other.

While Churchill was keen to support Greece, Wavell saw it as a diversion of resources that he preferred to use in his campaign in the North African desert. As a result, the RAF role in Greece was never large, but aircrew in Greece saw a fair bit of action.

The winter war was fought with Blenheim fighters and bombers, and Wellington bombers. From November, 80 Squadron RAF provided fighter support with Gloster Gladiators. They coped, as did their Greek allies, while they were fighting Italian forces. February 1941 saw the arrival of 33 Squadron RAF from Egypt with Hurricane fighters, working out of mountain bases 3,000 feet [914m] high.

The highest-scoring RAF fighter pilot of the entire war, 26-year-old South African 'Pat' Pattle, had been in the thick of the fighting with 80 Squadron in the Libyan Desert, scoring his first 17 kills on a Gloster Gladiator. When he was promoted to lead 33 Squadron in Greece, he gave this appreciation of the Hurricane as he converted over:

'The pilots of 80 Squadron had all flown Hurricanes before in the Western Desert, but needed plenty of practice with them before they could be risked on operations. It was no use going into battle until one was thoroughly acquainted with all the peculiarities of the Hurricane, and capable of using its advantages. The Hurricane also had some disadvantages when compared with the Gladiator, and these had to be taken into account too when deciding on the tactics of aerial combat ...'

Pattle's first impression when he lowered himself into the cockpit of the Hurricane was of the heavy, solid-looking metal all around him. It would certainly absorb much more punishment than the Gladiator. He revved the engine and straight away liked the obvious power hidden away at the back of the instrument panel. He liked the speed of the take-off too, and the fast climb, while the power of the Hurricane in a dive was breathtaking.

In level flight the Hurricane was as steady as a rock and he knew it would make a splendid gun platform from which to aim the guns. Now he had twice the number of guns, and double the rate of firepower. He would not need to keep the enemy plane in his sights for so long to create the same amount of damage. Neither would he have to wait to get in so close to the target, for the cone of fire of the eight guns did not converge so tightly as the Brownings on the Gladiator.

But he missed the quick loops and the tight turns of the Gladiator. The Hurricane could do everything that a Gladiator could do in the way of aerobatics, but it took a much bigger volume of sky in which to do it. A turn in the Hurricane, for instance, was wide and slow compared with the fast wing-over of a Gladiator. On the other hand, the speed of the Hurricane in moving in a wider arc was much faster, and the resulting physical drain on the pilot greater. Pat found himself blacking out almost every time he made a change of direction and soon his legs became stiff and sore.

In March 1941 the Italians started a new ground offensive in Greece, and the air fighting intensified.

A hotchpotch of RAF aircraft were involved in the fighting, and losses were high, increasing dramatically after the *Luftwaffe* entered the fighting on 6 April with large numbers of Bf 109s, delaying their attack on Russia to help out the faltering Italians.

In ten days the *Luftwaffe* reduced the RAF to 22 Blenheim bombers, 14 Blenheim fighters, 12 Gladiators, five Lysanders, and 18 Hurricanes. British ground forces were in full retreat, complaining loudly of having no air cover.

By 20 April, *Luftwaffe* bombers and fighters were bombing and strafing with almost no opposition. Just 15 Hurricanes fought an overwhelming German force over Athens. The RAF claimed 22 kills, but lost two, with another pilot later dying of burns.

One of the losses was 'Pat' Pattle, DFC and bar, credited that day with his 50th victory. He was shot down going to help one of his fellow Hurricane pilots under heavy attack.

Within three days, only one airfield in mainland Greece was still flying Hurricanes. *Luftwaffe* Bf 110s attacked it that evening, and another 13 Hurricanes were wrecked on the ground. A day later the last RAF aircraft left for Maleme in Crete.

The Germans went on almost immediately to attack Crete, with a full airborne assault that was a success, but won at heavy cost to themselves, against just a handful of Hurricanes. There were also six Gladiators at Heraklion, five Fulmars at Maleme, seven Sea Gladiators and seven Blenheim fighters – little protection against the Ju 87 Stukas, protected by swarms of Bf 109s. One solitary Hurricane survived to fly back to Egypt.

By the beginning of May the Greek evacuation was over. Of the 62,500 troops deployed in Greece, 50,700 had been evacuated. British soldiers and sailors were bitterly abusive of the RAF for not being visible, but the RAF claimed 231 kills, as well as many 'probables' and those destroyed on the ground. It lost 72 aircraft in combat, 55 were destroyed on the ground and 82 were abandoned – 148 aircrew were killed.

The *Luftwaffe* appeared in the desert at the same time as it appeared over Malta, and with similar results. The Bf 109 had evolved quicker than the Hurricane, and the relative parity of the Battle of Britain the previous year was gone. However, the desert air force had more aircraft than the defenders of Malta – nine squadrons of Hurricanes took part in Operation Crusader, the relief of Tobruk, at the end of 1941.

When the Germans became embroiled in the battle they brought with them the deadly Bf 109F. Hurricanes were increasingly assigned to ground attack and reconnaissance roles and the pure fighter mission was handed to Spitfire Vs.

The rifle-calibre bullet of the 0.303 inch Brownings – the original armament of the Hurricane Is – was completely ineffective against German tanks. Although the 20mm cannon was devastating against soft skinned vehicles, tanks remained impervious to anything except a direct bomb hit. Something stronger was needed.

On 18 September 1941, a Mk II Hurricane with two 40mm Vickers S guns was delivered to Boscombe Down for service trials. It sailed through approval and became the Hurricane IID, with an additional 368lb (167kg) of armour added for the protection of vital areas. Operations began in June 1942 with No 6 Squadron who quickly adopted the tin opener as their mascot for their tank-busting endeavours. Two 0.303 inch machine guns were left in the wings of the IID to enable sighting of the main cannon, which had only 15 rounds per gun. The weight and drag of the guns and their fairings had a significant effect on the performance of the Hurricane, sacrificing 40 mph (64 kph) from the maximum speed.

Sea routes through the Mediterranean had been closed by the fighting, and aircraft of all types were shipped to the Gold Coast, assembled in western Africa, and then flown overland to Egypt. On 14 October 1941, Last Witness Billy Drake took command of 128 Hurricane Squadron at Hastings in Sierra Leone to protect convoys re-fuelling in West Africa. Their main enemy in the region were the Vichy French based at Dakar.

Billy Drake:
'I arrived in West Africa and eventually we put the Hurricanes together

that arrived in crates. It took about a week to assemble them and make them operational. Our job was to ensure the Vichy French up north did not interfere with the large convoys coming through Freetown.

'On one occasion, a Sunday, the authorities thought there was a twin-engined French aeroplane coming towards us. I was detailed to intercept. There appeared to be no rear gunner. I formatted with, and looked at the pilot of this aeroplane, and I suggested to him, using signs, that he should land. He took no notice. He was not going to do what I told him to do. I had the unpleasant job of getting behind him and shooting him down. I think he was probably on a reconnaissance in Sierra Leone.'

Drake was then posted on to the desert in the Middle East where he met Keith Park who asked, 'What the f**k are you doing here?' Park had him posted to a Kittyhawk squadron as a 'supernumary', flying as number two to another squadron leader in 260 Squadron. Drake then took over 112 Squadron, also flying Kittyhawks in May, 1942. They were painted to look like Sharks (the Americans copied the British with this insignia, not the other way around) and Drake became known as 'Shark Leader'.

During that period, Last Witness Bill Swan had missed being posted to the Far East because he was struck down in Egypt with amoebic dysentery. When fit to return to full flying duties, he was posted as a 21-year-old sergeant pilot to 33 Squadron on Hurricane Is, arriving on 31 March 1942.

Swan was thrown into the fighting throughout that year, and survived the experience before finding his true skills as a test pilot. On his own admission, he could have been a pacifist – there are few fighter pilots who would have put up with the sort of treatment one Controller put Swan through.

Bill Swan:
'I was sent out on patrol because something was moving on the other side of the line in the Western Desert, and they had to have an aircraft showing up on whatever detecting devices they had. I was expected to patrol between Tobruk on the north end, and a fort in the Qattara Depression to the south. I had been up for a long time and realised my fuel was low and I was desperate to get back to base.

'I called Control on the R/T and told them I was running short of fuel and wished to return. They said, "Sorry, you must stay there, it's essential we keep an aircraft airborne there."

'I said, "I am running out of fuel!" But they told me I had to stay.

'Inevitably, I ran out of petrol and force-landed. I looked for a salt pan and a bit of level ground, decided that wheels up was going to be safer than wheels down. I recovered the crystals from the radio set, picked up my water bottle and other survival gear, and decided not to go south to the Qattara Fort, though it was nearer than the road and in our hands.

'I knew if I went north I would be sure of hitting the road, so I started walking. By the time darkness fell I was still in the desert and realised I would be out there all night. I had to stop. I found a damaged German truck which had been abandoned. The side wings were solid, long flat wings which were about the size of a bunk bed, and they had canvas covers normally protecting the petrol cans.

'I decided I would sleep there, and then looked up to see a light. It appeared to be a vehicle. I scrambled through a barbed wire fence, climbed up a slope and there was the road. I had stopped just short of the tarmac highway that ran east-west along the coast. I flagged down what turned out to be a South African Air Force vehicle, and explained what had happened.

'I asked them, before we left, if they could show me where I was on a map, so we could recover the aeroplane. As they turned around we saw that the barbed wire fence I had just come through had the skull and cross-bones of a minefield! I had walked, for however many hours it was, through a minefield.

'When I got back to base, nobody would admit to having given the order for me to stay out there. Instead, I got an endorsement for it in my logbook, a black mark. They called what happened to me "inexperience."

'"This pilot is held responsible for the accident to Hurricane Z4940, in that he failed to check fuel contents gauge" … an absolute lie … "and as a result had to force-land, wheels-up, rendering the aircraft Category 2. Owing to extenuating circumstances the accident is classified as 'inexperience', particularly as the pilot was new to the desert and was not acquainted with the location" …just not true!

'I should have told Control exactly where they could put their order for me to stay there. That was where my inexperience was, not in flying.'

On 18 June 1942, No 6 Squadron, armed with Hurricane IIDs, each with two 40mm cannon, attacked an armoured column of tanks and halftracks at Sidi Rezegh, leaving 18 vehicles destroyed for no loss. To make the RAF's support of the ground battle more effective, liaison officers were posted to the army to direct attacking aircraft and to advise planners on the capabilities of ground attack missions.

Trials were carried out with rockets, which would prove even more deadly and versatile than the 40mm cannon. The rockets were effectively steel tubes packed with a solid propellant, tipped with a 60lb (27kg) explosive charge. Hurricanes were capable of carrying eight of these devastating weapons, which could be fired in pairs or in salvo. They could be used with deadly effect against ground installations, vehicles and even shipping. The

Hurricane was the first aircraft to carry this widely-used weapon into action. By October 1942 there were 22 Hurricane squadrons in the Middle East, of which four were equipped with the 'Tank Busting' IID.

In the ding-dong fighting that characterised the desert war in North Africa, the fighting moved back to El Alamein in the Summer of 1942, as Field Marshal Erwin Rommel headed east for Cairo. Increasingly outclassed in aerial combat, Hurricanes were now deployed ever more against ground targets.

Bill Swan:

'Most of my operational trips were sweeps, looking for targets on the ground or for other aircraft. We ran into the odd Italian plane. One that I went after was so manoeuvrable that I couldn't get anywhere near it, it eventually just got away because of manoeuvrability, not speed.

'I came close around that period to what is known now as a "friendly fire" incident. Some of our Blenheims had been out over a target in the Mediterranean and were coming back to land on our aerodrome. I had been on an op, and was also flying back, eastwards. This was in a period when Rommel was pushing us back. The Blenheims were coming from the direction of Malta and flying in the same direction as me.

'I thought that the plane I had seen was German. The tactic, when you were on your own, was to get down below a ridge so you were covered for 180 degrees. I could see the tip of this aeroplane's tail, nipping along, and I thought it was a twin-engined Messerschmitt 110. I thought the sun was in the south and if I get up-sun he wouldn't see me. So I went up into the sun, intent on flinging myself at him.

'As I turned to go towards him he started firing at me, and put a bullet through the two sides of the hood! As I was about to reply I saw a big roundel on its side – a Blenheim.

'I met the pilot when we were on the ground and he thought I had been a Bf 109. Looking into the sun, he couldn't see very well. I went back to my cockpit and put a cleaning rod through the two holes where the bullet went through.

'I could not get my head back far enough to miss it, so how did the bullet miss me? That was the nearest I have come to being killed.'

Last Witness Billy Drake led 112 Kittyhawk Squadron from 26 May 1942 to January 1943 in the western desert. This included the retreat to El Alamein and then the advance in October under Montgomery. Drake was shot down once more but landed among tanks operated by 11 Hussars. He won an 'immediate' bar to his DFC on 16 July 1942, an award in the gift of C-in-C Fighter Command, Sholto Douglas. Four months later he was awarded a DSO 'Just for being a good guy. We had air superiority by then and I went on a lot of ground attack missions' and went on to become the highest-scoring Kittyhawk fighter pilot of the war.

Drake's RAF squadron was seconded to work with American Kittyhawk pilots in the desert. The Americans were experienced flyers but had little or no operational experience. It was with them he won an American DFC. He went on to fly Spitfires and then Typhoons. But Drake did have a week working with Greek Hurricane pilots, and took some responsibility for breaking down class barriers in the desert between commissioned officers and NCOs.

Billy Drake:
'All my sergeant pilots were members of the pilot's mess, they were not members of the sergeant's mess. Only a few other squadrons accepted this fact. It was, to me, common sense to do this. I am half Australian and not as undemocratic as a lot of other people. I said, "If a pilot is a pilot, you didn't segregate them. They should always be in the same mess." I did it because I thought it was the correct thing to do.'

Last Witness Peter Ayerst, exhausted after the Battle of France, spent the following year in England as an instructor passing on his fighting skills – though taking time off to shoot down a Heinkel 111 in August 1940 at the height of the Battle of Britain. In July 1942 Ayerst was one of 20 pilots sent to the Middle East, arriving in Cairo on 22 September. He was sent to 33 Squadron flying Hurricanes IICs that were armed with four 20mm cannon.

Peter Ayerst:
'When we got to the Middle East the Hurricane had been improved tremendously from the ones we had in France. It had a three-bladed airscrew to start with. Of course, it was also designed especially for the hot temperatures of the Middle East, with a big cooling area. It was a good aircraft and we did a lot of damage. We used to get involved with Bf 109s quite often and never felt at any real disadvantage.

'We were really supporting the 8th Army in 1942. Montgomery had taken it over, and he said he wanted air cover for his troops. The line then was at El Alamein, only 30 miles [48 km] long, from the Mediterranean coast down to the Qattara Depression. Nothing could operate in that depression area, it was total soft ground, and any vehicle that went there went straight down.

'We were patrolling in Hurricane Mark IICs over the troops at about 10,000 feet [3,000m] for an hour at a time, before we were relieved by another aircraft. The Germans were trying to use the JU 87s to dive bomb our troops over that short front line. These dive-bombers would come in at about 8,000-9,000 feet, [2,400-2,700m] and they had a fighter escort above them, Bf 109s.

'We allocated one squadron against the dive bombers and one squadron against the fighters. We had four Hurricane squadrons, and sometimes we would operate the whole four, two and two. We generally gave the army chaps very good protection.'

Bill Swan was a sergeant pilot in the same 33 Squadron that summer, and found one of the best teachers possible:

'In combat, I thought I would cope. In your teens and twenties, you tend to be a bit cocky, and I think I was. I learned a lot during my short time with the squadron. One of my tutors was Lance "Wildcat Wade", a Texan who had joined the RAF, among the highest-scoring Hurricane aces of the war.

'He told me, "Don't ever get shot down for lack of attention. How many panels are there on the hood of a Hurricane? Include the windscreen. If you take one four-second look – a proper look at distance – through each of those panels, then check your instruments, you are checking frequently enough to see another aeroplane before it comes within firing range."

'I enjoyed the maths of that suggestion, and that's what I did when I was flying. I always did the mirror first, then all the panels individually, check controls and the instruments, then the mirror again and you're back flying within a minute. Nothing ever gets near enough to shoot you before you have seen it. That lesson from Lance Wade was probably the most valuable lesson I was ever given, and it got me through the summer of 1942.'

Peter Ayerst:

'On 9 October 1942, I was credited with a 109 and a Feiseler Storch, two in one day. We did a strafe at two or three airfields at the Dhaba, about 60 or 70 miles [96 or 112 km] to the west of where we were based on the Alamein Line.

'There were freak weather conditions over the German side. Though it was the desert, they had torrential rain and we didn't get it. The airfields at Dhaba were absolutely water-logged. How our chaps got this information, whether it was a photo reconnaissance aircraft, or the Long Range Desert Group got it, I don't know.

'We had our four squadrons in the wing taking part, that is, 33 Squadron, 213, 238 (which I was in) and one from the South African Air Force. We flew out from the coast, ten miles out to sea and then turned due west until we saw Dhaba on our left. There is an escarpment up there.

'We could see some aircraft on the ground there so we turned in, all four squadrons spread well out. As we came up the escarpment – I was flying with the wing commander leading the whole thing – there were tents. We could not weave because we were too closely packed together, so we had to fly straight. Right in front of me I saw a ridge tent, halfway up the escarpment. It was only about 300 feet [91m] above sea level. I saw the flaps of this tent come up and a chap leant out with shaving cream all over his face.

'I didn't have to weave, he was straight in front of me. I gave him a quick squirt. Then we attacked the airfield. There were too many of us, though we destroyed a lot of aircraft. Fifteen 109s jumped us as we went in at zero feet, and there was bags of panic.

'I was hit in the fuselage behind the cockpit but I destroyed one 109, one Feiseler Storch and one tent. We lost nine pilots on that do, but they weren't all killed. A number of them crashed on the other side where the ground was so soft, and they were picked up later. Next day we sent out aircraft to have a look around, and we found one or two; six got back. We lost, at the final count, three chaps.'

Graham Leggatt moved into the main struggle against the German *Afrika Korps* after he left Malta on 1 April 1942 in a Sunderland flying boat to go to Egypt. He had a couple of weeks' leave during which he joined the Aden Defence Flight, and remembers flying a Hurricane in the cool early morning light. Then he was posted to the air forces gathered west of Cairo to throw Rommel out of Egypt.

Graham Leggatt:

'I was with 73 Squadron all the way from El Alamein right the way through to Tunisia, 2,000 miles [3,200 km], and I was on that all the time flying Hurricanes IICs. Most of the work was ground attack. It was thought there would be a lot of air activity, by day and by night, and that we would need night-fighters to deal with this. But the Hurricane was not a night fighter and never could be. Even on bright moon-lit nights, you could be quite close to a Ju 88 and not see it.

'The Battle of El Alamein was a fantastic affair. Some of the more experienced senior pilots on the squadron were agitating to be given something more tangible to deal with. Hunting non-existent German aircraft in Hurricanes at night was rather a waste of time. I think in the whole time I was with 73 from El Alamein to Tunisia, I did not get a shot at an aircraft.

'The Germans, extraordinarily enough, put in very little effort to night bombing in the battle area. They did a certain amount on the fringes, but it never amounted to much. It seemed to be just patrols.

'When we realised that the Germans were not going to do much in the way of night bombing in the battle area, it was decided to make Hurricanes available to the army as required, or independently if the RAF wanted a job to do. So we were really given the choice of the task, or even seeking out targets that could be hit by a Hurricane at night.

'We finished up with rather limited success, one or two people managed to set a few things on fire. On the whole, night fighting was not terribly productive.'

Peter Ayerst:

'Over the night of 23 and into 24 October, we were involved in "The Push", the beginning of the Battle of El Alamein. I did two trips that day. One was a patrol of the line, protecting the army push in the north, up near the coast. We were intercepted by 15 109s and Macchi 202s. The 109s were seen above but they did not attempt to attack. On the second trip, a terrific dog-fight ensued. I damaged a 109, everyone was okay, bags of action on the ground

'In November when we broke the German line, I did two trips in one day. One was patrolling the line where we met 30-plus Stukas, and 20-plus Bf 109s and 109Gs. There was very heavy anti-aircraft fire followed by a Stuka Party. I had several squirts at 109s and probably damaged two. Sergeant Cornwall got one.

'The second trip that day, on a patrol of the line, there were several 109s around which attacked 33 Squadron, who were "top cover". They were useless attacks but there was plenty of activity on the ground.

'A day later I got a 109, but was shot down myself by flak. We were scrambled for a Stuka Party. We missed the Stukas but caught up with the Bf 109 escorts. There were at least 12 of them. My logbook says I destroyed one of the 109s and damaged another, but I was shot up three times by heavy ack-ack, and numerous times by light ack-ack. I force-landed five miles [8 km] on the German side of the line, but near the Australians. There was an area, almost neutral, between the two armies.

'It was the heavier flak that knocked a hole in my starboard wing. It also damaged the tail-plane and the engine. I was streaming glycol. I hadn't got full power, nor full control and I was still well over the German lines. All the German troops were having a go at me with everything they had got. It was about 5.30 in the afternoon, and there was a period of twilight at that month; daylight would be gone in half an hour. I was weaving around trying to avoid all this fire, losing height and I saw a track ahead of me. I made a successful crash landing, immediately leapt out and threw myself to the ground, because the Germans were still firing at me.

'I think, as I didn't move, lying on the ground, they thought they had got me. It got dark and I resolved to start a quick walk back towards our lines. I was shaking myself down when I heard a vehicle coming up very fast.

'I thought, "Oh my God, here come the Germans. Now I shall be a prisoner of war."

'Instead, an Australian voice rang out, "Anybody there?" I shouted, yes, and this Australian Major pulled up. He had his jeep and a driver. We tore off at a hell of a speed, going east.

'After about 25 minutes, the Major said to me, "You know that track you crash-landed on? You could not have landed anywhere else. It was all mined."

'It took me three days to get back to my unit. They thought I had had it. I was made a member of the "Late Arrivals Club". I was even awarded a certificate!'

After the 8th Army won their great victory at El Alamein, cannon-armed Hurricane Mk IICs took a heavy toll of the retreating German and Italian forces. The short range of the Bf 109 always reduced its effectiveness during periods of rapid movement, and by now the Germans were outnumbered in the desert.

Peter Ayerst:

'Eleven days later, we had moved 450 miles [724 km] behind the German lines, into the desert, where we stayed for four days. There were two squadrons in the wing, ours (238) and 213 Squadron. We took 18 aircraft in all. All the supplies came in by air. RAF transport aircraft brought all our ground crews in, our fuel and our food.

'We slept in the open, no cover whatever. We were about 150 miles [241 km] from the Germans to the north of us. When we first started strafing the road which followed the coast, along which they were retreating, they didn't know where we were coming from. After three days of strafing they began to get some idea of where we were.

'On the fourth day, they sent a recce aircraft over. They were getting ready to pounce on us, and the whole wing moved out of the area. While we were there, we destroyed a hell of a lot of vehicles. This was south of Benghazi around to El Agailya, and the German vehicles were nose to tail getting away. They presented a wonderful strafing target.

'The whole squadron would go in, fly all the way down the line strafing them, turn around and come back and have another go. In all, there were four strafing runs and I cannot tell you how many vehicles we destroyed. There were a hell of a lot of them.

'On one of these runs I destroyed a Ju 52 transport aircraft. I destroyed a petrol bowser, a six-ton lorry and three three-ton lorries damaged. That was my last trip on 16 November 1942.'

Had it not been for the development of the rocket projectile, Hurricanes would have been progressively phased out of front line service in the Desert/Mediterranean theatre from mid-1943 onwards. The squadrons equipped with Hurricanes now became ground support specialists.

The German *Afrika Korps* was finally driven out of Africa on May 8, 1943. Tank-busting Hurricanes with 40mm cannon, and Hurribombers, played a significant part in the victory.

Chapter Fifteen

HURRICANES FOR RUSSIA, SEA HURRICANES AND 'HURRICATS'

By March 1941 Hurricane production from all sources reached almost 100 per week, including an average of 10 per week from Canada. When the Germans invaded the Soviet Union on 22 June 1941, its armies were thrown back towards Moscow and the Russians were desperate for modern fighters.

Within days the British and the Soviets entered into a formal military alliance, and the Hawker Hurricane was the first Allied aircraft to be delivered to the USSR. Britain's decision to aid the Soviets meant sending supplies by sea to the far northern ports, Murmansk and Archangel.

As the convoys had to sail within range of enemy air attack from the *Luftwaffe* based in Norway and Finland, it was decided to deliver a number of Hurricane IIBs to provide protection, flying with two RAF squadrons, 81 and 134. These comprised 151 Wing RAF, headed by Wing Commander H. N. G. Ramsbottom-Isherwood of the RNZAF. The first 24 cannon-equipped Hurricanes were shipped north in the carrier HMS *Argus*, and arrived at Murmansk-Vaenga airfield, six miles North-East of Murmansk, on 7 September 1941. Merchant ships carried 15 boxed Hurricanes and ground equipment to Archangel, where the fighters were assembled.

The Hurricane proved well suited to conditions around Murmansk. The British, Australian and New Zealand ground crew and aircrew were mostly veterans of the Battle of France and Battle of Britain, and highly experienced. They brought with them a modern radio and radar air control system.

In addition to protecting convoys, the Hurricanes also acted as escorts to Russian bombers. During the following month, the Royal Air Force provided air cover to Soviet troops trying to hold off enemy forces from Murmansk and the Murmansk railway. In their two months in Russia, RAF pilots shot down 15 German aircraft for the loss of one Hurricane. As with the RAF in the Western Desert, Hurricanes in Russia were often used as a ground attack aircraft, armed with rocket projectiles.

The RAF pilots carried out their final operational flight on 8 October 1941, and at that point they started handing their aircraft and equipment over to the Soviet Air Force. This move was completed by 22 October and the British returned home by 7 December. After the RAF direct role had ended, the Hurricanes remained behind and became the first of thousands of Allied aircraft that were delivered to the Soviet Union.

The 1941 expedition to Murmansk achieved three objectives from the point of view of the British government:

> It provided vital aid to the Soviets at a critical moment.
> It introduced the Soviets to the use of modern technology, control systems, and fighter tactics.
> It showed the Finns in particular that offensive action against the Soviets would result in direct military confrontation with the Western Allies

A total of 2,952 Hurricanes were eventually sent to the Soviet Union between 1941 and 1944 from British and Canadian production. These included 210 Hurricane IIAs (with some Mk I conversions), 1,557 Hurricane IIBs, 1,009 Hurricane IICs, 60 tank-busting Hurricane IIDs and about 100 Hurricane IVs. The Russians adapted some Hurricanes to carry American 0.50 inch (12.7mm) machine guns, and a few were modified to two-seaters for training.

Yet the Soviets appeared to be anything but grateful for the generous aid offered by the Western Allies:

> 'From: British Military Mission, Moscow
> To: The War Office   20 June 1943
> Personal for C.I.G.S. for Martel
> Russians furious that they are not getting new Spitfires. They consider that excuse for giving them part-worn Hurricanes cannot apply to Spitfires. Mission has no knowledge of reasons for this action. This lack of liaison is jeopardising present improved relations.'

It seemed there was no acknowledgement of the sacrifices made by the Western Allies to get thousands of fighter aircraft to the Soviets for no cost to them at all. The British sent a reasoned, if pained, reply:

> 'Secret Cypher Telegram – Immediate
> From: Air Ministry
> To: 30 Mission, Moscow

Following from Chiefs of Staff
The Russians have repeatedly complained that a proportion of the aircraft
supplied have been reconditioned and it has been explained many times
both in writing and orally that we are only adopting the same procedure for
supplies to Russia as applies to our own units in all theatres.
In supplying aircraft to our own units, no distinction is made between
those that are new and those that are reconditioned and we cannot modify
this system in favour of the Russians. Reconditioned aircraft have as full an
operational life as new aircraft.
Out of 150 Spitfires shipped to Russia 90 were new and the remaining 60
were reconditioned.'

After the war, hundreds of surviving Hurricanes were reported to have been
dropped down empty mineshafts, because Stalin did not want his people to
know about aid from Britain. Recent attempts have been made to salvage
these aircraft, but the price demanded by the Russian 'Mafia' is too high.
They remain in their frozen graves.

Development of a fully adapted Sea Hurricane began in earnest after the
disastrous Norwegian campaign highlighted the need for a modern fighter
for the Fleet Air Arm. Hawker converted a repaired Hurricane in January
1941 and the decision was made to go ahead with full production shortly
afterwards. Refurbished ex-RAF Hurricane Is were fitted with catapult
launch points, an arrestor hook and other associated naval equipment by
General Aircraft Ltd.

Last Witness Eric Brown:

'The Sea Hurricanes differed only from a standard Hurricane in having an
arrester hook, and catapult spools, two things that stuck out either side of the
aircraft – like knobs on Frankenstein's neck, but around the centre of gravity – to
hoist the Hurricane on to the catapult. These were four very solid pieces of metal.

'I did the first deck landings with Hurricanes on escort carriers to
see if they were fit to operate on the smaller ship. They were okay and no
special technique was needed. The little worry that concerned us a bit was
the bounce of the undercarriage, which might bounce the aircraft over the
arrester wire and into the barrier.

'One had to ensure a three-point landing was done, and one could not
just land on the two main wheels. In all, in Hurricanes, I did 200 landings,
with no incidents, from a total of 2,407 deck landings.'

The Sea Hurricanes did not have the wing folding capability typical of carrier-
borne aircraft. The Sea Hurricane IA and IB, armed with eight Browning machine

guns, was powered by the Merlin III. When the cannon-armed Hurricane II was converted for naval use it was known as the Sea Hurricane IC.

In June 1942, Sea Hurricanes from 801 Squadron on HMS *Eagle* provided top cover for *Harpoon*, the essential supply convoy heading for Malta. Leaving Gibraltar, the convoy came under almost constant attack from the Germans and Italians. Sea Hurricanes, and Fulmars from HMS *Argus* did an outstanding job of defending the convoy, with No 801 Squadron claiming six Italian planes.

The most famous action involving Sea Hurricanes took place in August 1942 when another large convoy attempted to fight its way to relieve the embattled defenders of Malta. Three Fleet Air Arm Squadrons, 800, 801 and 885 embarked on fleet carriers HMSs *Eagle, Victorious* and *Indomitable*. The German and Italian enemy made a huge effort to prevent the convoy reaching the island and deployed several hundred bombers and fighters against it. HMS *Victorious* was lost to a U-boat and eight British fighters were lost for the destruction of 39 enemy aircraft. The arrival of the convoy bolstered the defences at a critical time and had a major effect on the course of the war in the Mediterranean.

Subsequently, the Supermarine Seafire and American-built naval fighters gradually replaced the Sea Hurricane in squadron service from mid-1942. By the end of the war Sea Hurricanes had all but disappeared from the Navy's inventory.

In the summer of 1940 Winston Churchill was confronted with a serious crisis. Nazi Germany employed a formidable weapon against convoys bringing food and supplies from America to Britain – the Focke Wulf FW 200 Condor. Churchill called it the 'Scourge of the Atlantic' and it was the first German military aircraft capable of flying within range of the East Coast of the United States.

The Condor was a four-engine monoplane that started life in 1937 as a 24-seat civilian airliner, but was soon seen by the Luftwaffe as an ideal maritime reconnaissance aircraft that could carry a bomb load. By December 1940, 36 Condors were scouring the Atlantic, and in 1941, 53 more were built. A major threat to Allied shipping, 116 ships totalling 323,016 tons were sunk by Condors during April 1941 alone, and in a matter of months they had sunk nearly one million tons.

They also became the eyes and ears of the U-Boat fleet, reporting the locations of convoys. There were areas in mid-Atlantic where Britain could provide no protection to their merchant convoys against German aircraft, which could spot allied shipping and direct U-Boats to carry out attacks at will.

With a five-man crew, Condors were heavily armed and extremely tough. Last Witness Eric Brown won a DSC for shooting down two Condors. Though he did not achieve these kills in a Hurricane, he did pass on his intelligent technique to others, as an effective counter to the Condor's power:

Eric Brown:
'I was flying an American Wildcat with 0.5 inch ammunition when I got those Condors. In both cases they were head-on attacks. They were not quite pioneer attacks, but I had worked it out, because the Condor was one of the most heavily-armed aircraft of World War Two, and it did not seem to have a blind spot. I worked out that the dorsal turret on top could not depress beyond a certain area without shooting its own bits off.

'Similarly, the gondola underneath – they both had cannon, the upper and the lower – could not elevate beyond a certain range, otherwise it would again shoot its own bits off. The pilots up front only had two fixed guns, and to aim those it would have to move the whole aircraft.

'So if you came in very, very flat, not a shallow dive, but absolutely flat, you could get into a blind spot. And it worked. I was not shot down, and they were.'

Many battleships of the period were equipped with steam-powered catapults to launch spotter planes. It was proposed that such catapults be put on the decks of merchant ships to launch a fighter aircraft. No existing catapult was powerful enough to launch a heavy fighter like a Hurricane, and the proposal to remedy this was put to the research unit at the Royal Aircraft Establishment at Farnborough. Within a week they developed a rocket-sled to get the Hurricanes airborne.

The catapult, the largest existing at the time, was powered by a cluster of 13 solid-fuel rockets. The rockets had to instantaneously reach a speed capable of getting the plane off the deck, but the power of the rocket couldn't be too great, because the acceleration might break the pilot's neck. The first manned test flight went well. The major problem with the catapult was that, once launched, there was no way the pilot could return and land on the ship. It was possibly a suicide mission.

Eric Brown:
'Hurricats, as they were known, essentially had only one life. They were mounted on catapults on merchant ships, to protect the convoy. The Hurricat was positioned on the catapult but was not fired off unless the enemy aircraft was actually sighted. A report of an enemy aircraft approaching was not enough to send it off, because it was a one-way passage.

'Once you got off it was usually out of range of land, and after you had engaged the enemy, whatever the outcome, you were on your own. The only thing was to ditch. It sounds suicidal, and ditching was not fun in a Hurricane. Because of the huge scoop underneath, it ditched like a submarine. The other alternative was to bale out near one of the escort ships. In icy waters you might live three minutes.'

The specially modified Hurricanes, or Hurricats, used in this role were piloted only by volunteers. The first battle between a Hurricat and a Condor occurred on 3 August 1941. The Hurricat pilot was Robert Everett, and his brave flight was to be the first test of this new tactic.

Everett had been born in Australia in 1901, so was relatively old to be a fighter pilot in the Second World War. He had won the 1929 Grand National at Aintree as a jockey, riding the 100-1 outsider *Gregalach,* and enlisting when the war began, he had volunteered for an extremely dangerous mission, to test in open combat the extraordinary rocket invention that hopefully could take on the marauding Condors. The ship on which he was sailing, *Maplin,* was called a Catapult Armed Merchantman – a CAM Ship – part of the convoy OG70.

A marauding Condor came across the convoy equipped with Everett's Hurricat, and apparently failed to see the rockets' flames when it was launched. The German crew were taken by surprise but still managed, equipped with eight machine guns and a heavy cannon, to severely damage the Hurricat. As he was all that stood between the convoy and its destruction, Everett fired the last of his ammunition straight into the Condor's cockpit, bringing it down in flames, the first and only Condor to be destroyed by a Hurricat.

Everett had to find his way back to the convoy or risk being lost at sea. He was able to climb to 2,000 feet (610m) in the stricken Hurricane, high enough to find the convoy again, and landed the aircraft on the water close to the British ships. But the Hurricat flipped over on its back and quickly began to sink, with Everett still inside. He had sunk an estimated 30 feet (9m) before he was able to open the canopy and struggle to the surface in the freezing waters. He won the DSO for this act of bravery. His experience led to the issuing of instructions for pilots to lower the flaps and wheels, slide back the canopy, punch out the starboard escape panel and tighten their straps prior to ditching at sea … and pray.

Hurricats were credited with turning the tide of battle against the Condors. Now that Condors could be intercepted at sea, the Germans were less inclined to press home attacks or reconnaissance missions against convoys. More powerful catapults were installed and the Hurricanes were able to carry an extra 88 gallons (400 litres) of fuel in external tanks under each wing. This greatly increased their endurance and effectiveness.

Eric Brown:

'There were a total of 38 ships that could take Hurricats – more than that number of aircraft were built – and they all had wheels. If there was a possibility of nearby land, they could land it safely. The pilot who shot down the Condor got a medal, but I don't think any of the others did. In the two years that they were in service, only eight catapult launchings were made, and six enemy aircraft shot down with the loss of one RAF pilot. Twelve CAM ships were sunk through enemy action.'

CAM Ship pilots were drawn from both the RAF and the Fleet Air Arm; the Hurricane was the only aircraft used in this type of operation

Everett was killed the following year, 1942, crashing a Hurricane while on a flight in Wales.

Chapter Sixteen

SINGAPORE, HURRICANE RETREAT

The Fall of Singapore to the Japanese in 1942 was probably the worst military defeat in British history. Believed for decades to be impregnable, the island fortress of Singapore had a garrison of 70,000 that included 33,000 British troops and 17,000 Australians.

Last Witness Terence Kelly, then a 21-year-old sergeant pilot with the RAF's 258 Hurricane Squadron, watched it happen:

Terence Kelly:
'Singapore, Sumatra and Java fell not because of any vast preponderance of men and arms by the Japanese but because the men who should and could have fought them off lost their courage, were bust in morale or were cowards. These are different ways of putting the same thing, or rather nearly the same thing.

'There is a difference between being a coward, being bust in morale or losing one's courage even if, unfortunately, when it comes to defeating a cock-a-hoop enemy, the effect is the same. You don't defeat him. He defeats you. Had a Churchill appeared, the whole of world history would have been different, but there was not one on the island.'

The Second World War had become truly global when a Japanese task force attacked the American naval base at Pearl Harbor on 7 December 1941. The following day, Singapore was subjected to bombing by long-range Japanese aircraft based in Japanese-occupied Indochina. Other outposts of the British Empire were also attacked, including Hong Kong, and landings were soon made in Malaya by Japanese forces that headed south for Singapore.

The RAF operated biplane bombers at the time, and a hopeless American monoplane fighter called the Brewster Buffalo, swept aside by the under-rated Japanese air force. Initially, air cover for Singapore was provided by only ten Hurricane fighters of 232 Squadron based at Kallang Airfield. The other three airfields on Singapore, Tengah, Seletar and Sembwang were in range of Japanese artillery at Johore Bahru. This fighter force was judged to have performed well, but was outnumbered and often outmatched by the excellent Japanese Zero fighters.

Last Witness Eric Brown:

'The Japanese did not believe in their pilots acting defensively. Their aircraft had no armour. They were there to attack and kill … or be killed. The Zero, their most prominent fighter, had no armour for the pilot whatsoever. It didn't even have a bullet-proof windscreen or self-sealing fuel tanks. They were not easily shot down because it was a light and highly manoeuvrable aeroplane – more manoeuvrable than any allied aircraft, but once the Americans appeared on the scene with 0.5 inch ammunition, that was enough to kill a lot of these Japanese aircraft.'

During December, 51 Hurricane Mk II fighters were sent to Singapore, with 24 pilots, the nuclei of five squadrons. They arrived on 3 January 1942, by which stage the Buffalo squadrons had been overwhelmed. Like the Buffalos before them, the Hurricanes began to suffer severe losses in intense dog-fights.

On 20 January a formation of unaccompanied Japanese bombers was intercepted over Singapore, and eight were destroyed. Further raids the next day were escorted by Zero fighters. The Hurricane could fight the Zero on almost equal term at altitudes above 20,000 feet (6,100m) but was out-classed at the lower level where most combat took place. The Zeros began to take a heavy toll of the British fighters.

Terence Kelly:

'When we landed on the evening of 29 January 1942, at Selatar aerodrome on Singapore Island, within ten minutes of ordering a drink in the Mess we realised that the pall of defeatism was so thick you could have cut it with a knife.

'The following day, my friend Bruce McCallister and I went to take our Hurricanes out of their packing cases. Bruce was a pilot officer and one of the nicest men you could know. The aircraft had had a thin coat of oil put on them to protect them in the journeys across the oceans. We wanted them cleaned and made ready to fight. We were overseeing this with British ground staff, and a Japanese aircraft came over and started circling, very high, over the airfield. It did not drop any bombs, just went around in circles.

'The ground staff started to make for the jungle for cover. Bruce looked at me and he said, "We can't have this."

'He pulled his revolver, and said, "Take your revolver out, too, Terry."

'We had our two revolvers in our hands and we had to point them at the ground staff and say, "Stay there until we say you can go."

'That was the character of Bruce McCallister. I did not do much flying in Singapore, and nor did 258 Squadron. Theoretically we were going to get 48 Hurricanes. In fact we got only eight serviceable the first day. They took off – Red Campbell shot down a Japanese bomber – and Bruce McCallister was killed.'

During the period from 27 January to 30 January, another 48 Hurricanes IIAs arrived on the aircraft carrier HMS *Indomitable*. They flew to airfields code-named P-1 and P-2, near Palembang, on the island of Sumatra in the Dutch East Indies (now Indonesia). The staggered arrival of the Hurricanes, along with inadequate early warning systems, meant that Japanese air raids were able to destroy a large proportion of the Hurricanes on the ground in Singapore and Sumatra.

On the morning of 8 February, a number of aerial dog-fights took place over the west of Singapore. In the first encounter, the last ten Hurricanes were scrambled from Kallang Airfield to intercept 80 Japanese aircraft, flying from Johore to provide air cover for their invasion force. In two sorties the Hurricanes shot down six Japanese planes for the loss of one of their own. They flew back to Kallang halfway through the battle, hurriedly re-fuelled, then returned to it. Air battles went on over the island for the rest of the day.

By nightfall it was clear that with the few RAF aircraft left, Kallang could no longer be used as a base. The remaining Hurricanes, one flown by Terence Kelly, were ordered to withdraw to Palembang on the island of Sumatra, and Kallang became merely an advanced landing ground. The Japanese had full control of the skies. On 10 February, General Wavell ordered the transfer of all remaining Allied air force personnel to the Dutch East Indies.

One of the units sent to Sumatra was 258 Squadron, annihilated in the following few weeks. Of the original 22 pilots of 258 Hurricane Squadron in the Operational Records Book on 30 October 1941 – before the USA entered the war – eight were British, five New Zealanders, four Americans, three Canadians, one Rhodesian and one Australian. Of those, six were killed in action (plus one died from burns), three were killed in flying accidents, one died after the war from wounds received in action, and five became Japanese Prisoners of War. Only seven survived to fight through the whole war.

Most of the young pilots of 258 Squadron had no operational experience before the Japanese got to Singapore at the end of January 1942. Kelly went on to fly cannon-firing Hurricane IICs, initially operating out of P-1, ten miles north of Palembang, in Sumatra. His personal stories, there are few Last Witnesses left from that theatre of war, are an illustration of the tough fighting put up by the remnants of the Hurricane squadrons in their failed attempt to stop the Japanese occupying the whole of the Dutch East Indies and threatening Australia.

> *Terence Kelly:*
> 'We had no sooner arrived in Sumatra than, on the very first day, we were sitting "on readiness", and getting used to being there. Then we heard some aircraft coming and thought, "Good, it's some more Hurricanes coming up from Java." We only had a limited number of Hurricanes, and they had been sent off from HMS *Indomitable* in dribs and drabs. When we heard these aircraft, we sat there looking at them and the Japanese came down in a dive and started strafing us. These were Japanese Navy Zeros.
>
> 'That was our first experience of Palembang. We came to learn the Zero's advantages; that it was, at certain heights up to about 20,000 feet [6,100m], slightly faster than Hurricanes, and it had a definite advantage in manoeuvrability. But it was without armour, its fire-power was less, its ceiling was apparently lower – we never saw a Zero operating above 30,000 feet – and above all, it lacked the astonishing capacity of the Hurricane to absorb punishment.'

On 14 February, thousands of miles away in England, horror-struck and despairing at the collapse of Singapore and the successful Japanese attacks on Britain's Far East Empire, Winston Churchill estimated that, 'Our air force in Palembang, mainly Australian squadrons, consisted of about 60 bombers and 50 Hurricanes.'

The most aircraft Terence Kelly saw there was 14 serviceable Hurricanes.

But, unlike Singapore, morale among the retreating air force pilots in Sumatra was high, though most of their radio communications did not work.

The P-1 airfield was attacked by paratroops.

> *Terence Kelly:*
> 'When the Japanese decided to invade Sumatra, we were instructed to go and strafe this invasion force. We got the maximum number of Hurricanes we ever got in the sky at once. That was 14. We had no sooner taken off than we saw, below a very thin layer of cloud, a whole lot of Lockheed Hudsons going in the opposite direction to us. We thought, "That's marvellous."
>
> 'We headed to where we thought we should find the Japanese, but

never found the landing spot. We had rotten information, so turned around to come back and when we got near to our airfield, I suddenly saw some Japanese Navy Zeros. I had no R/T – this was not uncommon because everything was hurried – so I flew up to the front of the squadron and gesticulated to Squadron Leader Thompson, our C/O. He waved his hands in anger at what looked like rude gesticulations – there was nothing I could do, he was not going to take any notice of what I was doing – later I discovered that there had been a wireless instruction not to land back at our airfield, P-1, but to go to the jungle airfield, P-2.

'Anyway, I felt we should do something about these Japanese so I went back and Bertie Lambert, another one of the 14 flyers, had seen them as well. We rather took it on ourselves to do what we could about the Zeros. It was quite a busy time. I got chased all the way over Palembang Town with a Zero on my tail, and managed to avoid him by sliding between trees and things. Then I came back and there was another one up above me. So I pulled up to fire at him and he fired at me, and I managed to get him. I shot him down.

'By then I thought I couldn't have that much fuel left, so I had to land. I landed back at P-1 to find it deserted, like the story of a Foreign Legion fort. Everything laid for dinner, no people.

'I taxied off the runway and then I heard another Hurricane – it was Bertie Lambert – come in to land. Suddenly out of the jungle came a man called Micky Nash – the pilot on duty that day looking after things – I think the Japanese killed him later that day.

'He came up and said, "What the hell are you doing here? This place is surrounded by Japanese parachutists." What we had thought were Lockheed Hudsons were Japanese aircraft delivering parachutists. We had just enough fuel to get off and get to P-2. When I landed I found I had two gallons left.'

'One of the jobs we had to do was strafe the Japanese invasion forces which were coming down in great big long barge trains, about six or eight in a row, with about 200 Japs in each of them and just one gunner in the back.

'I remember flying with Art Donahue, an American who was a jolly good pilot and a very brave man, and we came upon this load of barges. There was a string of them heading upstream, keeping in close to the northern bank. They were packed with men like sardines in a tin, and because at this point the river ran straight, they were in a long, straight line. It was a remarkable sight. The soldiers gave the impression of being so tightly packed they could not have raised their arms to fire at us. The oblongs of upturned faces made a curious spectacle.

'We strafed them. It was carnage. The target was, to all practical purposes, helpless. I have never seen anything like it in my life.

'When you have 12 machine guns – we were flying Hurricane IIBs – and a line of barges straight in front of you, packed shoulder to shoulder with Japanese, it is an extraordinary experience shooting at them. We must have killed a great many.

'The flicker of defending gunners was like torches switched on and off, but no more than that. We had orbited to get straight in line and dived from perhaps a thousand feet. I really don't believe Donahue missed a barge, his guns raking the convoy from head to stern. The bullets made an unforgettable pattern. There was a pincushion of water ahead of the nearest barge which moved along so that, as the bullets raked through a barge, what one saw was the pinpoints of lights in the barge itself. This was the tracers striking and the pin-cushioning carrying along both sides of the barges, and then reappearing in between each barge, and so on along the line.

'It is impossible to conceive the horror and the slaughter wrought. Donahue received a bullet in the leg from one of the gunners and broke off the attack. I stayed a little longer and was unharmed.

'There were many things about the war in the Dutch East Indies that I never understood, but what was incomprehensible was that we were not ordered to repeat the attacks on the barges. I know we killed a lot of Japanese because after I was taken prisoner it was known that the Japanese were after the people who had done this, if they could find them.

'The Hurricane was a wonderful aircraft to strafe in. I can't imagine any aircraft more perfect for strafing. Another of the strafes I did was against an invasion force which landed east of Tayfel. Unfortunately, *en route* we met a Japanese sea-plane and everyone had a go at that. I gave up trying to shoot it down and went on to do strafing. I was the only one who did. I set a sea-plane on fire along the coast, did some shooting up of Japanese troops coming ashore in comparatively small boats.

'I never forgot in all my life, as I went over the beach, there was one Japanese soldier looking up at me. I was only 100 feet (30m) up. I remember his face. I did not have a go at him particularly, but I have never forgotten him.'

Last Witness Gawain Douglas, not yet in the fighting, had this view of the Hurribomber's capabilities:

'The Hurribombers turned out to be very suitable for strafing and bombing attacks. They had the speed, they had the agility and they could keep out of harm's way when there were Japanese fighters around.

'The Japanese army equivalent of the famous navy Zero fighter was better than anything we had as a combat fighter, but it depends on what you're looking for. It had just a couple of machine guns, it had no armour plating, it was lightly-built, its engine was not so powerful, but because it was so light and small it could go faster than us, and it could climb quicker.

'In fighting, you could get on the tail of another aircraft and it had more or less had it, it was bloody lucky to survive. But Zeros could always get on the inside of a turn against a Hurricane going at it. The Zero was quite a formidable fighter. The Spitfire was more agile, being lighter-built than a Hurricane, but neither the Spitfire nor the Hurricane were built for ground-attack.'

Terence Kelly:

'On 14 February 1942, we only had six Hurricanes available to 258 Squadron, but we had more pilots than aircraft. A ship was available to take some pilots (we were valuable commodities at the time) and we had to decide who should stay behind to fly the six aircraft we had left. We had one volunteer, the American Red Campbell. Harry Dobbyn, a Flying Officer, was nominated to stay as the CO.

'Someone else who was not from the squadron volunteered to stay. The rest of us drew cards. Bertie Lambert stayed, because he drew a low card. Healey also drew a low card. I drew the four of diamonds.

'With the exception of Arthur Shearing, an Australian who went back to Australia, the other Hurricane pilots went to Colombo. They were there in time for the only occasion when the Japanese attacked Colombo, the capital of Ceylon – now Sri Lanka – and then they went back into the fighting.

'Those who got away to Burma now had experience of the Japanese. They knew they could not out-turn a Zero. We did not know this at the beginning of the fighting. We had naturally assumed that a Hurricane could out-turn anything, but when they started fighting again, they had enough experience to survive. We lost one or two in the fighting in Burma – there was Scottie, sadly. He got killed when practicing camera-gun shooting, and the man who was doing it with him pressed the trigger of the real guns, instead of the camera guns, and killed him.

'Six of us were left in Java. Harry Dobbyn was killed on our first fixture with the Japanese after the rest of the squadron had got away. Red Campbell, he got shot down but managed to bale out – he had to butt with his head through the hood to get out because it got stuck in the grooves – you can't pull the hood backwards and forwards if the grooves have been damaged. This did something to his neck so he could do no more flying. That left just four of us.

'The Japanese kept sending over fighters and bombers every day to stop us strafing. When we got information that the Japanese were coming, we had enough time to take off and fly up to 30,000 feet [9,144m], above the level the Japanese aircraft could reach.

'When we saw the Japanese we would come down and have a pop at them. On one particular occasion, we had got to our height, and there were tremendous cumulous clouds to both sides of us. We saw the Japanese, and came down to have a go. I went first, it just so happened, and when I had had my poop, I kept the nose down in the dive. I looked back and saw the other three peeling off from where they were. It was so fascinating that I looked and looked, three of them against the cumulous clouds, and then the Zeros turning off to follow them.

'I looked for far too long. I decided to pull out but when I tried, I could not move my stick. It was absolutely solid, jammed solid. I was going vertically down, full bore, and I thought, "How the devil do you get out of this?" I did at least remember the one thing you could do, that there was a tail trimmer on the elevator. You could wind it back fractionally – you can't do too much or you will just pull the wings off – so I wound the tail trim back and just got it out of the vertical. Eventually I managed to get out of it, getting level at 15,000 feet [4,572m] from 30,000 feet, and looked at the air speed and I just didn't believe it. It was reading something ridiculously low. I discovered why – because it had gone around twice. I must have been flying at 650 mph [1,046 kph]. What a wonderful aeroplane to pull out of that.

'There were four of us left from 258 Squadron, and there was another group of New Zealanders who had a few Hurricanes. It was decided that we should give our Hurricanes over to them, and that every day we would take turns. We flew 24 hours on the Hurricanes and they flew 24 hours on. We used the same aircraft. We were told to get away, to escape, and pass our Hurricanes to 488 Squadron.

'Well, we couldn't get away, so we got captured.'

When Sumatra was overrun the surviving Hurricanes retreated to Java, and were joined by 33 reinforcements flown in from HMS *Indomitable*. The Japanese onslaught continued and soon there were no serviceable machines left. To prevent them being captured, the remaining grounded Hurricanes and their spares were burnt.

Hurricanes helped avert the threatened invasion of Ceylon and were, for a long time, the only effective Allied fighter in the whole region. When Burma was invaded there was a real danger that India would be next to be seized by the seemingly unstoppable Imperial Japanese war machine.

In the fighting in Europe, when a pilot was shot down and captured, in general the Geneva Conventions worked and they were made Prisoners of War – PoWs. The Japanese had not signed the Convention and had a great contempt for it, especially when they were winning and thought they were always going to win. When they captured Singapore, Japanese soldiers went into a general hospital and bayoneted to death 200 of its patients. What happened to Hurricane pilot Terence Kelly for the rest of the war underlines the risks run by young fighter pilots fighting the Japanese, and haunts comments of the Last Witnesses involved in such fighting:

Terence Kelly:

'Early on after the fighting stopped, the Japanese didn't believe it, they just did not believe that they had taken Java. There were so few of them and so many of us. I remember at a place called Gerute, where I went with somebody else to make arrangements for most of the ground staff, a thousand RAF people down at a sugar plantation, and when we got there, there were far more PoWs in Gerute than there were Japanese.

'The Japanese looked scared to death of us, even though they were the captors and we were the prisoners. At the time they all seemed to be reasonable people. Eventually they decided that we should go to Batavia (now Jakarta). They put us on a train, and gave us two packets of cigarettes each.

'When we got to the station in Batavia there was an RAF officer sitting on the side of the carriage with his legs dangling over the edge as we came in, and stopped opposite the Japanese officer. The Japanese officer really belted into him. They had us march through the streets of Batavia, a shambling mass of men, with Japanese on both sides shouting and yelling and kicking and so on, until we came to what was the native jail known as Boegloduc. They counted us in, and every sixth man was booted in. With each boot they made a mark. That's when we began to learn what the Japanese were really like.

'I was seven months in Java, and then two months going on boats to Japan. That was the worst part of my life as a prisoner of war. We were incarcerated in a ship's hold, 60 feet by 80 feet [18m by 24m], along with wet iron ore. It was soaking wet, riddled with rats, and illness gradually attacked us. The boat was called the *Di'Nichi Maroo*, it means Great Day, and was about 3,000 to 4,000 tons. It had a thousand prisoners and twelve hundred Japanese troops on it. We were down in the hold, and there were four holds on this ship. We set off, dressed for the tropics, up to Japan in winter.

'It was hot to start with, then it was wet and cold and the rain used to pour down through the open hatch. It wasn't too long before illness started to hit us, in the form of dreadful diarrhoea. The worst cases were taken up on deck and when they died they were thrown overboard. This went on for the whole voyage of about five weeks. By the time we got to Japan, I do not know how many we had lost from the boat, though it was not the end of the illness.

'We were about 350 men, 100 in my group, 100 in a second group and a third group of 150. In our group we had 8 die very quickly. In the second group they lost 23. In the group of 150, they lost 35.

'That was the state of our health when we arrived in Japan. It was absolutely appalling. On one Boxing Day my head was against a thin bit of plywood in the hut I was in. The other side of this bit of plywood was a man screaming his guts out every minute, then silence for a minute.

'I worked in a Japanese dockyards for more than three years, about 24 miles from a city called Hiroshima. The island we were on had little hills on it, so you would not see a bomb going off 24 miles away. You would not see the cloud for that matter. We saw the actual aircraft come over. We were accustomed by now to being bombed by the Americans. Tactin, the dockyard, was actually attacked twice, strafed very seriously, and we often saw formations of six hundred B-29s coming over in perfect formation.

'Then this particular morning, August 6, 1945, we saw one aircraft come over. We thought that was very odd, and no doubt we heard the atom bomb go off, but we were so used to hearing these huge explosions around us, we didn't know it was a single aircraft dropping an atom bomb.

'We learned quite soon afterwards, of course, because the war came to an end. There is no doubt that dropping the atomic bomb on Japan was the best possible thing that could have happened for the Far-East prisoners of war. If the Americans had not had the atom bomb, they would have had to invade Japan.

'When you think of the tremendous casualties that the Japanese and the Americans suffered in fighting their way back through the islands to Japan, the death toll of Japanese and Americans in an invasion of the homeland would have been unbelievable, a million men. Of course, they would not have had time to deal with us prisoners of war.

'There is no doubt about it, the moment Japan was invaded we would all have been exterminated. I am very grateful for the atom bomb.'

Chapter Seventeen

BURMESE DAYS

When Last Witness Tom Neil left Malta he had one important task to undertake:

'I went down to the local church and I lit a candle. I prayed to God that I would never have to fly a Hurricane again. His reply was to send me to Burma!

'I flew with one or two Indian Hurricane squadrons with the Arakan Wing in Burma. I didn't fly very much. I was there purely to test the water. I didn't go out there to fight. Those Hurricanes did a good job because there were no Japanese aircraft there to fight.'

Whatever Tom Neil's views, understandable after eight months hard fighting over Malta flying clapped-out Hurricanes against a superior Bf 109, Burma was where Hurricanes had a second coming. They turned out to be almost perfect for the terrain and the type of fighting that evolved.

It was not such a happy experience in the beginning, in 1942. The victorious Japanese Army, having consolidated its conquest of Singapore, advanced up through Malaya and deep into Burma, heading for India. Last Witness Eric Batchelar was 20 years old when he flew a 17 Squadron Hurricane from Egypt across India and down to fight the Japanese, arriving there in January 1942:

'By the time we got to Burma, the Japanese were operating from the other side of the Gulf of Matapan, from Moulmein, which was in reach of their aircraft range.

'They had every advantage over us. Numerically, they were enormously superior. We had no early warning, no radar. Half the time we were caught with our trousers down. Rangoon's airfield at Mingledon was attacked daily – either bombed or strafed by fighters. Very often it was a bit of a chance whether you managed to get off all right.

'The day after we arrived, just after an air raid occurred, we were in the thick of it. The first time I got engaged in a fight was with an Army 95, a nippy biplane. I had climbed up high and I happened to spot, low down below me in the hazy murk, a single Army 95. I recognised it straight away, it had a fixed undercarriage. I did everything by the book, got up-sun, set everything up, went down on the blighter – going far too fast – blazing away. Damn me, he twizzled around and had a good go at me at the same time. We did that two or three times.

'We had been advised right from the start that with these older Japanese aircraft, you did not want to mix it with them. They were too agile, so it was a case of dive and zoom. I did that three times, and each time we blazed away at each other. On the third attack I lost him completely in the awful heat haze we had out there, a haze that went up to 10,000 feet [3,048m] or more. I hope to God I did more damage to him than he did to me, because I had quite a few holes when I got back to base.

'Apart from air-to-air fighting, we were also doing escorts to the small light bomber force – the Blenheims. They flew across to Moulmein and tried to catch the Japanese on the ground on their own bases. We also did a few strafing sorties, some of which were hair-raising. Japanese flak was very effective.'

As Japanese troops neared Rangoon, 17 Squadron flew defensive patrols until the airfields were overrun. Burma's air defences had been initially entrusted to the 16 fat little Brewster Buffaloes of 67 Squadron RAF and the 21 Curtis P 40 Kittyhawks of the American Volunteer Group.

Eric Batchelar:
'In Mingledon there was a dreadful shortage of aircraft all the time. We never had sufficient aircraft, nowhere near enough. We were operating with an element of the AVG, the American Volunteer Group – Pershing's "Flying Tigers" – volunteer Americans who were flying Tomahawks. They were paid by the kill, so they were very keen chaps, and most of them were bloody good pilots. But we gradually had diminishing resources, losing friends virtually every day.

'One of our flight commanders, Watson, just went missing on a strafing sortie. We never did hear what happened to him. Life was so chaotic, we were surviving in the best way we could, living for the moment.

'Soon after I got there, the ploy was that we had to get the aircraft off the strip at night, otherwise they could be obliterated by a night bombing attack. We used to fly them out to roughly prepared strips in the paddyfields, and then go out before dawn the next morning to fly them in again. Life was terribly hectic, you never had a moment to think. We were pretty confident in ourselves, but we realised that, numerically and in every other way, we were fighting a losing battle.

'With diminishing resources, it was not long, about a month after I arrived there, that we had to start moving to rear bases up in the middle and the top of Burma, places like Prome and Bak and eventually to Magwe. By the time we got to Magwe there were only enough aircraft left to support one squadron, and 17 Squadron was chosen to remain there. The rest of us were evacuated by whatever means possible.

'I got a lift in a Blenheim out to Akyab, and from there I flew in an ancient old Vickers Valencia, in an open-cockpit all across the Sundamanns back to Dum-dum near Calcutta. We eventually reassembled, re-formed and re-armed at Dum-dum over the next six months.

'We felt then that the Japanese had over-stretched themselves, so we thought they would try bombing raids on Calcutta. Our first concern was the air defence of Calcutta. The only way we could do this, without radar, was to mount fighter night sorties, stacking up Hurricanes at 2,000 foot [610m] intervals all the way up to 20,000 feet [6,100m]. They patrolled as long as they could, in the hope that if anything came in, somebody – up or down – would make contact.'

By the end of May 1942, 17 squadron had re-assembled at Calcutta and in June received Hurricanes again for the defence of the area. The Hurricane squadrons in Burma were reinforced at a rate of 50 aircraft a month, despite heavy demands from Russia and the Middle East. There were difficult problems operating from rough jungle airstrips, with monsoon weather and limited ground support.

Eric Batchelar:
'I had occasion once or twice where I went down to strafe some activity that was going on at a jetty-point at Akyab. It was only when I climbed up and re-joined the rest of the formation – I had taken a section down myself to make the attack – and the rest of the flight closed up to have a look at me, that they saw holes in the back of my hood.

'One bullet had gone through, clipped the back of my helmet, and came out the other side. It was right where my head should have been, had I not leant forward to look through the gun-sight. The chaps had a great laugh, saying that if the bullet had gone in one ear and out the other, it wouldn't have hurt me anyway. It had been good marksmanship from the ground by the Japanese.

'It was not long before the end of 1942 that I was picked out from 135 Squadron to become a flight commander in 17 Squadron, taking over 'A' Flight. This is when Bush Cotton was squadron commander, and they had, like us, re-formed and re-equipped. Most unusually, they were operating from a long straight road right in Calcutta, known as the Red Road.

'It was the former approach road, with a slight camber on it and stone balustrades on either side, leading up to the Governor's Palace in the Maidan, the big central park area that comes right into the heart of Calcutta. This leads up to the main street, Chowringee; 17 Squadron were operating from this street in the heart of the city.

'It was a bit like operating from The Mall, leading up to Buckingham Palace, in London. I had the unique thrill of operating Hurricanes out of the middle of Calcutta for a couple of months, which was unforgettable. Coming in on finals you were flying through blocks of flats on either side, and landing on the camber was particularly tricky. The whole exercise may have been a morale-booster for the teeming local population, trying to keep them calm, to show them they had some form of defence.

'Came the time to move out from the Red Road, 17 Squadron was put out on this Acorn strip in the paddyfields. We sent detachments of aircraft, six at a time, out to the forward bases in Chittagong and Cox's Bazaar, front-line bases, for short-term detachments. Things had quieted down, it was probably the monsoon season.

'From a flying point of view, the monsoon was absolutely horrific. I would not recommend flying in it to my worst enemy. It was horrible. We flew whenever we possibly could, but some of the monsoon cu-nims went up to 20,000 feet [6,100m]. There was one occasion when there was a flight of six Spitfires, in transit back to Calcutta from the front area, and they ran into cu-nims.

'They were all destroyed, blown apart by the weather.'

After initial success with overwhelming air power, swarming all over the Hurricane defenders in Singapore and the Dutch East Indies, the Japanese air force had much of the life sucked out of it in big naval battles in the Pacific with the US Navy. The Japanese withdrew their air force back to begin defending the homeland. It became rare in Burma to come across large formations of Japanese in the air, but the intensity of the ground fighting did not lessen.

Eric Batchelar:
'We never had any radar assistance of any kind, we had poor HF radios in the aircraft, not terribly reliable and not long range. The areas we flew over, in long sorties up and over the Chin Hills and down into the river valleys on the other side, were poorly mapped, and anyway they were just vast expanses of jungle-covered hills. There were few landmarks, so navigation was always a problem.

'One of the most helpful features I found after a while was the contours of the hills, big things like that. You got to recognise the contours on the horizon, and had a rough mental knowledge of where you were and where you were going.

'Our targets were supply columns. The rivers were pretty vital means of supply for the forward Japanese land forces, in many areas the only means of supply. We had to keep going on them to catch them moving material up and down the rivers in Sampans.'

By June 1943 there were 16 Hurricane squadrons in Burma, including 11 Squadron, which flew the first tank-busting Hurricane IIDs in the region, carrying 40mm cannon. Japanese tanks were considerably smaller than Germans, and poorly protected against air attack with heavy cannon.

Eric Batchelar:
'We became aware of a change in the way we fought after we were moved from the Acorn strip to a place called Argatale, an airfield in the mid-to-northern part of Burma. It was from there that we mounted never-ending, long-range ground-attack sorties, up and over the Chin Hills to interdict the supplies on the rivers. The Japanese soon got used to this. We were the first to discover the trick they used of putting up trip-wires over the rivers, trying to catch us when we were flying low-level up and down them. We had to keep a sharp eye open for those.

'On most of the sorties, we usually found something to shoot up. Some of the trips were three hours or more, and we were getting back to base with very limited fuel supplies. It really was a bit nerve-wracking. The thought of being brought down by small arms fire, or mechanical failure, was always there. If you survived a crash landing, there was little prospect of continuing to stay alive in this awful jungle. We wore a harness with survival kits strapped to us, and a gun-belt with a revolver and a big jungle knife.

'In that particular phase, which went on for six months, we didn't lose any of our pilots, after which senior officers decided to pull us out and give us a rest, because they realised what a strain it was, doing that kind of work over that particular terrain.'

By now the Hurribomber's standard operation was 80 per cent close support of the army. Air superiority had been established, and the local Japanese troops were starving in the jungle, where IFF - Identification, Friend or Foe – was by coloured smoke.

Bob Doe:
'The Hurricane was very good at ground strafing. At one stage we were carrying two 500lb [227kg] bombs, and four 20mm cannon, and they were very effective. We didn't really see a lot of the results because we flew over the

jungle all the time. The army would tell us where to bomb, what to do and where to strafe. I only saw the effects of this on one occasion.

'All supplies came in through Akyab, and we were south of there. The ship that was carrying the fuses for our bombs had been misloaded, and as a result they had a thousand tons of coal on top of the bomb fuses. We ran out of fuses, and I got very cross about that, so I went to Group and protested at the armaments officer. He said, "Well, I have got some fuses here, but they are air-burst fuses, and they can't be fused safe."

'I said we'd try and use them. We had a get-together with the pilots and the armament chaps, and the pilots all agreed we needed to pattern bomb. We couldn't risk dive bombing with these fuses. We might put pressure in the wrong place and blow them up in the air.

'We only really got results when we bombed the headquarters of one of the Japanese divisions, and dropped our bombs smack on target next to the river. We went down afterwards to have a look, and found a completely flattened headquarters, and a launch in flames on the river. We wiped the whole lot out completely.

'The Hurricane was much better than the Spitfire for ground attack, because it was sturdier. A Spitfire was a dream machine, but it could only carry one bomb, against two for the Hurricane. We were pattern bombing, carrying 24 500lb bombs which were very effective.'

The Indian Air Force was supplied with Hurricanes, ending the war with eight Hurricane squadrons. They fought alongside RAF Hurricane units in the fierce battles of February 1944, to relieve the siege of Imphal.

Last Witness Bob Doe:

'I didn't like the way things were organised in England after the Battle of Britain. I didn't like this idea of 'Big Wings'. It took away a pilot's initiative. I liked to be able to do things my way, not the way I was told. That was why I volunteered for Burma. At that time I had two DFCs, and was an acting squadron leader, and I was sent to India.

'There, I formed 10 Squadron, Indian Air Force, and we were deployed at Risslepore on the north-west frontier. We were then posted down to Bihar where we were changed from being a fighter squadron to a bomber squadron – flying Hurribombers, Mark IIs with four 20mm cannon – and eventually posted to Burma, stationed at Rhamu, just inland of Cox's Bazaar.

'Our first operation was just before Christmas, 1944. We decided to have a party, and the ration was one bottle of beer per man. This was only if you were British, Indians didn't get anything. I accidentally returned all the Indians in my squadron as British for the drink ration. We did two operations that first day. The first one was bombing a Japanese storage dump, and then a short while later I was asked if we would go into the Calidan Valley, where the Eighty-First West African Division had been cut off by the Japs. They wanted aircraft there to help them break out. I went in first to tell them a safe place to build a runway, which had to be sheltered from the Japs by a hill, so that they couldn't shell us on the ground. We also wanted a flat approach, because we would have to fly in there with bombs on board, and start the aeroplanes using our internal accumulators, which one normally never did.

'I sited the runway alongside a river, flew back, and a week later we flew in with a squadron. I landed and a dust-cloud came up, I taxied to the end, and four Hurricanes taxied up with me, and then nothing else. I walked back into the dust, and found that a chung, an underground river, ran under the runway. It had collapsed, so my rear seven or eight aircraft were in heaps, down a hole. They were not badly damaged but as far as we were concerned they were a write-off. The West Africans just picked them up, took the guns out, and dumped the rest in a local river.

'They adapted the guns, which were very good against Japanese trenches; a 20mm cannon shell would penetrate where a 0.303 bullet would not. The West Africans went out of the way to give us cover, while we slept. They even gave us their parachutes – from dropped supplies – for our beds. They were wonderful.

'Around midnight the Japanese started shelling us, but the hill sheltered us. Eventually the divisional doctor came around and invited us to the only place they could black out, the local temple, and there he had some medical supplies, rum. We had a pleasant experience drinking that rum, and then went back and fell asleep.

'Next day I was woken at dawn with a big mug of sweet tea. We took off from what was left of the runway, hit our targets with bombs and strafing and the division managed to break out.'

The Hurricane's role was now defined as an army co-operation aircraft with missions usually conducted at tree canopy level. The system of calling up close air support by the soldiers at the front was perfected and greatly aided the 14th Army's advance back through Burma.

By contrast to the way young pilots with ten hours experience – such as Last Witness Bill Green – were thrown into the Battle of Britain in 1940, in 1944 there was a proper system, taking 18 months, to get flyers to the front line with enough skills to have a chance of surviving. Last Witness Colin Ellis had been a 16-year-old schoolboy in the East End of London looking up at the Battle of Britain in 1940, and had been taught to fly in Rhodesia before arriving in Imphal by lorry in September 1944. From Imphal, he and three companions were posted to 113 Squadron at Palel, at the southern end of the Imphal Valley. He did a sector recce on 6 October 1944, and two days later had his first operation flying a Hurribomber:

Colin Ellis:

'The war in Burma was so different from the war in Europe. In Europe, the fighter-bomber, such as Typhoons – successor to the Hurricane – was shot out of the sky left, right and centre. The Germans had such accurate low level and high level anti-aircraft guns. In Burma there was none of that, apart from going over towns like Rangoon. We never did that, because we were close support to the army.

'It was compensated for by the fact that the terrain – the jungle – was so vicious, as also was the climate. Flying in the monsoon, they never dreamt of doing that in peacetime, yet we went straight through the monsoon season. Thick cloud goes from ground level up to 30,000 feet [9,144m]. Apart from anything else, Thunderbolts and Hurricanes didn't have the oxygen, because there was no necessity for it. We normally never went above 6,000 feet [1,828m].

'The Hurricane was a very comfortable aircraft to fly. I felt totally safe in it. By comparison with the Spitfire, you could probably call the Hurricane a very good point-to-pointer horse, whereas a Spitfire is a thoroughbred race horse. At one time I thought the Spitfire was the finest thing I had ever flown, and it was a very nice aircraft, but I got more attached to the Hurricane.

'It was the sheer fact that it was such a reliable aircraft, easier to take off and land with its nice wide undercarriage, which suited the airfields in Burma, where the bulk of my flying took place. I can recall very few occasions when a Hurricane had to drop out and return to base because of engine trouble. Of course, that is down to the excellent servicing by the ground crew.

'Personally I never ever had a bullet hole in my aircraft. All the time I was flying, the Japanese were in retreat. The most offensive weapons they would have had were hand-held machine guns. There was no ack-ack, as it was known in Europe. Mind you, when you've got a great big engine roaring away, you don't know what's going on around you, or how much is missing you.'

Gawain Douglas, oldest of the Last Witnesses, had moved from a posh cavalry regiment and dropped a rank to fly in the RAF, but had been kept out of the fighting for three years following jaundice and malaria, working instead as an instructor.

In 1944, frustrated about not being able to fight, he beat up his airfield in a Tiger Moth, including a flight through hangars. The authorities were furious but he eventually won through, learning to fly a Hurricane at the end of September 1944, after which there were so many trained pilots that he had to wait, fearful he would never see action at all. In early 1945 there was a vacancy in 60 Squadron flying Hurribombers, and he joined on February 20, 'plastering the buggers' three to four times a day.

Gawain Douglas:
'When I moved to 60 Squadron, the CO there – a New Zealander – gave the impression of not wanting to fly any more. He had done plenty of good work in the past and now he was very happy to stay on the ground, and for me to take all the flights I wanted. I really hogged my hours in March 1945.

'The equipment we were getting was rejected or not wanted in the West. They were getting the newer stuff, anything older we got. We still had Hurricane IIBs which they were flying in 1942. Cost and availability was a factor. But we had a job to do and we did the best with what we had.

'Morale was incredibly good, despite having nothing to make it good. We were luckier than the PBI – the poor bloody infantry – living in muddy water-logged foxholes. We came back to a tented camp at the end of a runway that had been hewn out of nothing. It had PSP on the ground, perforated steel plating, where the ground was soft or dusty, otherwise an aircraft would sink up to its axles, so we ran on a metal-jointed runway put together like a Meccano set.

'There was no air opposition from the Japanese any more. There were a few high-flying reconnaissance aircraft, but there was never anything, even for Spitfire pilots to do in the way of air-fighting, so they were also fitted with bomb racks. Like the Hurricanes, they became Spit-bombers, carrying a 250lb [113kg] bomb. They had four cannon, the same as we did on the Hurricanes.

'Our job was to be called in by the army. Attached to every army unit there were former pilots. We would have their wavelengths and they would have ours, and when we were in the area they would call up, "We see you now. The part where the opposition is coming from we will mark with yellow puffs of smoke," or anything, in fact, that you could see above the expanse of trees. Then we knew exactly where they wanted the bombs placed.

'I never had any "friendly fire" incidents. When we came over, everything went quiet on the ground. We went in first of all with the bombs and plastered the area, and the effect was said to be that of a ground-attack earthquake, especially when medium bombers, higher up, also dropped their stuff.

'Our approach to the target depended on the bombs we were carrying. If we were carrying NITI's – Nose Instantaneous, Tail Instantaneous – nose hit the ground and it went Boom! Like that. We had to drop NITI's from a little higher up and get the hell out of it before we were blown up by our own bomb.

'Another bomb type had 11-second delays, and were more generally used, but that depended on the situation on the ground. We seldom used NITI's.

'There were only six of us in a flight. We would go in singly, not in pairs, following each other. We would make two or three passes, with a minute or two under fire. We dived from 2,000 feet [610m] from a mile [1.6 km] away, not in a steep dive, but the main thing was to get the bombs on the area we were targeting. By the time six aircraft had gone around the Japanese would have experienced a dozen bombs of very high explosives. In their foxholes it was enough to stun them – easy meat for the army which would immediately come in as soon as we stopped bombing. We were that close to our own army.

'From our point of view, you didn't see anything come up in the way of flak, but they were firing back as was proved by the casualties we sometimes had. In the air we heard nothing of the noise of the attack and didn't see much either. We saw buildings sticking up out of the jungle, and it was only really outside the jungle that we actually saw the target. I never saw the Japanese on the ground, except once or twice. They were all concealed. They were waiting, of course, fanatical little chaps. You'd be firing at them and they were firing straight back, even if they were going to meet their deaths. They were tough opponents.'

Graham Skellum, a 21-year-old sergeant pilot with 113 Squadron, started the first of 136 operations in Burma on 2 September 1944, flying Hurricane IICs with cannon. His logbook is full of B&S – Bomb and Strafe:

'I was always involved in ground attack. Our sorties lasted about an hour and ten minutes. With the air superiority at that time, we could land without any difficulty. In fact, I used to please myself by gliding my Hurricane into land. I didn't switch the engine off – it was just ticking over – but you could glide in the Hurricane when you got used to it.

'We used 11-second delay bombs, and over the terrain we were sent to, they were ideal. You could dive down to 200 feet [61m], release the bombs, and they wouldn't explode until we climbed away.

'Then we had cannons. We had to be careful firing the cannons, which we could not fire in long bursts. You could quickly get a stoppage, and when that happened, the wing that didn't have a stoppage swung around, you couldn't keep it straight.

'We seemed to move every six weeks, chasing the Japanese. There were no Japs to prevent us doing that, so it was obvious we were getting close to the end of the war. We dropped bombs on Japanese targets, then circled around and sprayed them with machine guns. Sometimes doing three flights a day; on the short distances, targets were often so close the ground crew could see the attacks.

'Getting hit didn't happen to me, I was fortunate. I didn't consider the danger. I was only 22, and at that age you think you're immortal, so you didn't worry about things like that.

'If you survive a war, it's not bad, is it? We were successful in what we did, and that's a good war. We only had occasional deaths. One was an officer who joined us, B. T. Smith. We used to call him "Big Time Operator" because he did a lot of talking. Then he didn't come back.

'There was Bruce Reid, a Canadian in "A" Flight. He was late taking off. He tried to catch up and did a roll to build his speed up but he had got two bombs under the wing and that stopped him pulling up and he hit the ground. It didn't blow up because he hadn't made the bombs live but he hit the ground because the bombs prevented the aircraft from climbing.

'There was one youth, I think his name was Bailey, he crash-landed a Hurricane. Never got to the target, and he put down on one of the rivers in Burma. When it was not the rainy season, there was lots of sand on the bends. He put down on one of those sandbanks without a really good explanation. A couple of months later he was dismissed from the RAF for LMF – Lack of Moral Fibre – so not everybody put up with the fighting conditions there.

'But to me, the thought of coming home, having been dismissed for LMF, what do you do? What does your family do? You can't live with yourself, can you?'

Last Witness Tom Adams had spent half the war as an instructor in America, finally reaching the front line to make his first operational flight at the age of 22 after VE day, Victory in Europe Day, on 5 June 1945. Flying ground attack under army co-operation, he made 30 operational flights, and never met any Japanese aircraft.

Tom Adams:
'The hairiest moment for me was when flying over the Mawchi Road between Toungoo and Mawchi, firing at Japanese troops – they were not visible, you couldn't see them, but because of transports and that sort of thing, you knew they were there. Having fired into the bases of the trees, I pulled up to get over the hill … and the engine stopped!

'I was on the auxiliary fuel and the auxiliary tank had fallen off. A lightning switch to the main tank and I was all right, the engine re-started, but it was not the happiest of situations. Japanese soldiers were never likely to take kindly towards a downed British pilot who had just been strafing them. That really could have been quite difficult. It didn't occur to me at the time.

'The Japs were a different breed from everybody. They did not believe in surrendering. That was a difference really, and if you got into their hands, they were not going to treat you very well, were they? The Burma Railway showed their typical behaviour, and the prison camps that they had were ghastly. So it was as well not to fall into their hands. That was one of the differences between fighting in Europe and fighting in the Far East. Germans did behave badly on some occasions, but the Japs behaved badly on all occasions.

There were near-death incidents almost every day among the Hurricane squadrons, some of them with amusing conclusions.

Tom Adams:

'We took off together. I was on the starboard side of my section leader, Harry Smith, and we were staggered slightly. As I got to 150 feet [46m], only three wing lengths away, I found I was having to go slower and slower, just to stay in formation.

'Then suddenly Harry dipped down out of sight. I was left there, just off the stall, a mere 150 feet above the ground. Fortunately I was able to open the throttle and gain some speed, go around and come in and land safely. Harry landed quite successfully in an open space beyond the airfield, no problems with trees or anything. His engine had abruptly stopped, and he had had no power to stay up.

'After he landed, two men came running towards him – British Army men, there to protect the airfield. When Harry took his helmet off, one of them said, "Sergeant Smith!" Then he turned and ran like the wind. Harry, an ex-policeman from Essex, had apprehended this man before the war on some crime. Harry hadn't remembered, but the man had. Harry Smith was a good friend. One day he just never came back.'

There are always close calls in any war, but taking to a parachute over the Burmese jungle was particularly hazardous. Records published years after the end of the war showed that, of 176 pilots who bailed out or came down in Japanese-occupied territory or over the Burmese jungle, 166 were never located or seen again alive. Only ten survived. One was Last Witness Colin Ellis:

'We had crossed the enemy lines on the River Chindwin at 6,000 feet [1,828m], so we were over Jap-occupied territory. In the usual fashion, the Squadron Leader gave the order to form into line astern. This meant, instead of two groups of six, you became line astern, each of us in line and below the one in front.

'During that operation, I collided with my Number Two. I am still not sure why this happened, but my tail was chopped off and I immediately went into a flat spin. I could see the stick flapping around with no assistance, and immediately decided to get out. There was no way of controlling the aircraft. I went straight over the side.

'At the briefing at base before the operation, we went to collect our parachutes – normally we left our parachute in the cockpit – and my locker was empty because my parachute was being re-packed. I had grabbed the parachute from the next locker. I am 5 feet 6 inches tall [1.7m], and the chap whose parachute I grabbed must have been about 6ft 2 inches tall [1.9m]. All the lower parts of the harness worked perfectly well, but the shoulder straps were very, very loose. When I left the aircraft and was tumbling through the air, the shoulder straps fell off and the whole harness went right down to my feet. I came down head first.

'Every time you went on an operation you signed for a pouch which contained silk maps, rupees and all sorts of things. You usually stuffed that down your front, and that fell away from me that day.

'By the time I was down to about 1,000 feet [304m], upside down, hanging from my harness by my feet, the aircraft had crashed and was burning fiercely in country that was covered with jungle. Fortunately, as I came through the trees head first, I wasn't hung-up. Otherwise I would have been in a right pickle. I got out of the harness, and on an occasion like that you think there's a Jap behind every tree. It was not the case, the jungle was perfectly neutral. It would casually kill either nationality.

'I got away from the site because the aircraft was blazing. Any enemy who wanted to get there had a good marker. I travelled for about half an hour and then holed up in a dry river – they're called Chongs in Burma – and I sorted out my kit. We wore an escape kit, like a pair of overalls but with a lot more pockets. It had everything in it that I needed. We had about six compasses. One was a marching compass, then an ordinary compass, then a pencil that broke in the middle with a compass in it. I had a sensitised magnetised needle which, put it on a leaf on a pond, would rotate and give me north. We had fly buttons back then, not zips, and I could take two off, and one would spin around on the other and also give me a compass. I was well-equipped there.

'I knew more or less where I was – that's the beauty of being in the air force – being close to the front I had a complete knowledge of everything that was going on. It was hilly countryside with ridges going north and south, and I wanted to go west. I decided I would go up and down these ridges. If anybody was moving around in places like that, they kept to the valleys.

'From that time onwards it was climbing up one side, and sliding down the other. It took me five days to get back to our lines. At night, I had to sleep on the ground or any shelter I could find. I would pack up about four o'clock in the afternoon. I had emergency rations – Horlicks tablets and barley sugar – and worked out that if I rationed myself to two Horlicks tablets for breakfast plus a barley sugar, and repeated that at lunch, and in the evening I had at least 12 days of rations which I could rely on. But, in fact, I was not really hungry.

'As for water, I had a water bottle and sterilising tablets, so I could fill up in any stream, feed the tablets in, and after half an hour I could safely drink the water.

'I met no one until the late afternoon of the fourth day. I was coming down a dry riverbed with a little trickle in it, and turning one corner, I bumped into two Burmese. They were as surprised as I was. I got out my phrase book, part of the escape kit, and did the famous "take me to your leader" question.

'They looked after me. I slept that night on a bamboo platform under a grass "basha" hut. There were 13 of us, the head man, his wife and family. With the phrase book, I asked for guides to take me back. They provided me with two guides and we set off quite early the next morning, and climbed to the top of one of the ridges. It happened that the Japanese and the British were exchanging artillery fire, and we were just under the trajectory of the shells. I knew it was all right, but my guides didn't like it. They did not want to hang around, so I gave them one of the tins of rations that I had.

'I was getting a bit tired by now, the fifth day, and I thought I would go further downhill to hit the river. It was very wide, 200 to 300 yards [182 to 274m], but there was only water in the middle because the monsoon had gone through months ago. On each side there were sandbanks and it was easy to see across to the other side. I could see it was the West Africans who were pushing the Japanese back.

'I had not been walking very long when there was a burst of machine gun fire, and sand was spitting up all around me. I dived down into a gully and got out my head-dress, put it up on my kukri and waved it. This only attracted more fire. I stayed there for half an hour. I discovered a gully on my left and thought I would make a run for that, which I did, and I wasn't followed. I honestly think it was our people who were firing at me, because I was on the enemy's side of the river.

'I got back into the jungle and walked parallel with the river for an hour or so. I came to a point where it was obvious that the Japanese had had an encampment. Fortunately, they had retreated. I could see across the river, which was obviously the advance headquarters of the West African fighting troops. I shouted across.

'As it happens, they were already alert to keep a look out for a couple of pilots who had come down. They sent a boat across to collect me.

'The jungle just swallowed you up. There was no possibility of forced landing and getting away with it. You could get hung up in the trees and that was it, you had your lot. I was one of not quite six per cent, who survived. My number two, whose aircraft had chopped up my tail, was never found.'

Last Witness Gawain Douglas was lucky to survive the consequences of one trait of a Hurricane, that in some circumstances it leaked deadly carbon monoxide into the cockpit.

Douglas survived an extraordinary crash, hitting a tree at 300 mph (482 kph). That he lived at all was a tribute to the toughness of Sydney Camm's great fighter. It was the last flight Douglas made in a Hurricane:

'We had carried out an attack on a strongly-defended Japanese position at Mount Poupa, in central Burma and were headed for home. We were flying back at 4,000 feet [1,219m], beyond the range of small-arms fire. It was an easy flight back in an open formation. I wasn't worried about anything.

'My pilots told me later that they saw my aircraft go into a slight dive. They followed me down from 4,000 feet, wondering if I had seen something and was chasing it. As my aircraft dived, it started to turn right – because of the torque action of the Merlin engine – and it went into a very wide spiral dive, the radius of half a mile. They started calling me, thinking I had seen something Japanese, asking what I wanted – line astern? Should they stay with me? Of course, they were getting no answer at all from me.

'I had apparently passed out. It was later determined that a hole in the manifold had caused gasses to seep into the cockpit and over-power me. The aircraft continued its downward spiral at more than 300 mph, until the starboard wing hit a palm tree and was torn off. The aircraft went straight on but it was cart-wheeling and somersaulting at high speed across dried-up paddy fields, shedding bits as it went. The next bit torn off was the second wing, and then the engine cowling in front of the bullet-proof windscreen came away.

'Underneath the wheels and radiators were torn away, then the tail unit fell away, leaving just the cockpit, with me sitting in it. We were right way up, still skidding like a toboggan across these paddy fields, slowing all the time, and eventually it stopped.

'My pilots flew around in the circle, and thought I had had it. There were only bits and pieces of the Hurricane left, scattered over a mile and a half [2.4 km]. They could see me thrown over the engine panel, no movements, straps broken. There was no way, in their minds, I could be alive.

'They reformed and went back to base. They reported that they thought the CO had had it. They had marked on their maps where the incident had happened.

'I woke up on the ground. I don't know how long I had been unconscious, but I was lying on the ground with a circle of brown faces looking down on me. The people were friendly and there was a Burmese girl who was a student at one of their colleges and could speak some English. They were able to tell me where the nearest RAF airfield was, and said they would try and get me to a road where I could be shipped back as some of our transport had been seen moving up and down the previous day. It was late afternoon, and it was no use trying to get me to safety that day because the Japanese were in the area at night.

'The girl went away to see her father in a nearby village, to ask permission for them to shelter me. They ran great risks themselves doing so. He came back with them and I was brought into the house with the wife and daughter and other members of the family. I had a good night's sleep. I fell asleep almost immediately in this tiny room they had given me, despite the rather superficial injuries I had suffered. I had a lot of blood on my face from cuts, and skidding marks from where I had been rattled around unconscious like a pea in a pod.

'The doctor I finally spoke to said the reason I had lived through this event was probably because of the slow deceleration. If the aircraft had hit a bank or a tree or a big rock that stopped it instantly, I would have been flattened. But the cockpit section, which was quite strong, had survived all the bumps from the somersaulting.

'When they examined me in the hospital after I got back to base, they found carbon-dioxide in my blood. This was when they put two and two together. The Engineering Officer had come out to see what had happened to the aircraft, and where I was. He discovered the bullet holes in the manifold, so they knew then that's how it happened.

'As far as that accident was concerned, I didn't get pains in my neck for six years. I was in a shipping company after the war, and suddenly got terrible pains. I could not lie down at night. The pain was worse in a horizontal position. The doctors, when they looked at me, said, "When did you break your neck?"

'I told them I had never broken my neck and they said that lots of people had done it falling out of trucks and tanks and jeeps during the war. They fall awkwardly and they fracture their vertebrae. Two of my vertebrae had ground together during the crash and had since fused. All they could do was go in and chip away the ossification in my neck, and hope it wouldn't deteriorate.'

Chapter Eighteen

TYPHOON AND TEMPEST – CHILDREN OF THE HURRICANE

Pierre Clostermann, the French fighter ace and author of the best-selling *The Big Show*, missed the Battle of Britain, but was deeply involved in air fights against the Germans later in the war, first flying RAF Spitfires, later Tempests. His account of the poor operating performance of Hurricanes against the Germans in France at the end of 1943 dramatically illustrates how quickly aircraft performance was moving on.

Hawker Typhoons and Tempests, children of the Hurricane, were capable of more than 400 mph (644 kph), but some unfortunate RAF squadrons in Europe were still flying Hurricanes.

On 28 October, the RAF found the first evidence the Germans were building V-1 rocket sites launching 'Doodlebugs' as Vengeance Weapons aimed at London. The French coast between Boulogne and Cherburg was dubbed the 'Rocket Coast', and attacks against the launch sites were called 'No-ball' operations.

Pierre Clostermann:

'Gradually every kind of aircraft was mobilised and thrown against the "Rocket Coast", and 184 Squadron with its old Hurricanes was soon sent into the fray. With their four 60lb [27kg] rockets, the miserable machine dragged along at 200 mph. Exceptional nerve was needed against the German flak at ground level and at that speed.

'With childish levity and spite we poked fun at the pilots and their misgivings. These misgivings were all the more comprehensible as they were beginning to receive their new Typhoons and it was really a bit hard for them to get shot down just as their dreams were about to be recognised.

'We didn't laugh long at their expense. On 4 December 1943, eight Hurricanes had just crossed the French coast when ten Bf 109Gs attacked them. 184 Squadron, with Squadron Leader Rose at their head, defended themselves tooth and nail. Weighed down by their bombs and with only eight 0.303 inch guns against the Germans' three 20mm cannon and two 13mm machine guns, the Hurricanes hadn't much hope of coming through. Six Hurricanes were brought down and the other two crashed on landing, both their pilots seriously wounded by enemy bullets.

'And we laughed quite on the other side of our faces when it was decided that in future the Hurricanes would be escorted at ground level by Spitfires!'

Clostermann, from a covering Spitfire, described what happened to the clapped-out old Hurricanes on 20 December 1943, 16 days later, in a No-ball attack with 15 light flak guns defending.

'The Hurricanes began their dive, slap into the machine-gun bullets. The tracer bullets formed a wall of steel and explosive round the target.

'The inevitable happened. Powerless, I watched the tragedy. Flight Lieutenant Roughhead, just as he let go his salvo of rockets, was hit and killed instantly. His disabled Hurricane recovered with incredible violence and zoomed vertically upward, its propeller stationary. At the top of the trajectory one wing wilted, the aircraft hung as on a thread suspended in space, motionless, then went into a spin.

'As in a nightmare I saw Warrant Officer Piece's Hurricane literally mown down by a burst of 37mm. The tail came off, the machine crashed into a wood, scything down the trees, scattered jets of burning petrol.

'The other two Hurricanes attacked simultaneously. Struck by a direct hit, Sergeant Clive's machine exploded and was soon nothing but an inchoate mass of flame, dragging a long trail of black smoke.

'By a miracle, Bush the Australian was luckier; he succeeded not only in placing his eight rockets in the control room but even in extricating himself from the barrage of flak, in spite of the enormous gash in his fuselage, not to mention two bullets in his thigh and one in his side.

'I sat there, petrified, flying mechanically. Everything had happened in a fraction of a second.'

The Hurricane had two successors, the Typhoon and the Tempest, both designed by Sydney Camm. The Typhoon was credited with a vital role in the success of the Normandy Landings after June 6, 1944. The Tempest was rated the fastest piston-engined aircraft ever flown in the RAF.

The Typhoon, designed as a fighter interceptor but which evolved into a fighter bomber, first flew on 24 February 1940, and went into service in 1941. It was designed to be a direct replacement for the Hurricane fighter, but several design problems were found – in some early models the tail fell off! In May 1940 the prototype suffered a mid-air structural failure at the join between the forward fuselage and rear fuselage, just behind the pilot's seat. Hawker's chief test pilot, Philip Lucas, could see daylight through the split. Instead of baling out, Lucas chose to fly back to base and land the stricken Typhoon. He was later awarded the George Medal.

Despite these serious failings, the Typhoon won the support of distinguished pilots such as Roland Beamont. Through their dedication it established itself in new roles such as night-time intruder and a long range fighter. From late 1942 the Typhoon was equipped with bombs; from late 1943 rockets were added to the Typhoon's armoury.

Using these two weapons the Typhoon became one of the war's most successful ground attack aircraft.

Even before the new Hurricane was rolling off the production lines in March 1937, Sydney Camm had contemplated a private venture replacement, a big fighter designed around the powerful 24-cylinder Napier Sabre engine, developing more than 2,000 hp.

The Sabre-powered aircraft, with a chin-mounted radiator, combined traditional Hawker techniques – Sydney Cam's aircraft always showed their parentage – with more modern building techniques, allowing easy access on airfields to all the complicated parts that made up a modern fighter aircraft. The thick, strong wing allowed plenty of room for fuel and heavy armament, and under-pinned the Typhoon's quality as a steady gun platform.

Although the new fighters were expected to reach top speeds of 460 mph (740 kmh) in level flight it soon became apparent that once 400 mph (644 kmh) was reached the thick wings created a large drag rise, preventing any further speed increases. In a dive at speeds of over 500 mph (805 kmh) this led to buffeting and trim changes. Tests showed the Typhoon could reach 410 mph at 20,000 feet (6,100m), although the climb rate and performance above that level was disappointing. Instead of a sliding or lifting canopy the Typhoon was first produced with forward opening side doors, complete with wind-down windows, along with a transparent 'roof' hinged to open to the left.

The Typhoon 1A was armed with twelve 0.303 inch Brownings, soon superseded by four 20mm cannon on the Typhoon IB.

The loss of entire tail sections of some early aircraft occurred mainly during high-speed dives. It was caused by a combination of factors, including vibration leading to metal fatigue, and a weak transport joint just forward of the tail-plane. Typhoons were modified and did gain the trust of many pilots, but some tail failures occurred right up to the end of the aircraft's operational life.

They cost at least 25 aircraft and the lives of 23 pilots.

From early 1943 the wings were adapted to carry 45 gallon (205 litre) drop tanks, the same as those fitted to long range Hurricanes. They increased the Typhoon's range from 690 miles (911 km) to up to 1,090 miles (1,754 km), enabling Typhoons to range deep into France, the Netherlands and Belgium.

As production continued, the Typhoon's role changed from a low-level interceptor fighter to a fighter bomber. Bomb racks capable of carrying 500lb (227kg) bombs were fitted to the wings from October 1942. By mid-1943, all Typhoons off the production line were capable of carrying bombs.

The larger tail planes of the Hawker Tempest were fitted from June 1944. These improved the handling characteristics of the Typhoon when carrying 1,000lb bombs. Originally they were only used on 'Bombphoons'.

In June 1943 Hawker fitted a Typhoon with steel 'Mark I' rocket rails, four under each wing. Trials showed that the combination of the RP-3 rocket and the stable, high-speed platform of the Typhoon was promising. Carrying eight rails and rockets reduced the top speed by 38 mph (61 kph), with no adverse handling effects. By D-Day, 2 TAF – the Second Tactical Air Force – was able to field 11 RP Typhoon squadrons and seven 'Bombphoon' squadrons.

Once Typhoons started operating from forward landing grounds in Normandy, dust clouds stirred up by propeller-wash contained 80 per cent of hard, abrasive material which damaged the Sabre engines. Sleeve valves were subject to excessive wear, and some engines only lasted three take-offs! To fix this a 'dome deflector' was designed at great speed by Napier and fitted on most Typhoons within a week. In operational service these mushroom-shaped filters, which became red hot, could be blown off the air intake at high speed whenever a Sabre engine backfired. They were soon replaced by drum shaped filters, with 'cuckoo clock' doors in front able to cope with engine backfires.

When the Typhoon entered fighter service it was found that carbon monoxide could seep into the cockpit, to repeat the type of problem that had nearly killed Gawain Douglas. Longer exhaust stubs were fitted in the Typhoon, and Pilot's Notes recommended flying with oxygen on at all times, no matter how low the pilot was flying.

The Sabre engine was also a constant source of problems, notably in colder weather when it was very difficult to start.

Not until the end of 1942 did the Typhoon begin to mature as a reliable aircraft, when its good qualities eventually became apparent. It was extremely fast, tough and capable. During early 1943, Typhoon Squadrons on the south coast were finally effective in countering the *Luftwaffe*'s 'tip and run' low-level nuisance raids, shooting down a score or more fighter-bomber FW 190s. During a daylight raid by the Luftwaffe on London on 20 January 1943, five FW 190s were destroyed by Typhoons.

As soon as the aircraft entered service it was immediately apparent the profile of the Typhoon resembled a FW 190 from some angles, and this similarity caused more than one friendly-fire incident with Allied anti-aircraft units and other fighters. This led to Typhoons being marked up with high visibility black-and-white stripes, applied to all Allied aircraft on D-Day, although this did not help one Last Witness later in the war.

There was soon no demand for the Typhoon as a pure fighter, and it was developed as a fighter-bomber, much like the Hurricane had been. The powerful engine allowed the aircraft to carry a massive load of bombs equal to that of light bombers of only a few years earlier. The 'Bombphoons' were joined by 'Rocketphoons'. In October 1943, 181 Squadron made the first Typhoon rocket strikes. Although the projectiles were inaccurate and it took some skill to aim properly, as an official report put it, 'the sheer firepower of just one Typhoon was equivalent to a destroyer's broadside.'

Going into 1944, 18 rocket-equipped Typhoon squadrons formed the basis of the RAF's ground-attack arm in Europe. Though they were not outstandingly accurate, the 60lb rockets, backed by the Typhoon's four 20mm cannon, proved highly effective against targets like unarmoured vehicles, road transport, trains and small sea craft. Great things were expected against the heavily-armoured German tanks, but only the thin-walled engine compartment, or the tank's tracks, were vulnerable to the rocket attacks. Analysis of destroyed tanks after the Normandy battle showed a 'hit-rate' for the air-fired rockets of only four per cent

The Typhoon IB, modified with a four-blade propeller and teardrop Perspex canopy, distinguished itself in the Battle of Normandy. By D-Day, on 6 June 1944, the RAF had 26 operational squadrons of Typhoon IBs. It became the most effective RAF tactical strike aircraft on raids deep into Europe prior to the invasion, and in direct support of the Allied ground forces after D-Day.

'Overlord's' Commander, US General Dwight Eisenhower, was full of praise.

'The chief credit in smashing the enemy's spearhead must go to the rocket-firing Typhoon aircraft of the Second Tactical Air Force. The result of the strafing was that the enemy attack was effectively brought to a halt, and a threat was turned into a great victory.'

The top-scoring Typhoon ace was Group Captain John Baldwin, CO of 123 Typhoon Wing, who claimed 15 aircraft shot down between 1942 and

1944. Typhoon pilots claimed a total of 246 kills. Typhoon production, almost entirely by Gloster Aviation, was 3,330 machines. Yet once the war in Europe was over, the RAF was quick to remove the aircraft from front line squadrons. By mid-1946, the Typhoon was no longer in use as an operational aircraft.

Hawker developed an improved version which Sydney Camm intended to call the Typhoon II, but the differences between it and the Typhoon I were so great that it was effectively a different aircraft. This became the Tempest, which went into service with the RAF in January 1944.

The Typhoon II new design was finalised by October 1941, and the name changed to Tempest in January 1942. More prototypes with various experimental changes were ordered, because there was such huge demand for engines. Six prototypes were ordered with different engines, so if there was a delay in the delivery of one type of engine, another could take its place. The engines were a Sabre IV, two Centaurus IV's, a Griffon IIB, a Griffon 61 and a Sabre II.

The first Tempest prototype flew on 2 September 1942. This aircraft retained the Typhoon's framed canopy, a car-type door, the Sabre II engine and the characteristic 'chin' radiator. It soon had a bubble canopy, and tailfin area twice that of a Typhoon.

The Tempest was a great improvement over the Typhoon in sheer performance. Test pilots at the A&AEE reported in February 1943 that they were impressed by 'a manoeuvrable and pleasant aircraft to fly with no major handling faults.' The Air Ministry had already ordered 400 Tempests in August, but production of the new Sabre IV engine ran into protracted problems and delays, and as a result the second prototype, with the Sabre IV did not fly until 24 February 1943. This prototype also had the older Typhoon cockpit and vertical tail-plane. Elimination of the 'chin' radiator did much to improve performance and the Tempest Mark I was the fastest aircraft Hawker had built to that time, reaching 466 mph (750 kph).

Meanwhile, Hawker went into production with the Tempest V with a Sabre II engine. The first rolled off the production line on 21 June 1943, delivered with a long-barrelled 20mm cannon. Later production aircraft used the short-barrelled 20mm cannon, which eliminated the protruding barrels.

Some of the assets of the Tempest V were its high cruising speed, nearly 400 mph (644 kph) in level flight, good acceleration, and excellent climbing and diving speeds, especially at low to medium altitudes. All of these are vital in aerial dog-fights.

The first Tempest Mark II flew on 28 June 1943 powered by a 2,520 hp Centaurus IV radial engine driving a four-blade propeller. The radial engine installation owed much to examinations of the captured FW 190s, and was clean and effective. One adopted feature was the use of individual exhaust stubs, laid out in a row down either side of the fuselage. In spite of the promise of a more reliable power-plant than the Sabre, problems continued with overheating, unreliable and leaking exhausts, insufficient crankshaft lubrication and propeller reduction gear seizures.

Physically, the weight of the Tempest II with the heavier Centaurus engine – 2,695lb (316kg) versus 2,360lb (164kg) – was offset by the absence of a heavy radiator unit, so the Tempest II was only 20lb (9kg) heavier overall than the Tempest V. Performance was improved; maximum speed was 442 mph (711 kph) at 15,200 feet (4,633m), and climb rate to the same altitude took four and a half minutes compared with five minutes for the Tempest V. The ceiling was increased to 37,500 feet (11,430m).

The first production Tempest II was rolled off the line on 4 October 1944, a long-delayed 15 months after the prototype's first flight. With the end of the Second World War in sight, orders for the Tempest II were trimmed or cancelled; after 50 Tempest IIs had been built at Bristol's Banwell facility, production was stopped and shifted back to Hawker.

A total of 452 Tempest IIs were built, mostly by Hawker, powered generally with Centaurus V engines, and of that number, 300 were completed after the war. The Tempest II, despite its slightly improved performance and better reliability, never saw combat. Tempest IIs produced during the war were intended for combat against Japan, but the Pacific war ended before they could be deployed. The RAF passed 89 Tempest IIs to the Indian Air Force in 1947, while another 24 went to the Pakistani Air Force.

The Tempest V was in the hands of operational squadrons by April 1944. Number 3 Squadron was the first to be fully equipped, closely followed by 486 (NZ) Squadron, the only non-RAF unit to be equipped with the Tempest during the Second World War. A third unit, 56 Squadron, also moved to Tempests, where they formed 150 Wing RAF under the command of Wing Commander Roland Beamont.

In June 1944 the first German V-1 flying bombs were launched against London and the Tempest's excellent low-altitude performance made it ideal for dealing with these small fast-flying unmanned missiles. Tempest squadrons racked up a healthy percentage of the total RAF kills over the flying bombs, knocking out 638 of a total of 1,846 destroyed by aircraft.

The Tempest was also deployed in support of the Allied armies advancing across northern Europe. In December 1944, the first month of operations, 52 German fighters were downed and 89 trains destroyed, for the loss of 20 Tempests. Following the Ardennes Offensive, 'The Battle of the Bulge', on 1 January 1945, Tempests bore the brunt of low-to-medium altitude fighter operations for 2 TAF.

Last Witness Bill Green, then 27 years old, was involved in this fighting. Green, whom we last saw shot down twice in Hurricanes during the Battle of Britain, had managed to get back into the front line after years of effort.

Bill Green:
'I genuinely felt guilty that I had been shot out of the sky twice on Hurricanes, even if the first time was by our own flak, before I had an opportunity to prove to myself – and my son, I had a son by that time – I couldn't bear the thought of finishing the war without proving myself to him.

'The bravest thing I did throughout the whole of the war was struggling, battling, lobbying to get out of Training Command, which was worse than getting out of jail. Many people were happy to stay there because it was a cushy job, training other people to go and face the horrors of war.

'Eventually, after a lot of hard lobbying, I used the old boy's rules. I knew a Canadian, Buck Ryan, who got posted to the famous 56 Squadron, flying Tempests, and he got me a posting to his Squadron. If they asked for you, you would get the posting. If you asked to go, you had no chance.

'I did a conversion to Typhoons, and then a conversion to Tempests, which were wonderful aeroplanes. They had everything. I had three hours on the Tempest and then went over to Holland to join 56 Squadron, and later in the morning I went straight into action. That went on until 22 February 1945.'

In the Ardennes Offensive, 900 German aircraft attacked 15 Allied air bases in Belgium and France, destroying 194 RAF and USAAF aircraft. It was a costly victory, because the Luftwaffe lost 300 of their own aircraft, and 255 air crew.

Bill Green:
'During the Battle of the Bulge and the Ardennes Campaign, we were in Volkel in Holland, and the wing commander flying was going nuts. The Americans in the Ardennes were screaming for air cover. Eventually, with the cloud at about 500 feet [152m], maybe less, we said we would go down. It was ridiculous, we were so low that there was no way we could help them. We got over Belgium and the tops of the slag heaps were disappearing into the clouds, so the CO turned back.

'We went back, but 486 New Zealand Squadron, part of 122 Wing, flying Tempests, they said, we'll go down, and they did. Eight aircraft went down.

Six of them were shot down by American ground fire.

'That was a deadly evening in the Mess. There were apologies flying left, right and centre but it was a bit late.'

For a while, in March 1945, a strict 'No, repeat, No ground attacks' policy was imposed; this only applied for a few days.

Bill Green:
'My squadron was involved in strafing anything of a military nature on the ground that moved. I cannot say I was good at it, though I did a lot of operations, at least once a day, sometimes twice. German ground flak was devastating.

'On one occasion we were being led by somebody who should not have been leading us – he got blind drunk every night and drank until he dropped – and I didn't rate him sober, much less half-sober. He was our leader at the time. We went out on a foray and there was a train between two forests. The train was stationary, and when we came back it was still there. I thought, that had got to be a decoy.

'But he ordered us to attack it and personally led that attack, and of course, all hell broke loose. The woods were full of flak guns, and it was like rain. The Germans were virtually asking us to attack the train. I always went in at about 50 feet [15m] – the lower you were, the safer you were. The flak was going past me just like hailstones. I had my head well down out of sheer self-preservation. I could not believe I would not be hit, and I wasn't hit. I should have been riddled.'

Given the trigger-happy state of American ground forces, and Bill Green's history with Hurricanes, there was a certain inevitability about what happened to him less than three months before the war ended.

Bill Green:
'I got shot down for the third time on 22 February. We were involved with some Americans flying Mustangs, and friendly fire did for me. I could see this American Mustang and he could see me, but before I could do anything there were flashes at his leading edges and instantly my wing was hit.

'There were six holes in the port wing, each about an inch and a half wide, through which I could see a blue flame. There were no flames outside. I kicked on rudder and dived down to about 400 feet [122m] to avoid any further damage from the American. I was watching the instruments to see if I could assess the damage, and mentally going through the getting-out procedure.

'Suddenly, I felt heat searing my face. Time to get out.

'The technique in the Tempest involved a hood release toggle, and you simultaneously pulled the toggle and the pin of your Sutton harness, which held you in the aeroplane. At the same time, you kicked the stick forward. One minute you are strapped in to a giant fighter aircraft doing 400 mph, the next minute you are not strapped in, the hood has gone, the aeroplane has gone into a vertical dive and you are shot out over the tail-plane, hoping you won't hit it. I didn't.

'First thing I saw was the pack of my parachute, seemingly about 12 yards [11m] away, and my mind instantly went back to 1940. I knew I was not very high off the ground, so I pulled the rip-cord, it opened up and that was it.

'The Germans captured me immediately. I hit the ground and the first thing you had been taught to do was to pull the parachute together and bury it. If they found it, they would look for you. I put my hands up to pull it down and a voice shouted "Halte!"

'You would normally expect troops being attacked by aircraft to be hostile to a pilot they shot down, but they were not hostile. Then again, they hadn't shot me down, an American had done it for them. We were in the middle of a wood.

'The German said, "Are you armed?"

'I said, "No."

'He said, "You can put down your hands. I speak English better than you do. I was educated at Cincinnati University, in the USA."

'I thought, "Yanks again!"

'He marched me to a farmhouse and that began my three or four months of incarceration, an exciting and dangerous time. I think the Germans knew that their time had come. We were addressed by a German officer in perfect English, as we were being en-trained for PoW camp. He said, "If we get into a railway station, get on the floor, don't let the civilian population see you. They are very hostile because of the damage you people have been doing."

'And indeed, they were hostile.'

The top scoring Tempest pilot was Squadron Leader David C. 'Foobs' Fairbanks DFC, an American who joined the RCAF in 1941, and suffered the same fate as Bill Green. When he was shot down and made a PoW in February 1945, he had destroyed 11 or 12 German aircraft (and one shared).

Tempests scored a number of kills against the new German jets, including the Me 262. Hubert Lange, a Me 262 pilot, said: 'The Messerschmitt 262's most dangerous opponent was the British Hawker Tempest — extremely fast at low altitudes, highly manoeuvrable and heavily-armed.'

Some were destroyed with a tactic known to 135 Wing as the 'Rat Scramble'.

When a Me 262 was reported airborne, 'Rat Scramble' Tempests took off. They did not intercept the jet because they did not have the speed, but instead flew towards the Me 262 base at Rheine-Hopsten. They planned to attack the jets on their landing approach, at their most vulnerable, travelling slowly, flaps down and incapable of rapid acceleration.

The Germans responded by creating a flak lane of over 150 quadruple 20mm (0.79 in) guns at Rheine-Hopsten, to protect the approaches. After seven Tempests were lost to the flak at Rheine-Hopsten in a single week, the 'Rat Scramble' was discontinued.

The last piston-engined fighter in RAF service was a Tempest VI. A total of 1,702 Tempests were built

However well her children did, the last Hawker Hurricane was built before its descendents really began to show their paces in Europe. 'The Last of the Many' came off the Hawker production lines at Langley, in Slough, Berkshire and made its first flight on July 22, 1944.

It is still flying.

Chapter Nineteen

HURRICANE FIGHTER ACES

Fifty-eight pilots achieved ten or more victories flying Hawker Hurricanes. The top-scorers came from all over the world to fly and fight in Sydney Camm's great aircraft, and include an American, a Canadian, two Poles, two South Africans and a Czech.

The Last Witnesses account for three of the top-scoring pilots.

Billy Drake claimed four destroyed and one probable in the Battles of France and Britain, though shot down and wounded himself. He shot down a Vichy French aircraft over Sierra Leone in 1941 flying a Hurricane II, but thereafter flew Kittyhawks and later Spitfires and Typhoons, ending the war as a Wing Commander with a total score of 24.

Tom Neil, who features strongly in the Battle of Britain and Malta chapters, achieved most of his 18 claimed kills in Hurricane Is.

Bob Doe scored his first 12 victories in the Battle of Britain on Spitfires, but thereafter led Hurricane squadrons and later Hurricane wings through the rest of the war. He was credited with 14 kills and two shared.

The highest-scoring RAF pilot of the war, the so-called 'Ace of Aces', with most of his kills on Hurricanes, is almost the least known. This is possibly because he scored his first 17 victories – unbelievably – on the biplane Gloster Gladiator.

Geoffrey 'Pat' Pattle was born on July 23, 1914 in South Africa, and joined 80 Squadron in the Middle East and later Greece in 1940. He and his fellow pilots made mincemeat of the Italian CR42s biplanes and of the Fiat G50 monoplanes they came up against when Italy entered the war in June 1940. He had 17 solid claims – all against Italian aircraft – flying a Gladiator.

On 20 February 1941, Pattle took a flight of six Hurricanes into battle in Greece, and he operated there for the rest of his short life. On 12 March, having won a bar to his DFC, Pattle was promoted Squadron Leader and left 80 Squadron to command 33 Squadron. In the eight weeks between acquiring Hurricanes and getting killed, Pattle destroyed 25 aircraft in the air, including 13 'destroyed' against the Luftwaffe. These included five Bf 109s, three Bf 110s, three Ju 88s, a He 111, a Do 215, five 'probables' and five destroyed on the ground. He was shot down at the age of 26 on 20 April 1941, overwhelmed by large numbers of German Bf 109s and 110s.

Until recently he was virtually unknown. He is credited with 41 kills but he could, said his fellow pilots, have honestly claimed 60.

Geoffrey 'Sammy' Allard was born in York in 1912 and joined the RAF as a Halton apprentice in 1929. In 1936 he was accepted for pilot training and graduated as a sergeant pilot. 'Sammy' Allard fought in France with 85 Hurricane Squadron and shot down at least ten enemy aircraft. He was awarded the DFM and promoted to Flight Sergeant. He fought in the Battle of Britain, and shot down a total of 19 destroyed, five shared kills and two 'probables'. Commissioned in August, 1940, he flew to the edge of exhaustion, and was famously found after landing following a hard day's fighting, so exhausted he was asleep in his cockpit. Pilot Officer Allard, DFC, DFM and bar, was killed with two other Battle of France pilots in March 1941 when a nose panel came off their Douglas Havoc on a routine flight and jammed the rudder; they spun in.

Douglas Bader was born in London on 10 February 1910, and graduated from RAF College Cranwell in 1930, just having failed to win the Sword of Honour. In 1931 he had both legs amputated, one above, one below the knee, after a flying accident, and was invalided out of the RAF, working for Shell Oil. In 1939 he used his Cranwell connections to be accepted as a fighter pilot, and made his first two kills with 222 Spitfire Squadron. At the end of June 1940 he was posted CO of 242 Hurricane Squadron. He claimed 12 victories in the Battle of Britain on Hurricanes. By the time Bader was shot down in his Spitfire V in August 1941 (possibly by accident by a fellow RAF pilot called 'Buck' Casson of 616 Squadron), Bader had claimed 22 ½ kills, then the fifth highest score in the RAF. He remained a PoW for the rest of the war, led the Victory fly-past in 1945, and retired to work for Shell Oil. He was knighted in 1976, and died of a heart attack in September 1982.

Frank Carey, who became famous as the 'Cockney Fighter Ace', was born on 7 May 1912, in London, the son of a builder. He joined the RAF as a 'Halton brat' at the age of 15, was selected as a sergeant pilot in 1935 and became an aerobatics expert with 43 Hurricane Squadron display team. He was commissioned in 1940, and flew in the Battle of France, scoring 14 kills before being shot down and wounded. After being listed as 'missing, believed killed' he escaped from France along with 'three other derelicts' in a biplane Bristol Bombay, to find he had been awarded a DFC and bar to add to his DFM. He flew through the Battle of Britain until 18 August, when he was shot down again and more seriously wounded. Later in the war he was sent to Burma, and by the war's end he was a Group Captain with 25 kills and at least two shared, awarded a CBE, DFC and two bars, DFM and AFC. After a successful career in the RAF and afterwards, he died at the age of 92 in December, 2004.

Michael Nicolson Crossley was born in Warwickshire on 7 May 1912, educated at Eton College and was a flight commander with 32 Hurricane Squadron when the war broke out. He shot down six German aircraft by the beginning of June, 1940 – including four Bf 109s – and claimed another 10 by 18 August, though he was twice shot down himself that month. Known as the 'Red Knight' – he commanded Red Section of 32 Squadron – Crossley was credited with 20 kills and two shared kills, all on Hurricanes. He had won the DSO and DFC before being taken off operations in 1943, suffering from tuberculosis. He later won the OBE, was invalided out after the war, and went to live in South Africa where he died in 1987.

Jean Demozay was born in Nantes, France, on 21 March 1916, called up for military service in 1938 and invalided out a month later. When war began he was seconded to 1 Hurricane Squadron as an interpreter, supposed to be on non-combat duties. With the fall of France he escaped to England and passed himself off as a real fighter pilot, flying under the name 'Moses Morlaix' to stop German reprisals against his family, still in France. He was sent on a Hurricane II conversion course and scored three kills that winter flying as a 'Jim Crow' with Unit 421. He moved to 242 Squadron for three more kills, also on Hurricane IIs, then moved to Spitfire Vs with 91 Squadron. By the end of the war he was credited with 18 destroyed, two probables and four damaged. He was killed in a flying accident in December 1945.

Josef Frantisek, a Czech pilot who became the highest-scoring fighter pilot in the Battle of Britain, was born in Moravia, Poland on 7 October 1914. He joined the Czech Air Force in 1936, fled to Poland in 1938, escaped to France after the German invasion and claimed 11 victories – not confirmed – flying with the *Armee de l'Air*, winning a Croix de Guerre. He escaped to England, was assigned to 303 Polish Squadron, but was deemed too dangerous and stroppy to fly in formation. He operated as a sergeant pilot and a loner, and in the next 30 days he shot down 17 destroyed and 1 probable, to be awarded the DFM. He was killed the day after his 26th birthday on 8 October while landing at Ewell in Surrey, either because of battle fatigue and exhaustion, or manoeuvring to impress a girlfriend. Frantisek was the first foreigner to win a DFM and bar.

Jim Hallowes was born in Lambeth, South London on 17 April 1912, and became a 'Halton brat' in 1928, qualifying as an RAF aircraftsman metal rigger in 1931. In 1935 he was selected for pilot training, and when the war broke out he was a sergeant pilot with 43 Hurricane Squadron. Hallowes won his first DFM in June 1940 over France, after his engine stopped and he was in flames, shooting down a Bf 109 before he parachuted out; he and his German opponent landed in adjoining fields. By September, 1940 Hallowes was credited with another 10 or 12 enemy aircraft. He was awarded a bar to his DFM, commissioned, and thereafter he flew mainly Spitfires with 165 and 222 Squadrons, one of which he commanded. He was later awarded the DFC. Credited with 22 kills, Hallowes retired from the RAF in 1956 as a Wing Commander, and died on holiday in Tenerife in October, 1987. In recent years he had become friends with Julius Newmann, a German pilot he shot down over the Isle of Wight in 1940.

Petrus Henry Hugo, known as 'Dutch' Hugo, was born on 20 December 1917 in Cape Province, South Africa. He came to England in 1938 to join the RAF, and was sent to France to fly Gladiators with 615 Squadron in December 1939. Eight days after the *Blitzkreig* started the squadron received nine Hurricanes, and flying one of these two days later, Hugo shot down a Heinkel 111. He was wounded twice in the Battle of Britain, where he had seven victories in a Hurricane, and later moved to lead a Spitfire Wing in the Middle East. His score at the end of the war was 22 destroyed, four probables and 13 damaged, and he had a DSO and three DFCs. After retiring as a Group Captain, he was last heard of in East Africa in the 1950s.

Karel Kuttelwascher, 'Old Kut' was born in Czechoslovakia on 23 September 1916. He flew first with the Czech Air Force, then with the French, then as a Sergeant pilot with 1 Hurricane Squadron but missed the Battle of Britain. His first victory was on 8 April 1941 on convoy patrol from Croydon, downing a Bf 109; he shot down two more in the next eight weeks. In 1942, flying night-fighter, four-cannon Hurricanes IICs – without radar – Kut specialised in haunting German airfields in France and knocking down night bombers either landing or taking off. On one occasion he got three in four minutes. He had 18 confirmed victories, won a DFC and bar and the French *Croix de Guerre* and after the war became a pilot with BEA. He died in 1960, only 44 years old.

James 'Ginger' Lacey, born in Feb 1917 in Yorkshire, had a grammar school education and joined the RAFVR in 1937. He worked as a flying instructor until he became a sergeant pilot with 501 (County of Gloucester) Squadron. In the thick of it from the opening May 10, 1940 *Blitzkreig* that led to the fall of France, he was shot down a total of nine times! Between 12 August and 30 October he shot down 16 German aircraft, with four probables and seven damaged, including destroying the Heinkel that bombed Buckingham Palace on 13 September 1940. By September 27 he had 19 destroyed. On 4 October 1940 he crash-landed after being shot down by another Hurricane, having won a DFM and bar. He was commissioned in 1941 and his full score by the time the war ended was 28 destroyed, nine probables and five damaged. He remained in the RAF, retiring in 1967, then ran an air freight business. He died in May, 1989

Archie McKellar, born on 10 April, 1912 in Paisley, Scotland, worked for his father as a plasterer after leaving school in 1930. He was commissioned as an Auxiliary Air Force officer in 1936, joined 602 Hurricane Squadron, and on 28 November 1939 he was part-credited with the destruction of the first German aircraft – a He 111 – downed over British soil in World War Two. McKellar moved to 605 Squadron as a flight leader in early 1940, and fought all the way through the Battle of Britain, first with 13 Group, then with 11 Group. On 15 August 1940 he destroyed three He 111s and probably destroyed a fourth in one combat. On 9 September, operating out of Croydon, he shot down four enemy aircraft in a single fight, one Bf 109 and three He 111s. The first Heinkel exploded, downing the second, and McKellar destroyed the third in one single 12-second burst. On 15 September he destroyed two Bf 109s, a Dornier 17 and claimed a He 111 as a probable. That night he took off and shot down a He 111, earning a bar to his DFC. On 7 October he shot down five Bf 109s, four in less than 10 minutes in one battle, and won the DSO. His total was 21 destroyed, three probables and three damaged. Archie McKellar, DSO, DFC and bar, died on 1 November 1940, last seen as his Hurricane dived out of clouds and into a garden. A Bf 109 crashed nearby.

Stanislaw Skalski, the highest-scoring Polish fighter pilot of the war, was born on 27 November 1915, at Kodyma near Odessa in the Russian Empire.

He won his wings in 1938, and by 16 September 1939, became the first ace of the war by claiming seven kills with the Polish Air Force. Skalski escaped to England and joined 501 Squadron (Bill Green's squadron) on 27 August 1940, at Gravesend. In the Battle of Britain, flying Hurricanes, he was credited with four kills and one shared kill before being shot down and badly burned on 5 September, spending six weeks in hospital. In 1941 he was transferred to the all-Polish Hurricane 303 Squadron, where he went on to form 'Skalski's Circus' and shoot down a further 13 by the end of the war. He was credited with a total of 22 ¼ in all, became the first Polish pilot to lead an RAF Squadron, but was imprisoned by the Russians as an alleged spy when he went home when the war ended. Skalsi lived under a sentence of execution for three years but was released in 1956. The winner of a DSO and three DFCs, Skalski was made a General in the Polish Air Force in 1988. He died in Warsaw in November 2004.

Maurice Michael 'Mike' Stephens was born in Ranchi, India, on 20 October 1919, son of an Army officer. He graduated from RAF College Cranwell in 1940, and was posted to 3 Hurricane Squadron to fight in the Battle of France. He won two DFCs in a month for shooting down eight enemy aircraft, became a Squadron Leader at 20 years of age and was posted to the Middle East in 1941. On 9 December he shot down a Bf 109 while in flames himself, then baled out wounded and burnt. He landed within 300 yards (914m) of enemy lines, beat out his flaming clothing, and managed to get home. This won him a DSO. Stephens moved on to Spitfires in August 1942, fighting in Malta where he was again wounded. His total score was put at 17 kills, three shared kills, one probable and five damaged. He survived the war, retired from the RAF in 1960, and died on 23 September 2004.

Robert Stanford Tuck, whose epic duel with three Bf 109s featured in Chapter 1, was born on 1 July 1916, in Catford, London (16 days before Last Witness Gawain Douglas). Tuck joined the RAF in 1935, and became a highly skilled display pilot, twice surviving near-death collisions in the air. He flew through the Battle of France with 92 Squadron on Spitfires, but was then sent as a famous ace to command 257 Squadron flying Hurricanes. He claimed a total of seven kills, four probables and two damaged in his Hurricane period. He was shot down by ground fire on a 'rhubarb' over Boulogne in northern France in January 1942, spending the rest of the war as a PoW. At his capture he was credited with 27 kills, two shared kills, six probables and six damaged, and had won a DSO, DFC and two bars and an AFC. After the war he became a mushroom farmer, and was a technical adviser for the film *The Battle of Britain*. He died in May 1987.

Witold Urbanowicz, the second-highest Polish scoring pilot of the war, was born on 30 March 1908 in Olzanka in Poland, graduated as a pilot in 1932, and in 1936, by now a fighter pilot, he shot down a Soviet reconnaissance aircraft that had strayed into Polish air space (officially reprimanded, but unofficially congratulated by his CO). He escaped to France in 1939 when Poland was invaded, was then invited to join the RAF, and within eight days of becoming operational he shot down a Bf 109 and a Ju 88. Flying with 303 Polish Hurricane Squadron, by the end of October 1940 he had 15 confirmed kills and one probable, to put him among the top ten Allied aces. After being awarded a DFC and working as Second Air Attaché to the Polish Embassy in the USA, he was invited to join the USAAF in China where he fought with the 'Flying Tigers', claiming two Japanese Zeroes. After the war, returning to Poland, he was charged, like Skalski, with being a spy but sentenced to prison, not to death. When released he fled to the USA, was made a Polish General after the wall came down in 1989 and died in New York in August, 1996.

William 'Cherry' Vale was born in Chatham, in Kent on 3 June 1914. He joined the RAF as an aircraftsman fitter in 1931, trained as a pilot in 1936, and was commissioned in 1940 to join 80 Squadron, flying Gloster Gladiators with Pat Pattle. He scored his first ten kills in Egypt and Libya against the Italians, flying a Gladiator. Sent to Crete to fly Hurricanes in 1941, between 3 March and 12 June, Vale claimed another 20 kills against the Germans, although this included three Vichy French destroyed. Some records were destroyed when Crete fell, but Vale's score seems to have been 30 destroyed, three shared kills and six damaged. He survived the war as a Squadron Leader with a DFC and bar, but was killed in a motoring accident in November, 1981.

Lance 'Wildcat' Wade, the highest scoring American pilot in the RAF (who taught last Witness Bill Swan to fight), was born in Broadus, Texas, in 1915. He joined the RAF in Canada in December 1940. He was posted to Egypt in September 1941, flying Hurricane Is, and had achieved his first five kills, mainly against Italian pilots, by 24 November. In 1942, flying Hurricane IIs he had reached 13 kills, acquired the nickname the 'Arizona Wildcat' because of his aggressiveness in the air (for the geographically-challenged, Arizona is, after all, *next* to Texas) and had twice been shot down and walked out of the desert. He won a DFC and bar before being sent to the USA, resisting urgent invitations to fly with American squadrons. When he returned to battle in Italy in 1943, he flew Spitfire Vs and raised his total kills to 23 and one probable. By now sporting three DFCs, and CO of 145 Squadron, 'Wildcat' Wade was killed in a flying accident on 12 January 1944. He was awarded a posthumous DSO

Vernon 'Woody' Woodward, the second-highest scoring Canadian pilot of the war, was born in Vancouver, BC, on 22 December 1916 and grew up a crack shot with a rifle. He joined the RAF as a pilot in August 1938; of the 123 Canadians who were part of that expansion, 80 would die, many of them as bomber pilots. In June 1939, Woodward was posted to 33 Squadron in Egypt, flying Gloster Gladiators and, when Italy entered the war in June 1940, he ran up a score of five kills and two probables on Gladiators before converting to a Hurricane. In March 1941, 33 Squadron was sent to defend Greece and Woodward served under Pat Pattle; he was in the great fight over Piraeus in which Pattle died. With a score of 18 confirmed kills, four shared kills, two unconfirmed kills, three probables and 11 damaged, he won his last victory in July, 1941, before being sent to Rhodesia as an instructor. He ended the war with a DFC and bar, made a career in the RAF, retired in 1963, and eventually went back to his birthplace in Vancouver for a quiet retirement. He died there on 26 May 2000.

Chapter Twenty

AFTER THE WAR

A total of 14,533 Hurricanes were built. Including the Sea Hurricane, it was the most versatile single-seat warplane to emerge from the war.

The overwhelming majority of the Hurricanes, nearly 10,000, were built by Hawker at Langley in Berkshire, with its sister company Gloster Aircraft Co making 2,750 of the rest. Austin Aero Ltd built 300. The Canada Car and Foundry Company, in Fort William, Ontario, Canada – whose Chief Engineer Elsie McGill became known as the 'Queen of the Hurricanes' – produced 1,400 Hurricanes.

But when the war ended Hurricanes rapidly disappeared from the inventory of the RAF. The last unit, 6 Squadron based in Palestine, surrendered their Mark IVs in October 1947. Less glamorous than fighting icons like the Spitfire and Mustang, few Hurricanes were preserved to reach the 21st century. One reason was that construction techniques employed 70 years ago have made restoration a very difficult operation. After the war, surplus military aircraft of all types were hastily junked.

The majority of the remaining Hurricanes were simply burnt.

The cost of World War Two in blood and treasure was high.

The RAF lost 22,000 aircraft, the USAAF 18,000 and the Luftwaffe 57,000.

RAF Fighter Command lost 3,960 pilots.

A further 1,215 were wounded, and 601 became PoWs.

In all, 4,970 fighter aircraft were lost. This was the cost of defending Britain against her enemies. Carrying the fight to her enemies was much more costly; RAF Bomber Command lost 55,573 air crew, killed or missing.

Trafford Leigh-Mallory did not survive the war. He rose within the RAF until he was sent out to take over British air forces in the Far East with the rank of Air Chief Marshal. On 14 November 1944 he was killed in a Liberator crash on his way there.

In an irony of history, he was succeeded by Keith Park, who had scored as notable a victory in Malta (against the same opponent, 'Smiling Albert'

Kesselring) in 1942, as he had in the Battle of Britain in 1940. There was no job available for Keith Park in the RAF after the war. Seventy years later, with the erection of Park's statue in London as acknowledged victor of the Battle of Britain, it is tragic that the quiet New Zealander was never to know, when alive, such recognition.

The Hurricane's formidable designer, Sydney Camm, went on to create one of the most beautiful of all jet fighters, the Hawker Hunter, and the progenitor of the VTOL Harrier, the P1127. In 1953 he was knighted for his contribution to British Aviation. Camm once said the main requirements for an aircraft designer are 'a knowledge of aerodynamics, some elementary maths, and an eye for beauty.' He was planning the design of an aircraft to travel at Mach 4, four times the speed of sound, before he died in 1966.

Camm received the British Gold Medal for Aeronautics in 1949, was elected President of the Royal Aeronautical Society in 1954 and received its highest honour, the Gold Medal, in 1958. In 1966, Sir Sydney Camm was awarded the Guggenheim Gold Medal, the leading American aeronautical award, which had to be presented posthumously. He died at the age of 72, universally honoured.

Yet at some deeper level, according to Last Witness John Ellacombe, Sydney Camm harboured a resentment that his war-winning Hurricane fighter never had the glamour or the status of its supremely beautiful rival, the Spitfire:

'After the war, I was commanding the air fighting development squadron, flying different marques of Hunter and I used to go down and see Sydney Camm.

'He would always say, "Sit down and listen to what I have to tell you!" and rant away for about half an hour, an absolutely fascinating man.

'He told me how angry he was because the Hurricane was built to a specification which said you had to have two batteries of guns so they could re-load them quickly. The specification called for 90 gallons of fuel – the Hurricane actually had 94 gallons – and a wide undercarriage so you could land on rough fields. The Spitfire did not have all these features.

'He said the Hurricane was exactly right for the mission which they asked for in that specification. Yet all the credit for winning the Battle of Britain went to Reg Mitchell for his faster aeroplane, and not to Sydney Camm!'

A handful of Hurricanes were sold abroad post-war, the Irish Air Corps flew Mk Is and IIs alongside the Seafires they had also bought. Forty reconditioned Hurricanes were sold to Portugal and remained operational until 1950. Several returned to England where they became stars in the 1951 film *Angels One Five*. Reconditioned machines were also supplied to Persia, whose order for 16 Hurricanes in 1939 had been interrupted by the war after the delivery of only two machines. Forty Hurricane IICs were handed over to the Fighter Training School at Dosham Teppeh.

What of the Last Witnesses? In the last 70 years they have got on with their lives, some with memories dimming, others with recollections of their experience on Hurricanes so vivid they could have been gathered yesterday. Individual aircraft can come back to haunt them.

Bob Foster:

'Some years ago, a chap called Peter Basher called me and asked, "Did you fly with 605 Squadron?" I said yes and he asked if I ever flew an aeroplane with a certain registration and if he could come to see me about it.

'He came along, I looked up my logbook, and saw R4118. I said I had flown it many a time and he told me he thought he might have traced this aeroplane.

'I didn't hear much for two or three years. He said he thought he knew where it was but he wouldn't tell me. Then he phoned and said, "Okay, I've got the aeroplane back now."

'It turns out he was travelling around India and he happened to be at Benares University. In the back yard of the university was the wreck of an old aeroplane, just lying there. His friend said he thought it was a Hurricane fuselage. They searched around the wreck, found a number, did some detective work, and found out it had been a Hurricane made by Gloster Aircraft in 1940.

'It was delivered to 605 Squadron that August, and Basher built up its history from there. After three years of negotiation he managed to get this aircraft out of India where it had been rotting away since 1947. It had no engine, but he rebuilt it, and it is now flying around. It used to be my aeroplane. Its code is U-PW. It was restored by Peter Basher, and then sent to a place in Suffolk where they finished it off.

'I was flying that aeroplane when Bunny and I shot down that Ju 88. Other people used it, a chap called Archie Milne had a Bf 110 destroyed. The aeroplane had two or three confirmed kills and two or three damaged. I flew it over Eastbourne when we damaged a Heinkel. It's really an historic aeroplane.'

Bob Foster was credited with 2 ½ kills during the Battle of Britain, in which he felt that August was the worst month. He went on to 54 Squadron as a flight commander, and then to Australia as part of No1 Fighter Wing, based in Darwin until the end of 1943, which he found 'boring'. Flying Spitfires Vs, he shot down five Japanese aircraft and won a DFC. In 1944 he went into RAF public relations and was sent to Normandy to look after war correspondents.

He is currently Chairman of the Battle of Britain Association, of whom there are fewer than a hundred left alive.

Bob Doe went one further than finding an old aircraft, he found an old adversary:

'There was one occasion where we had a big dog-fight over the Isle of Wight. In a dog-fight I had made a rule, never to fly in a straight line for more than 10 seconds. I would have a snap-shot at anything that went across in front of my nose. A 109 came across, I had a quick snap-shot at it, and I know I hit it because a bit fell off it. This 109 then turned over and headed for the sea.

'I pulled out to the side of the dog-fight to watch it. When he got down close to the sea he turned and headed for home. I thought, you're not getting away, my friend, and I went down after him. It took me a long time to catch him and we were in the middle of the Channel when I did. He didn't realise I was there, I am sure of that. Eventually I got close enough and I had a quick burst at him, and astonishing things happened. His wheels came down, his engine stopped and his hood came off.

'I thought, no way could I go on shooting at a man who was as defenceless as this. It just was not in me to do that. I flew up alongside him and wished him luck. I knew there was an awful lot of sea out there, and then I headed for home, now very short of fuel.

'I saw him crash into the sea behind me. But he was picked up by his own side! Many years later I did a film called *Churchill's Few*, and described this situation. Someone took a copy of this film and he had friends in a flying club in Germany. He went out there and showed the film to the flying club. One of the Germans said: "That was me!"

'He turned out to be Adolf Galland's second in command, Rolf Pingel. I had a lovely letter from him, and eventually I had a lovely letter from his wife, thanking me for not shooting him down. She said that, without that, "I would not have had my lovely grandchildren."'

Bob Doe ended the war with a DSO and two DFCs and took a permanent RAF commission, until he retired as a Wing Commander in April 1966. He wrote about his wartime experiences in *Bob Doe – Fighter Pilot* in 2004, and was extensively quoted in Stephen Bungay's *The Most Dangerous Enemy* about his role in the Battle of Britain. He was also quoted in one BBC documentary saying, 'I wasn't fighting for the King, I was fighting for me Mum – I didn't want the Germans over here.'

Mike Croskell, having married his nursing sister sweetheart, went on to be an airline pilot amassing 17,000 hours on commercial aircraft.

Billy Drake survived being shot down in the Battle of France and went on to become the highest-scoring Kittyhawk pilot of the war. He led a Typhoon Wing in 1944, and ended the war on Eisenhower's staff, giving media a daily briefing on the war situation in the air. He served as an Air Attaché in various British consular posts, and retired from the RAF in July 1963 as Group Captain with a DSO, two British DFCs and an American DFC. He worked as an estate agent in the Algarve, and later chauffeured Rolls Royces until he was 85. Billy Drake wrote of his experiences in the book, *Billy Drake, Fighter Leader.*

Peter Ayerst's last sortie with 238 Squadron was on 18 March 1943, still flying Hurricane IICs. He was awarded his DFC in November 1944, having claimed nine destroyed, two probables and four damaged. Ayerst became a test pilot with Alex Henshaw at Hawkers in February 1945, but came to regret having left the RAF, so he signed on again, serving until 1973.

He joined his brother-in-law's firm of Chartered Surveyors, and spent three years helping the company to expand into Europe. His daughter married an Iranian prince, and Ayerst used his Iranian contacts for business introductions, but got out of Iran in 1979 because of the Islamic Revolution. He remained a go-between, facilitating contracts in the Middle East, and in 1991 he set up Ayerst Environmental to cope with asbestos problems. He is still connected with the company. At one point after the war, like Bob Doe, he met up with his old enemy.

Peter Ayerst:
'When we were fighting the Germans, our motto was, the only good Hun is a dead one. They were our enemy, they were trying to shoot us, they would have killed us if they had had half a chance. We were very anti-German at that time.

'The Heinkel crew that I shot down on 14 August 1940 all became prisoners of war and were sent to Canada. I met them 46 years later.

'It was started by a Welshman trying to find any aircraft that had been anywhere near the Welsh borders. He was picking up bits of aircraft and found some reference numbers on them. He then knew a Heinkel had come over, so he wrote to *Luftwaffe* HQ in 1986, and asked for the names of the German crew. He wrote to them all, and invited them over to Britain. Then he got hold of me. I had never met him before. He booked the Germans into a hotel near Chester, we went out and had a beer together. They were over for four days and they were a very good crowd.

'The navigator said, "Peter, in a year's time we are going to have another re-union but this time it will be in Germany and it will be in my house. Can you come?"

'I went, and they made a wonderful fuss of me. We met up three times, and I went twice to Germany.'

Colin Ellis completed 99 ground attack operations in Hurricanes, and 22 on Thunderbolts. His last Hurricane mission was on 4 April 1945, and he left the RAF the following year. He started civilian life as a draughtsman in a shop fitting company, and went on to work in design and layout, to become part of teams building new stores. He never went back to flying but in 2009 he retired after 21 years as secretary of the local RAF Association.

Eric Batchelar notched up 700 hours on Hurricanes, went on to teach air fighting, and emerged from the war with a Mention in Dispatches and a permanent RAF commission. He had a lifetime flying all the fast jets the RAF used, from Vampires, Venoms, Meteors, Javelins, Hunters and on to the Lightning, thoroughly versed in jet aviation.

He retired from the RAF in 1972 as a Group Captain at the Ministry of Defence, 'flying a desk' and went on to a 20-year career as a Planning Inspector for HMG.

There was one 'delightful period' between May 1958 to May 1960 when Eric Batchelar was in a position to air-test weekly both the Spitfire and Hurricane for the BBMF, the Battle of Britain Memorial Flight:

> 'When I went back to flying the lovely dear old Hurricane, it didn't seem as if there was anything to do! The cockpit was so basic, and yet when you got it off the ground the old feel came back again and it was simply lovely to fly.
> 'I was thrilled to bits to fly them again.
> 'Part of the enjoyment was going back to what I had flown as a young man. I think we all had great confidence in the ability of the Hurricane to stand up to damage. It was the best friend I could have had at the time. I loved it, a wonderful bit of machinery, it did its work extremely well, it looked after us. I would not have missed it for the world.'

Gawain Douglas came back from his 300 mph crash to be given command of 34 Squadron, RAF, promoted Squadron Leader flying Thunderbolts, which took over many of the ground-attack duties of the Hurricane in Burma as the war came to a close.

> 'Thunderbolts flew like bricks. They weighed seven tons, they had a high wing loading, they were not designed for low-flying and especially not for dive-bombing, but we did not have anything else. That was it. The CO I was replacing – when I was sent to 34 Squadron – had been killed "mushing in". He dropped a bomb, and while his aircraft's nose was pointing upwards it was still going down and hit the ground. This happened to many pilots flying

Thunderbolts. Hurricanes did not do that. But I liked flying them. They were marvellously comfortable aircraft to fly, cleaner that a whistle.

Inside, Hurricanes were awful. Junk used to get underneath your feet under all the girders, and when you flew upside down, all the shit fell on top of you, mud off an airman's boots, old nuts and bolts and whatever else. The Thunderbolt had a beautiful plywood floor. You could take a thermos flask and put it beside you.'

Gawain Douglas was awarded his DFC after the war ended, and went into shipping, and then construction, spending six years building dams in Pakistan. As an Army officer in the British Raj before the war, he had learned Urdu and Pashto, a useful skill in organising the labour forces there. He spent his career wandering the world, including the USA and Chile, always in construction, and married a number of times. He came back to England in 1993 to live in Kent, and in 1999 he met Anne, who was to become his fourth wife. He had first met Anne when he was 24 and ADC to Lord Erskine, the British Governor General of Madras in southern India. Anne's father headed the bodyguard to Lord Willingdon , a previous Governor General of Madras who went on to be Viceroy of India. Anne was 17 in 1938 when Gawain Douglas met her, and he was the first man in whose arms she ever danced.

The fortunes of war being what they were, it was ten years before they met again, when Anne was 27 and Douglas 34 and both were married to other people. 52 years after they last met, and 61 years after they *first* met, in 1999 they met again.

A year later, in 2000, they married each other. They live quietly in Lewes in Sussex.

John Ellacombe went on to be a Mosquito pilot, winning two DFCs, and was involved in some of the most daring Mosquito raids later in the war. Afterwards, he was awarded a permanent commission in the RAF, and rose to senior rank as an Air Commodore before retiring.

'I was in about 30 combats in Hurricanes in the Battle of Britain. Sometimes we were bounced by Bf 109s and, of course, the Hurricane could out-turn the 109. Much later on I met General Gunter Rall, the great German fighter ace, and he was interested in talking tactics. He said, "We couldn't out-turn the Hurricane, so we took the two guns under the wing off, so we could pull tighter turns, and we still couldn't out-turn the Hurricane. We could out-turn the Spitfire very easily."'

Tom Neil left Malta on Boxing Day in 1941, returning to England in early March 1942, via the Middle East, South Africa, West Africa and Canada. Later, he joined the 9th US Air Force, as a Flying Liaison Officer with the 100th Fighter Wing.

Post D-Day, Neil did some operational flying in France and, in March 1945, went to Burma to fly operational sorties with No 1 Indian Wing. He flew an Empire Test Pilots' course, and added to the two DFCs he won in 1940, when he was awarded the US Bronze Star, and the AFC.

Tom Neil retired from the RAF in 1964, as a Wing Commander. He is officially credited with 12 victories, four shared, with two 'probables' and several damaged.

His book about the Battle of Britain, *Fighter in My Sights* was published in 2001, and republished in 2010. It is quite brilliant.

Terence Kelly flew his last Hurricane in March, 1941, before becoming a Japanese PoW on Java. As a result of more than three years imprisonment, he became fluent in Japanese, and therefore more able to understand the people who imprisoned him. He went on after the war to become a writer, and his many books include *Hurricane Over the Jungle, Battle of Palembang* and *The Genki Boys*. But as with many young men who went through the Japanese PoW experience, it did not make him like the Japanese more.

'I remember too much about the behaviour of the Japanese that was unacceptable and unforgivable ever to like them. Something has been built into you after three and a half years of their behaviour towards us – the things that happened – the fact that you couldn't trust them.

'There were long-term consequences to being so close to Hiroshima when the atomic bomb went off. I started getting sores on my face. I used to go along to have treatment for skin cancer at RAF Halton to start with. They started cutting all these things out, and took this piece of face away, and then that piece of face, and it's on my arms and chest and so on. They recur. The RAF accepted that they occur because of Hiroshima. It could also occur because of having to work, as we had to work for the Japanese, in the blazing tropical sunshine as we were made to do in Java. The RAF at Halton decided, though, that it was Hiroshima, because they had not met so many people who had the same diseases.

'I keep getting them all the time now.'

Captain Eric 'Winkle' Brown CBE, DSC, AFC RN is the most highly decorated officer in the Fleet Air Arm, He commanded the Enemy Aircraft Flight, test-flying captured German aircraft. Brown flight-tested 53 German aircraft, including the Me 163 rocket plane and the Me 262 jet plane. Fluent in German, he helped interview Werner Von Braun, Hermann Goering, Willie

Messerschmitt and Dr Ernst Heinkel after the war. He holds the world record for the most aircraft carrier landings, 2,407, including 200 in Hurricanes, and is listed in the *Guinness Book of Records* as holding the record – 487 types – for flying the greatest number of different aircraft. He doesn't think this record will ever be beaten. In his 91st year he is official advisor to the Royal Navy on Britain's two new aircraft carriers … if they ever get built.

> **Eric Brown:**
> 'Without the Hurricane we would have lost the Battle of Britain. At one stage it was called the "stop-gap" aeroplane, it always seemed to fill in when we were short of sterner stuff, in performance. The country owes a huge amount to the Hurricane.'

Peter Hairs went on after the Battle of Britain to teach flying in Canada in 1943 as part of the Empire Air Training Scheme. He ended the war in India with a (Military) MBE and a Mention in Dispatches, remained in the RAF after the war, and retired in 1966.

Bill Green, having survived being shot down three times, returned from PoW camp to reclaim his beloved wife Bertha Biggs, and developed a successful business career, which ended as Managing Director and Chairman of Crown Paints.

Graham Leggatt, following the 'Great Italian Turkey Shoot' just after the Battle of Britain, was shot down over Malta on 21 December 1941. He went on after the war to hold a permanent RAF commission, from which he retired as a Squadron Leader in May 1958.

William Swan ended his fighting career in the Middle East by being appointed a test pilot, which he felt was his niche. After the war he went into publishing. He has a son who is now an RAF fighter pilot.

Graham Skellum, who gave up a reserved job as a postal worker to fly fighters as a sergeant pilot, went back to Stoke on Trent after the war as a commissioned officer. Skellum went into buying and selling, financial services, and helping his mother as a sub-postmistress. He later went into the hire-purchase business. In 1971 he bought a house in Portugal, and let it out to holidaymakers. In his words, 'I survived.'

Tom Adams, who flew 'clapped out Hurricanes' in Burma, went on to become a successful chartered accountant in 'civvie street.'

There are said to be a dozen Hurricanes still flying. Among them is the only flying version of a Hurricane IV, which is in Canada. This Mark IV KZ321, later G-HURY, was built by Hawker Aircraft Ltd. at the company's Langley, Slough factory some time after 1942. It was stored until entering service with 6 Squadron RAF at Grottaglie, Italy, in March 1943.

When the squadron was transferred to the RAF's Balkan Air Force four months later at Canne, Greece, the Hurricane operated from various detachments in Greece, Italy and Yugoslavia. The squadron ended up in Proks, Yugoslavia, where it remained until VE day, before moving to Palestine and Nicosia, flying Hurricanes. KZ321 was abandoned in what is now Israel when the squadron converted to Tempest VIs on 15 January 1947, having been the last RAF unit to operate Hurricanes.

Recovered from a Jaffa scrap yard by Doug Arnold's Warbirds of GB Ltd, KZ321 was returned to the United Kingdom in 1983 where it was stored at Blackbushe and Biggin Hill. It was then acquired by The Fighter Collection of the Imperial War Museum at Duxford in 1991. Restoration was started by Hawker Restorations Ltd. in Suffolk in 2001, returning the aircraft to zero hour condition using original and refurbished parts. It was registered as G-HURY, painted in the authentic RAF markings of 6 Squadron. Its first post-restoration flight was in 2003 and was thereafter flown by The Fighter Collection. Vintage Wings acquired and registered KZ321 in Canada as CF-TPM in May of 2006.

Two historically important Hurricanes are still maintained in airworthy condition by the RAF Battle of Britain Memorial Flight (BBMF) at Coningsby, Lincolnshire. The last Hurricane to remain on RAF strength, LF363, a Mk IIC, was issued to 63 Squadron but transferred to No 309 Squadron, a Polish unit at Drem, soon afterwards. There then followed numerous moves to training and development units until 1951 when LF363 could be found alongside the Gloster Meteors of 41 Squadron. In September 1952 she was refurbished by the manufacturer and delivered to the Station Flight at Waterbeach. After a brief career in films including *Reach for the Sky* she returned once again to the RAF in 1957 when the BBMF was established at Biggin Hill in Kent. She later was used in the epic *Battle of Britain* film.

On 11 September 1991, *en route* to the annual Jersey air display, engine failure caused the pilot, Squadron Leader Martin to divert to RAF Wittering. While still 100 feet above the ground the engine failed completely and the aircraft plummeted onto the runway performing several cartwheels before being engulfed in fire. Martin suffered a broken ankle and burns, fortunately the aircraft came to rest on its belly and he was able to escape.

None of the wooden or fabric components survived, the engine was torn from its mountings, the propeller was destroyed and the outer wing leading edges were crushed. The RAF carefully stored the wreckage for three years. In August 1994 the BBMF was given authority to sell one of its three Spitfires XIXs to fund the Hurricane restoration programme, undertaken by Historic Flying Ltd. The restoration took four years before she was able to take to the air again in September 1998 in the hands of Squadron Leader Day. It now carries the colours of the famous 56 Squadron, in which Last Witness Bill Green fought.

The other BBMF Hurricane, PZ865, also a Mk IIC, was the last Hurricane ever built, and first flew on 22 July 1944. She was bought back from the Ministry of Supply by Hawkers and christened the 'Last of the Many'. Painted in blue and gold livery she was entered in the King's Cup Air race of 1950 and, despite a heavy handicap, finished second. In the 1960s PZ 865 was used as a chase aircraft in the low speed trials of the P1127, an aircraft that would eventually evolve into the Hawker Harrier. Like her sister LF363, she also had a film career before joining the BBMF.

PZ865 is currently painted to represent Hurricane IIC BE581, 'Night Reaper', the aircraft flown by the Czech fighter ace Flight Lieutenant Karel Kuttelwascher DFC during night intruder operations from Tangmere in 1942 with the RAF's No. 1(F) Squadron (See Chapter 19, Hurricane Aces, 'Old Kut').

Bill Swan:
'I recently saw PZ865, in night fighter black, down at Chayleigh, which had been a Polish base. The farmer made the field available for flying again, and they had an air show there. My younger son is a fighter pilot, he bought a ticket and I went down with him. I sat in the Hurricane cockpit. As a former Hurricane flyer I automatically did the undercarriage lock-down check.

UMPFFTT – You don't forget it.

As I sat in the aircraft my hand automatically went to the controls – Undercarriage, Mixture, Pitch, Flaps, Fuel, Throttle, Trim – check them on the aircraft sitting on the ground before you touch anything, because how many pilots have just got into the cockpit and started, with the undercarriage lever being moved from down to up, and put the wheels up while the aircraft was still on the ground?

This happened so often, and it certainly was drilled into me.

Get this in your head!

Never sit in an aircraft until you have checked UMPFFTT!'

Hurricane Data

Hurricane Customer Nations

Belgium, Canada, Finland, Free French, Holland, India, Ireland, Persia, Poland (one a/c only), Portugal, Romania, South Africa, Soviet Union, Turkey and Yugoslavia.

Photographic evidence confirms the use of several captured Hurricanes by the Luftwaffe and Regia Aeronautica.

Dimensions

Wing span:	40 feet all versions
Wing Area:	258 sq. feet
Length:	31 feet 5.5 inches Mk 1. All other Marks 32 feet 2.25 inches
Height:	13 feet 1.5 inches

Performance

Version	Merlin Engine	Max Power (hp)	Max Weight (lbs)	Max level speed(mph)	Range internal fuel (miles)	Ceiling(feet)
Prototype	C	1,025	5,272	315	440	34,500
Mk I	II or III	1,030	6,220	328	425	32,800
Mk IIA Tropical	XX or 22	1,260	6,450	342	470	34,000
Mk IIC	XX or 22	1260	7,300	330	460	36,000
Mk XII Canadian	Packard 29	1,300	Not known	330	460	Not known
Mk IID A/T Cannon	XX or 22	1,260	7,550	280	420	35,500
Mk IV	24 or 27	1,620	8,450	330	430	32,500
Mk V	32	1,700	9,300	326	Not known	Not known
Sea Hurricane IB	III	1,030	7,410	290	505	30,000
Sea Hurricane IIC	XX	1,280	7,618	301	452	34,500

Armament and stores

Version	Fixed armament	Stores
Mk I	8 x .303 Browning machine guns	None
Mk IIA	8 x .303 Browning machine guns	2 x 44 or 90 gal tanks
Mk IIB &	8 or 12 x .303 Browning machine guns	2 x 44 or 90 gal tanks or

Mk XII		2 x 250lb bombs or 2 x 500lb bombs
PR Mk I, IIB & IIC	None (photo recce versions)	3 x F24 cameras or 4 x F24 cameras
Mk IIC & Sea Hurricane IIC / XIIC	4 x 20mm Oerlikon or Hispano cannon	2 x 44 or 90 gal tanks or 2 x 250lb bombs or 2 x 500lb bombs
Mk IID	2 x .303 Browning machine guns	2 x 40mm Vickers cannon
Mk IV & V	4 x 20mm Oerlikon or Hispano cannon or 2 x .303 Browning machine guns	2 x 44 or 90 gal tanks or 2 x 250lb bombs or 2 x 500lb bombs or 2 x 40mm Vickers cannon or 8 x 3in rocket projectiles

Production Figures

Company	Location	Figures	Marks
Hawker Aircraft Ltd	Kingston, Brooklands & Langley	10,030	All except Mks X, XI, XII (Canadian production)
Gloster Aircraft Ltd	Hucclecote	2,750	I, IIA/B/C
Austin Motor Ltd	Birmingham	300	II
Canadian Car & Foundry Co	Canada	1,451	I, X, XI, XII (licence built versions of Mk I and II)
Avions Fairey	Belgium	1	I (planned production cancelled by German occupation)
Total all versions		14,533	

Note: - Some sources quote total production as 14,670

Index

BIBLIOGRAPHY:

Mackworth-Praed, Ben, *Aviation – The Pioneer Years*, Studio Editions, 1990
Arthur, Max, *Symbol of Courage – A History of the Victoria Cross*, Sidgewick & Jackson 2004
Baker, E.C.R., *Ace of Aces*, New English Library, 1973
Baker, E.C.R., *The Fighter Aces of the RAF*, New English Library, 1962
Barnett , Corelli, *Engage the Enemy More Closely*, Penguin Books 1991
Bishop, Patrick, *Fighter Boys – Saving Britain 1940*, Harper Perennial 2003
Bowen, Ezra, *Knights of the Air*, Time-Life Books, 1980
Bungay, Stephen, *The Most Dangerous Enemy*, Aurum Press, 2001
Clostermann, Pierre, *The Big Show*, Chatto & Windus, 1951
Cotton, 'Bush', *Hurricanes Over Burma*, Crawford House Publishing, 1995
Crosby, Francis, *Fighters & Bombers of the World*, Anness Publishing, 2006
Deighton, Len, *Fighter*, by Jonathan Cape, 1977
Doe, Bob, *Bob Doe, Fighter Pilot*, CCB Aviation Books, 2004
Forrester, Larry, *Fly for Your Life, The Story of Bob Stanford Tuck*, Cerebus, 1956
Glancy, Jonathan, *Spitfire – The Biography*, Atlantic Books, 2006
Green, Rod, *Spitfire & Hurricane Package*, Michael O'Mara Books
Holmes, Tony, *Hurricane Aces 1939-40*, Osprey Aerospace, 1998
Iveson, Tony & Milton, Brian, *Lancaster – the Biography*, Andre Deutsche, 2009
Johnson, Johnnie, *The Story of Air Fighting*, Arrow Books, 1985
Keegan, John, *The Second World War*, Arrow Books, 1990
Kelly, Terence, *Hurricane Over the Jungle*, William Kimber, 1977
Legrand, Jacques, *Chronicle of Aviation*, Chronicle Communications, 1990
Neil, Tom, *A Fighter in My Sight*s, J&KH Publishing, 2001
Richey, Paul, *Fighter Pilot*, Arrow Edition, 1991 (originally 1941)
Shankland, Peter & Hunter, Anthony, *Dardanelles Patrol*, Mayflower Paperback, 1971
Thomas, Hugh, *Spirit of the Blue, A Fighter Pilot's Story*, Sutton Publishing, 2004
Turner, John Frayn, *VC's of the Air*, Airlife, 1993
Welham, Geoffrey, *First Light*, Penguin Books, 2002
Winton, John, *Carrier Glorious, The Life and Death of an Aircraft Carrier*, Cassell, 1986
Yoeman, Christopher & Pritchard, David, *Fighter Pilots in Portrait*, Rabbit Squadron, 2009